on track ...
Peter Hammill

every album, every song

Richard Rees Jones

sonicbondpublishing.com

Sonicbond Publishing Limited
www.sonicbondpublishing.co.uk
Email: info@sonicbondpublishing.co.uk

First Published in the United Kingdom 2021
First Published in the United States 2021

British Library Cataloguing in Publication Data:
A Catalogue record for this book is available from the British Library

Copyright Richard Rees Jones 2021

ISBN 978-1-78952-163-4

Typeset in ITC Garamond & ITC Avant Garde
Printed and bound in England

Graphic design and typesetting: Full Moon Media

on track ...
Peter Hammill

every album, every song

Richard Rees Jones

sonicbondpublishing.com

Acknowledgements

Thanks to Seán Kelly, Boris Lulinsky, Andrew Wales and the other members of the Top of the World Club for always fun and stimulating Hammill-related discussions, for useful insights into several songs, and for saving me a place at Café Oto.

Hello to friends in Vienna: John Stewart, Geraint Williams, Nicholas Ward. Here's hoping for a reunion sometime.

Hello across the ocean to Duane Capizzi, the world's most dedicated Hammill, Brötzmann, Braxton and Parker fan.

Eternal thanks to Peter Hammill for the music, and for a Sunday afternoon walk in Freshford after the flood.

Love and kisses, always and forever, to Maeve and Emma.

This book is dedicated to Ben.

as though he never knew the meaning of the words until just now

on track ...
Peter Hammill

Contents

Introduction

In 1988 Peter Hammill played a concert at the Gardner Centre, the arts centre on the campus of Sussex University where I was a student. At the time, I hadn't heard a note of his music, but was attracted by his vaguely Gothic-sounding surname (Hammer horror?), although not sufficiently so as to actually buy a ticket for the concert. Strangely drawn to the event, though, I found myself loitering disconsolately in the foyer of the Gardner Centre that evening, half-hearing the music coming from the auditorium, wishing I was inside.

Suffering no such hesitation on the occasion of Hammill's next visit to the Gardner Centre two years later, I duly secured tickets for my then-girlfriend and me. I was impressed, but what really sealed the deal for me was another concert the following summer. By that time, having left Brighton and lost the girl, I found myself in Bristol and gravitated towards a fine record shop called Revolver. Chatting to the people behind the counter, they informed me that Hammill was playing that week in his home town of Bath. I took the train there and saw him play a magnificent show in a tiny upstairs venue called The Loft. Accompanied by violinist Stuart Gordon and saxophonist David Jackson, it was this immensely powerful concert that made me a Hammill fan for life.

The strange thing about this journey of discovery was that I made it without being aware of Hammill's past with Van der Graaf Generator, my introduction to whom came later. For this reason, Hammill has, for me, always been a solo artist first and foremost, and the leader of VdGG second, with his solo albums and performances being those that capture the essence of what makes him great for me. It's also the case that, unlike many hardcore Hammill fans, my favourite of those albums are the angsty, riffy records he made in the late 1970s and early 1980s (roughly speaking, the run from 1977's *Over* through to 1983's *Patience*). This has remained true even since VdGG reformed in 2005, as exciting as that reunion has proven to be.

Hammill is by some distance the most important musical figure in my life, the one to whom I've turned over and over again through the past thirty years, the only artist who embodies everything that I find thrilling and true about music. What, then, have I learned over these thirty years? That Hammill's lifelong preoccupations – reason, memory, the unravelling of time and the choices we make – are deep, troubling ones. That there is something primal and atavistic about the way he confronts them in song. And that fifty years after he began, his music remains as visionary and essential as ever.

Although Hammill is a gracious and talkative interviewee, I have only rarely quoted his words on specific albums or songs given in interviews over the years. I have, however, quoted extensively from the 'artist's notes' that he wrote about some albums on his website; from the sleeve notes to the albums that were remastered and reissued on Virgin in 2006-2007; and from the *Sofa Sound* newsletters and journal entries, also on his website, where he writes detailed notes on each new album as it is released.

An index to this book can be downloaded from my website viennesewaltz.net.

Fool's Mate (1971)

Personnel:
Peter Hammill: vocals, acoustic guitar, piano
Guy Evans: drums, percussion
Martin Pottinger: drums
Hugh Banton: piano, organ
Rod Clements: bass, violin
Nic Potter: bass
Ray Jackson: harp, mandolin
David Jackson: saxophones, flute
Robert Fripp: electric guitar
Paul Whitehead: tam-tam
All songs by Peter Hammill, except where noted
Recorded at Trident Studios, London, April 1971
Produced by John Anthony
UK release date: July 1971
Cover: Paul Whitehead

Hammill's début solo album is an anomaly – a collection of short songs recorded over four days in 1971, but mostly written years earlier. The album was recorded in the midst of a feverish blast of VdGG activity, with the *H to He, Who Am The Only One* album having been released just a few months prior, and the group's masterpiece *Pawn Hearts* soon to follow.

With the group gigging relentlessly in the UK and western Europe for virtually the whole of 1971, it must have been something of a relief for Hammill to retreat to Trident Studios, with a trusted cadre of musicians gathered around him, to finally realise a cache of songs that had been living inside his head for several years. As Hammill told an interviewer at the time: 'I just feel that they are a part of me still, and that in a way they are something that I have to exorcise.'

Nevertheless, *Fool's Mate* is very far from being a work of juvenilia. Like favourite children, one or two of the songs have remained as staples of Hammill's live sets throughout his performing career. Others, tuneful and optimistic, bear the unmistakable traces of the late 1960s environment in which they were birthed – that brief moment when psychedelic pop was beginning to evolve into underground rock. Here and there, too, we find elements of the savage intensity that was to characterise Hammill's entire approach to songcraft, tenderness laced with anguish and turbulence.

Musicians on the album included Hammill's VdGG bandmates Banton, Evans, Jackson and Potter, lending a baleful VdGG influence to several tracks on the album. Also on board were Ray Jackson and Rod Clements from Charisma labelmates Lindisfarne, not to mention Robert Fripp of King Crimson on electric guitar, who was known to Hammill having played on *H to He, Who Am The Only One*. Together they give the album a quirky, diverse sound that renders it unlike anything else in Hammill's back catalogue.

The title *Fool's Mate* refers to the quickest possible checkmate in the game of chess. As a long-time chess aficionado (*cf.* the title of VdGG's *Pawn Hearts*, the back cover of *Chameleon in the Shadow of the Night* and the photograph on the inner gatefold of 1985's *The Margin*), Hammill is attentive to the beauty and difficulty of this game, to say nothing of the way in which victory is achieved through the gradual attrition of one's opponent's options, a progressive besieging leading to annihilation. In its knotty complexity and its troubling entanglement of situations, Hammill's music approximates to the reality of chess. We see the earliest traces of that here.

'Imperial Zeppelin' (Hammill, Smith)

One of two tracks on *Fool's Mate* with lyrics by Hammill's VdGG co-founder Chris Judge Smith, 'Imperial Zeppelin' is a barnstorming opener to the album. Gleefully proposing a Utopian existence above the Earth, the song imagines piling on board the eponymous airship to 'have love a mile above', while the Earth seethes with hate below. The occupants of the craft plan to throw the seeds of love overboard, a notion that, Hammill acknowledges in a note in his first book of lyrics *Killers, Angels, Refugees*, 'as a romantic fiction, remains appealing.' Jackson lets rip on sax around Evans' formidable drumming while Fripp adds fractured lead guitar to the organ-led middle section.

'Candle'

Written as early as 1966, this funereal song is powered by grim acoustic riffing from Hammill and by Ray Jackson's spiralling mandolin work. The lyric is a trifle overcooked, but Hammill's voice convincingly conveys a sense of raw abjection. John Anthony's production situates Hammill's wounded vocals in a hazy middle ground, as if on the verge of being extinguished. 'For the life I was part of breathes its last, and not only life but hope has gone away,' mourns Hammill, while Jackson's delicate mandolin propels the song gradually upward.

'Happy'

Banton, Evans, Jackson and Potter are all present and correct here, but despite this, 'Happy' is probably the least VdGG-like song in Hammill's catalogue. A light and relatively trivial exercise in romantic affirmation, this is the kind of song Hammill probably had to write, but by the time he came to record it had already left well behind. David Jackson's flute threads its way elegantly through the song, while Hugh Banton's vigorous organ work lends the song an air of authority I'm not sure it deserves.

'Solitude'

One of the album's key tracks, 'Solitude', is a devastating piece of work, showing an extraordinary level of maturity considering that Hammill was not yet twenty when he wrote it. This is true even when you take into account that the first and last verses are based on the poem 'Feldeinsamkeit' ('Alone in Fields') by the German poet Hermann Allmers, which probably came to Hammill's attention due to its setting by the composer Brahms. Drawing on Allmers' Wordsworthian notion of Romantic solitude, Hammill finds himself 'far from grime, far from rushing people' and retreats into 'a tiny peace' from which he is able to sense 'the lovely white clouds glide across the sky.' Hammill's guitar work is remarkable, with splintering notes and grinding chord progressions adding to the sense of extreme willed solipsism that hangs blackly over the song. His vocals, meanwhile, catch a note of intense regret that detonates at key moments during the song. Most strikingly, Ray Jackson lends the song a warped folk-blues sensibility with his weaving harmonica lines, stalking the piece in restless counterpoint to Hammill's urgent acoustic riffing.

'Vision'
One of Hammill's most enduring and best-loved songs, 'Vision' has long been a staple of his live performances. It's not hard to see why, since it is at once simple, heartfelt and shimmeringly beautiful, with Hammill's devotional voice rising like shafts of moonlight above Banton's gorgeous piano. Hammill has never sounded more enraptured than he does here, never more dazzled by the pain and breath of love. 'Vision' is a sublime appeal to transcendence, a love song fully entitled to take its place among the greatest love songs ever written.

'Re-awakening'
Another song on which Hammill is backed by the other members of VdGG, 'Re-awakening' is an arresting, energetic workout that seems to stand at that pivotal moment where late '60s optimism was shading into the darker, more uncertain times of the early '70s. Finding that 're-awakening isn't easy when you're tired', Hammill proposes as a response to 'curl up, slide away and dream your life out.' If that sounds like the polar opposite of Timothy Leary's famous exhortation to 'turn on, tune in, drop out', it's a conclusion that's hard to resist in the face of Hammill's commanding vocal performance, not to mention Jackson's astringent blasts of sax and Banton's luminous organ work.

'Sunshine'
'Sunshine' is an interesting footnote in the VdGG story, being one of two tracks on the group's first demo tape, which ultimately led to them being signed by Mercury Records in 1968. That embryonic version, which survives, was cut by the first line-up of the group. The version on *Fool's Mate*, as you might expect, is considerably more polished, with David Jackson parping away happily on saxophone and Robert Fripp contributing whacked-out lead guitar. The song itself is bouncy and euphoric, unlike anything else Hammill has ever written and reminiscent of early Bowie in its goofy cheerfulness. Yet with the curious reference to 'E-S/M attractions' in the lyric alongside sentiments like 'I'm ready

to be led', 'How sweet it would be to be chained by your side' and 'for you I'd get hooked and float six inches mud-free', one can't help wondering if there's something more going on here than meets the eye.

'Child'
Even when accompanied only by himself on guitar, Hammill has never been any kind of folk singer. Eschewing the cyclical force and repetition of traditional music, he works with dramatic chordal voicings that fragment and bleed into one another. 'Child' is a fine early example, a dreamlike ballad that sees Hammill's languorous vocal floating hazily over vapour trails of acoustic guitar. David Jackson's tender flute and Robert Fripp's miraculous electric guitar add to the flickering nocturnal ambience of this beautiful song.

'Summer Song (in the Autumn)'
Out of the five or six tracks on *Fool's Mate* that feature the other members of VdGG, most of them don't actually sound like VdGG songs. 'Summer Song (in the Autumn') is the exception, an imposing cut that makes a powerful impression despite being the shortest song on the album. Although Jackson is absent, the song is possessed by the collective consciousness of the group, with Hammill's uncannily pure alto reaching for the sky amid Banton's magisterial organ and Evans' hugely impressive drumming. Hammill adds seething piano stabs to this bleak tale of depression and suicide, rounding out the song's grim portrayal of a mind on the brink of collapse.

'Viking' (Hammill, Smith)
Chris Judge Smith, co-founder of VdGG, penned the text of this historical curio. Like Smith's other lyrical contribution to the album, 'Imperial Zeppelin', the song forsakes Hammill's imagistic force and psychological acuity in favour of a queasily drawn imaginary scenario. Drawing on the 13th century Icelandic Vinland sagas, the song depicts a crew of longshipmen returning home from their long explorations. Hammill's vocal is oddly inert, none more so than when he recites a list of various Vikings. Ray Jackson's harmonica and Fripp's lead guitar add much-needed colour, but aren't enough to lift the song above the mundane.

'The Birds'
Another song that Hammill has returned to frequently in live performance. As with 'Vision', its longevity is not hard to understand, for this is a song haunted by sadness and loss, its emotional impact undiminished by the years. Hammill evokes a world without pity, where the passage of the seasons is thrown into disarray and where the pain of lost love is reflected in unforgiving coldness and death. Hammill's deeply affecting vocal traces its way through Banton's rapturous piano, while Evans lays down intricate fills and Fripp takes a radiant solo.

'I Once Wrote Some Poems'

The album ends on another high note with one of Hammill's strongest early songs, a wracked solo confessional that would not have sounded out of place on his later masterpiece *Over*. In barely two minutes, Hammill's vocal progresses from an agitated whisper to a spectral calm and finally to a barely controlled rage, accompanied by weighty chords and angry slashes of guitar. Savagely intoning that 'I never wrote poems when I bit my knuckles and Death started slipping into my mouth', the commitment and intensity of Hammill's performance leave you thunderstruck.

Bonus tracks

The 2005 reissue adds five bonus tracks, namely demo versions of 'Re-awakening', 'Summer Song (in the Autumn)', 'The Birds', 'Sunshine' and 'Happy'.

Chameleon in the Shadow of the Night (1973)

Personnel:
Peter Hammill: vocals, guitar, piano, Mellotron, harmonium
Guy Evans: drums, percussion
David Jackson: alto and tenor saxophones, flute
Hugh Banton: organ
Nic Potter: bass
All songs by Peter Hammill
Recorded at Sofa Sound, Sussex and Rockfield Studios, Monmouth, February and March 1973
Produced by John Anthony
UK release date: 4 May 1973
Cover: Paul Whitehead

If *Fool's Mate* was essentially a retrospective collection of songs written while Hammill's career was still in its embryonic stages, *Chameleon in the Shadow of the Night* represents a dramatic step forward, a definitive statement of where he stood at the time as a singer, songwriter and musician. A mix of introspective solo acoustic numbers, dynamic rockers and one genuine prog epic, the album incorporates a range of approaches that were to recur throughout Hammill's career.

Like many of Hammill's early solo records, the gestation of *Chameleon* is inextricably linked to the story of Van der Graaf Generator. The songs that would go to make up the album were mostly written in 1971-72, during a time of tumultuous change for the group. The touring commitments that had seen them travel hectically across Europe throughout 1971 continued well into 1972, as they carried out heavy promotional duties for the *Pawn Hearts* album which had been released in October 1971. By August of 1972, however, they had split – 'blown apart,' in Hammill's words, 'by the intensity of the work.'

Chameleon contains at least one song, 'German Overalls', written in direct response to the boredom and stress of that constant touring. What is more, '(In The) Black Room' had been written for the group and had been played by them in the final throes of touring before the split. Since the other members of the group all play on the album, it's clear how closely related the two entities 'Hammill' and 'VdGG' were at this point – as, indeed, they were right up to VdGG's reformation in 1975.

The other reason why *Chameleon* was an important album for Hammill lies in the manner of its recording. Believing, not unreasonably, that he would not always have the benefit of record company patronage, Hammill decided to seize control of the means of production. He bought a four-track TEAC tape recorder, installed it in his home in the Sussex village of Worth, and set to work. The solo acoustic parts were all laid down on the TEAC, which may account for the low-fidelity sound quality of much of the album. Crucially,

15

however, home recording was a method that would serve Hammill well in the years to come, protecting him to some extent from the vicissitudes of the commercial record industry.

The group parts, meanwhile, were recorded at Rockfield Studios in Wales with VdGG's regular producer John Anthony at the controls. When it came to choosing a set of musicians to flesh out the songs in the studio, there was only one option. Banton, Evans, Jackson and Potter were so perfectly attuned to Hammill's creative visions that they were able to function equally as well as his backing group as they had as his VdGG bandmates. Together they made Hammill's first true solo album, a record that stands both as a rich collection of songs and as a waypoint to his future direction.

'German Overalls'

A strange yet wholly characteristic number to open the album. The curious title is a punning translation of 'Deutschland über alles', the first line of the German national anthem, which since the end of World War II is no longer sung. The song itself was inspired by a gruelling tour of West Germany, which VdGG undertook in May 1971, including stops at Mannheim and Kaiserslautern (referred to in the song as 'K-town', the nickname given to the city by US servicemen). The text grimly recounts the penury and fatigue that ultimately led to the break-up of the group, with an anguished vocal performance set to churning waves of acoustic guitar. Banton and Jackson have walk-on parts in the narrative, and Jackson also appears musically, his squally sax interventions lending weight to Hammill's increasingly disturbed singing. The song is also notable for the first appearance of what Hammill describes in a sleeve note as a 'junk shop harmonium', its dread overtones framing the Gothic imagery of the 'cathedrals spiral skywards' section.

'Slender Threads'

This is the first of three solo acoustic guitar songs on the album. The lyric tells a story of breaking up and drifting apart, of recrimination and regret, narrated in the soul-baring confessional style in which Hammill was by now excelling. Raking pitilessly over the embers of a failed relationship, the song anatomises how 'we start out together, but the paths all divide', ending with a chilling image of 'the knife already turning in my hand.' There's nothing so comforting as a verse-chorus-verse structure here, and the words erupt like an affliction. His voice shifting between a sombre baritone and an eerie falsetto, Hammill sings with a strange English precision that intensifies the emotionally turbulent landscape that the song inhabits. His guitar, meanwhile, swoops and glides around the contours of the song, avoiding any hint of fulfilment or resolution.

'Rock and Role'

One of the most sheerly enjoyable songs on the album, 'Rock and Role' is a key track in Hammill's development as a musician. Throughout his career, Hammill has shown a love for three-chord power and simplicity that sets him well apart from most of the artists normally labelled as progressive rock. There's a seam of raw energy running through his work that puts me in mind not only of the punk acts that were to follow but also of early '70s fellow travellers like Hawkwind, an association later acknowledged by Hammill: 'in terms of the noise, the rawness and energy level during their live performances [VdGG and Hawkwind] weren't that far away. The anarchic element and the sonic quality and rawness of punk was there.'

This aspect of his muse effectively starts here, Hammill having recently acquired a new Fender Strat that he quickly put to use on 'Rock and Role'. This cut fairly crackles with electricity, as Hammill's chiming rhythm guitar swarms around Jackson's majestic sax blowing, Potter's rock-solid bass and Evans' all-pervasive stickwork. The lyric is somewhat opaque, which hardly matters when the overall effect is as fresh and jubilant as this.

'In the End'

Hammill's piano playing is a remarkable thing, seen to full effect on 'In The End'. Dense clusters of notes hang defiantly in the air, shapeshifting in time with the rugged landscapes of the text and occasionally resolving into momentary but achingly beautiful threads of melody. This song is a long, emotionally draining depiction of a mind hemmed in by lacerating self-doubt, drawn in unsparing textual detail. And when Hammill sings lines like 'no more rushing around, no more travelling chess; I guess I'd better sit down, you know I do need the rest,' you're struck by the way the lyric explodes everyday utterances into blinding flashes of insight.

'What's It Worth?'

Like the earlier 'Slender Threads', this acoustic guitar song is played in an open D tuning, resulting in a slightly off-kilter sound that matches its wonky melody and baffling lyric. But it's a sly and bewitching tune, with Jackson's delightful flute darting like fireflies around Hammill's compelling vocal performance.

'Easy to Slip Away'

It's back to the piano for this essential cut, one of Hammill's greatest ever songs. On one level, it's a sequel to the VdGG classic 'Refugees' (from 1970s *The Least We Can Do Is Wave to Each Other*), taking up the characters of Mike and Susie from the earlier song and lamenting the loss of close friendships with them. As is well known, the characters are real; Susie is the actress Susan Penhaligon and Mike is Mike McLean, both of whom shared a flat with Hammill in London in 1968. But the song transcends the merely autobiographical with its terror-struck realisation of the fleeting, evanescent nature of time. Hammill's vocals reach new heights of intensity, his dark lamentations and shrieks of angry falsetto amplified by desperate hammerings on the piano. David Jackson

17

is a vital presence throughout, clouds of fervent saxophone orbiting Hammill's ever more bitter language. 'Easy to Slip Away' is a masterpiece, its harrowing insights impossible to unlearn or to forget.

'Dropping the Torch'

This intimate, desolate song drifts by on softly intoned vocals and twilit flickers of acoustic guitar. The lyric draws upon threatening imagery of imprisonment: walls, chains, the crushing of freedom. As the song goes on, hope seems progressively extinguished until, finally, an uncomfortable conclusion is reached: 'time ever moves more slowly; life gets more lonely and less real.' The claustrophobic encroachment of the text is reflected in the song's melancholic tone, with Hammill singing and playing as though trapped in some remote, airless cavern.

'(In The) Black Room/The Tower'

The album's one genuine prog epic, '(In The) Black Room', had seen life as a VdGG song in concert during 1971-72, and was slated for inclusion on the next VdGG album after *Pawn Hearts*. The group's demise in 1972 put paid to that, but a rough and ready rehearsal version survives on the 1981 *Time Vaults* compilation. The version on *Chameleon*, though, is the definitive one, with Banton, Evans and Jackson all present to summon the dark forces of VdGG. The piece is a frenzied interior journey of immense majesty; Hammill pushes his voice to its absolute limits, railing and burning in the throes of a soundworld rich in atmosphere and incident. Monstrous sax and organ riffs battle for supremacy against Evans' hyperactive drumming and Hammill's freewheeling piano runs, while the dynamic shifts that take place in the 'Tower' section ratchet up the tension still further. Lyrically, the song is a catalogue of typically Hammillesque oppositions: free will versus predestination, doubt against certainty, the rational and the speculative. References to the Tarot – the Priestess, the Star, the Fool and of course the Tower – heighten the sense of occult mystery that pervades the song, while the line about 'going to the feelies' is a reference to Aldous Huxley's *Brave New World*, in which the feelies are a kind of cinema involving touch as well as sight and sound. Such arcana, however, are less important than the overall gripping impact of this extraordinary song.

Bonus tracks

'Rain 3am'

A rare example here of a new, previously unreleased song being disinterred from the vaults. Originally released on the 1993 Virgin compilation *The Calm (After The Storm)*, the song was recorded at Worth in 1972. It was not specifically intended for inclusion on *Chameleon*, but fits perfectly here as a bonus track, being very much of a piece with other solo acoustic guitar songs of the period. Jackson's sensitive flute skips lightly through a filmic succession of nocturnal images, with a dying drunk and a lurking cat Hammill's only company. The oppressive imagery and slashing guitar make for a highly effective mood piece.

The 2006 reissue also includes live versions of 'Easy to Slip Away' and 'In the End'. Due to a lack of high-quality live recordings from the period, these are taken from a bootleg, *Skeletons of Songs*, recorded in Kansas City, USA, in 1978. This, however, is the best PH bootleg ever released, so the appearance of these two songs here is a definite bonus.

The Silent Corner and the Empty Stage (1974)

Personnel:
Peter Hammill: vocals, guitar, piano, Mellotron, harmonium, bass guitar, oscillator
Hugh Banton: organ, bass pedals, bass guitar, backing vocals
Guy Evans: drums, percussion
David Jackson: alto, tenor and soprano saxophones, flute
Randy California: lead guitar on 'Red Shift'
All songs by Peter Hammill
Recorded at Sofa Sound, Sussex and Rockfield Studios, Monmouth, September and October 1973
'Red Shift' recorded at Island Studios, London, April 1973
Produced by John Anthony and Peter Hammill
UK release date: 8 February 1974
Cover: Bettina Hohls

A 2014 poll held on an internet discussion group showed that *The Silent Corner and the Empty Stage* was by some distance the most popular of Hammill's solo works among fans, while 'A Louse Is Not A Home', the epic with which the album concludes, was the most popular song. Clearly, therefore, we are dealing with a major work here, and indeed the album represents a considerable advance on *Chameleon*. The production is fuller, the arrangements more imaginative and the full band songs – recorded again with VdGG as the backing group – are easily the equal of anything VdGG had released up to that point.

By the autumn of 1973, Hammill's home studio set-up had become more sophisticated, with further instruments, effects boxes and even an oscillator added to his armoury. As a result, the solo tracks recorded at Sofa Sound for *Silent Corner* – 'Modern', 'Wilhelmina' and 'Rubicon' – sound more fully realized than their counterparts on *Chameleon* had been, with 'Modern' in particular benefiting from a full panoply of studio effects.

The songs themselves had been written at various times over the preceding years, and were in some cases contemporaneous with material that had ended up on *Chameleon*. Indeed, 'Red Shift' and 'Modern' had originally been penned as far back as 1968 and 1969, respectively. Three albums into his solo career, Hammill was still working his way through a backlog of songs he had not yet recorded, sculpting and refining them into a body of work.

VdGG were still on hiatus, of course, but that didn't stop Banton, Jackson and Evans from once again convening with Hammill at Rockfield to lay down the full band songs 'The Lie', 'Forsaken Gardens' and 'A Louse Is Not A Home' with John Anthony at the controls. 'Louse', like '(In the) Black Room' before it, had been performed by VdGG during 1971-72 and had been intended for the next VdGG album. The odd man out was 'Red Shift', which had been recorded back in April 1973 at Island Studios in London and featured a scorching solo by Spirit guitarist Randy California. Taken as a whole, *The Silent Corner and the*

Empty Stage is one of the great Hammill albums, an unruly masterpiece from beginning to end, essential listening for anyone with the slightest interest in '70s progressive rock.

The cover was designed by Bettina Hohls, a German artist who had earlier lent her voice to a few songs by Ash Ra Tempel. The front and back covers were visually arresting, but the bizarre design on the inner gatefold was far from in keeping with the music. This was also the first Hammill album to feature his distinctive handwriting on the cover and inner sleeve.

'Modern'

The album kicks off in uncompromising fashion with a dangerous voyage through mythical civilisations. This is the one that illustrates how far Hammill's home studio set-up had developed since *Chameleon*. Recorded entirely at Sofa Sound, the song is a dense patchwork of sound that evokes the lost cities of Jericho, Babylon and Atlantis with ruthless stabs of guitar and frosty clouds of Mellotron. Hammill's voice reaches peaks of declamatory fervour as he rages that 'like the inmates of asylums, all the citizens are contagiously insane.' In a long, ghostly middle section, skeins of acoustic guitar pick their way through desolate harmonium before a mighty riff descends into the final verse. Hammill still performs this song regularly in concert, a testament to its enduring visionary power.

'Wilhelmina'

Hammill, not yet a parent himself, wrote this touching song for the daughter of VdGG drummer Guy Evans. An elegant piano melody glides through the song, making space for softly strummed acoustic guitar, spare touches of Mellotron and what sounds very much like a harpsichord. Hammill sings with deeply felt conviction and a rueful touch of misanthropy, warning that 'people all turn to children, spiteful children, and they're really so cruel.' Many years later, a considerably less jaded Hammill would revisit similar themes on 'Sleep Now' from the album *And Close As This*, this time dedicated to his own young daughters.

'The Lie (Bernini's St. Theresa)'

This incandescently powerful song was inspired by Hammill's time at Beaumont College in Old Windsor, a private school run by Jesuits. Interviewed about the song later, he described his religious education as 'a great confusion of sex and religion… I was into it from the point of view of being in love with all the female saints.' It's hardly surprising, then, that the song also takes inspiration from the Ecstasy of St. Teresa, a sculpture by the Italian sculptor Bernini that can be found in the church of Santa Maria Della Vittoria in Rome. From the transported expression on St. Teresa's face to her bare feet and parted gown, the sculpture is gloriously, transgressively erotic. Hammill sees 'rapture divine, unconscious eyes, the open mouth, the wound of love': a potent sexual charge refracted in the ice-cold marble of Bernini's masterpiece. Meanwhile, the Lie of the title (described by Hammill in the same interview as 'religion in the way that it is presented to you') subsists in the angst-ridden vocal delivery and in the air of tortured melancholy that afflicts the song. Hugh Banton adds devotional organ to the ritualistic knell of Hammill's piano.

'Forsaken Gardens'

Here's an intense, dynamic rocker with an addictive rhythmic drive and one of the most emotive lyrics Hammill ever committed to tape. One of the last songs to be written for the album, it has a tautness and economy which shows the direction in which Hammill's songwriting was heading at this point, away from the baroque richness of songs like '(In the) Black Room' and 'A Louse Is Not A Home' and towards a harder, leaner form of expression. This direction would ultimately lead to the barren forms of the first VdGG reunion album *Godbluff*, and indeed the reformed VdGG would occasionally play 'Forsaken Gardens' in concert (there's a live version on the 2005 *Godbluff* reissue). The song begins as a rapt setting for piano and voice before Jackson and Evans enter around the two-minute mark and blast the song wide open. The saxophonist blows with breathtaking verve and authority; as with VdGG, his skill lies not in soloing but in playing in and around the voice and other instruments, sounding like he is everywhere at once. The song's parting declaration that 'there is so much sorrow in the world, there is so much emptiness and heartbreak and pain' is one of the most upsetting moments in all of Hammill's work.

'Red Shift'

Hammill had studied Liberal Studies in Science at Manchester University, an interdisciplinary degree that aimed to give a broader education in scientific subjects, including sociological, economic, historical and philosophical aspects of science. It's not hard to discern the traces of this education in a song like 'Red Shift', with its disruptive assertion that 'the more that we know, the greater confusion grows.' The song itself is something of an outlier; with its steady, unhurried pace and clever, restrained use of effects, it's as Floydian as Hammill ever got. Jackson adds spaced-out sax to the mix, but the real star is Randy California, whose serpentine solo ushers in Hammill's final, shattering realisation that 'Red Shift is taking away my sanity ... I'm a song in the depths of the galaxies.'

'Rubicon'

A return to home recording, but (as in the case of 'Modern') things were getting more interesting here. Alongside acoustic guitar and voice, we hear the spacey hum of what Hammill described in the sleeve notes of the 2006 reissue as 'a single oscillator, unattached to any kind of synth.' There's also some nice springy bass guitar played by Hammill himself. The song's an unnervingly placid mood piece with an early iteration of a theme to which Hammill would later return on more than one occasion: 'I am a character in the play; the words I slur are pre-ordained, we know them anyway.' Beset by self-doubt and resignation, Hammill's voice drifts unsteadily through the song as though on the verge of exhaustion.

'A Louse Is Not A Home'

This monumental piece began life as a VdGG song, but it has rightly ended up as one of Hammill's most celebrated solo recordings. It's a nightmarish, edge-of-the-seat ride through the cracks of a consciousness that, near to breakdown, finds itself in a house in whose shadows 'lurks the spectre of Despair'. As the song progresses, the consciousness suffers agonising visions of cracked mirrors, moving walls and a faceless watcher before coming to an appalled understanding that 'nothing else exists except the room I'm sitting in.' The Gothic horror of these images recalls VdGG's 'House With No Door'; equally, it anticipates Chris Judge Smith's libretto for Hammill's 1991 opera *The Fall of the House of Usher*, on which the pair had begun working in 1973. The piece unfolds as if in the middle of a tempest, with hellish ensemble passages colliding into eerily quiet hymnal sections. Unleashing wave after wave of vicious imagery into the void, Hammill seems afflicted by some curse, an impression only reinforced by the glee with which he alights on the thrilling melody of the 'what is that but out of and into' and 'is it a sermon or a confession' sections. The group are on fire, with Jackson's malevolent sax coiling like tentacles around Banton's sublime organ and Evans' furious drumming.

Bonus tracks

The 2006 reissue includes live versions of three songs from the album. 'The Lie' is taken from the 1978 *Skeletons of Songs* bootleg, a real high-wire solo performance. 'Rubicon' and 'Red Shift', meanwhile, are taken from a 1974 Peel session, with Hammill accompanied by David Jackson on flute and sax, respectively.

23

In Camera (1974)

Personnel:
Peter Hammill: vocals, guitar, piano, Mellotron, harmonium, bass guitar, synthesizer
Guy Evans: drums
Chris Judge Smith: backing vocals, percussion
Paul Whitehead: percussion
David Hentschel: ARP programming
All songs by Peter Hammill
Recorded at Sofa Sound, Sussex and Trident Studios, London, December 1973–April 1974
Produced by Peter Hammill
UK release date: July 1974
Cover: Frank Sansom and Peter Hammill
Photography: Mike van der Vord

By the turn of 1973, Hammill had already recorded and released one exceptional album that year and had another one in the can. This astonishing burst of creativity showed no signs of abating as he embarked on the set of recordings that would become *In Camera*. What sets this album apart from *Chameleon* and *Silent Corner* is that while those albums contained significant elements of band recording, *In Camera* was an almost entirely solo endeavour. VdGG had split up the previous year and, despite the appearance of Banton, Jackson and Evans on both *Chameleon* and *Silent Corner*, there didn't seem to be any immediate prospect of the group reforming. As Hammill writes on his website, it was 'time to get serious about solo recording.'

Hammill laid down the backing tracks – guitar, bass and piano – at Sofa Sound and then decamped to Trident to overdub vocals, synthesizer and Evans' drums. The synthesizer, in particular, is worthy of note since this represents the first appearance of such an animal on a Hammill album (although Banton had used one on *Pawn Hearts*). 1973 had seen the release and global success of Pink Floyd's *The Dark Side of the Moon*, which included the dramatic use of an EMS synth on the track 'On The Run'. Nor can Hammill have been unaware of Tangerine Dream's *Phaedra*, released to great acclaim in February 1974, not to mention Brian Eno's use of the VCS3 synth on the first two Roxy Music albums. It's not surprising, therefore, that Hammill chose to incorporate a synthesizer (albeit an ARP, not an EMS) into several songs on the album. The ARP was programmed at Trident by engineer David Hentschel, later to forge a successful partnership with Genesis as their producer.

At this point in his career, Hammill was still reaching back into his past and finding songs that he had not yet perfected. 'Ferret & Featherbird' had been written as far back as 1969, while 'Tapeworm' dated from 1971. Otherwise, the songs were written in the studio, a methodology that would serve Hammill well on later albums.

In his sleeve notes to the 2006 reissue, Hammill notes that 'the stretch of style and subject matter on this CD is extreme.' Certainly, there's a wide range of approaches here, from the zesty riffage of 'Tapeworm' to the seething cauldron that is 'Gog', from the plaintive cry of 'Again' to the dense *musique concrète* of 'Magog (in Bromine Chambers)'. Yet despite the variety of styles on offer, the overriding impression is one of introspection. The soundworld is arid and enclosed, a reflection of the album's gestation as a purely solo project. Not an easy Hammill album by any means, but an important one nonetheless.

'Ferret & Featherbird'

This opening track was, Hammill relates in his notes to the album on his website, 'a late entrant to the lists ... something approaching a 'sweet' song was needed to balance the other stuff.' Indeed the vibe here is very different from the rest of the album, the song being a tender ballad that wistfully recalls how 'distance came between us long ago', only to conclude on the strangely hopeful note that 'time and distance make a love secure.' The song had been written as early as 1969, and an earlier version had been cut at the sessions for the début VdGG album *The Aerosol Grey Machine*. The double-tracked vocals are striking, there's a poignant quality to Hammill's voice that entirely fits the mood, and there's a rare glimpse of lap steel guitar threading its way delicately through the song.

'No More (The Sub-Mariner)'

Growing up as a boy in the late 1950s, Hammill (a sports fan to this day) would have been well aware of the sporting achievements of British racing driver Stirling Moss and England cricket captain Peter May. Equally, he would have been aware of (and may even have read the adventures of) Namor the Sub-Mariner, a fictional anti-hero from the world of Marvel comics. These diverse references to popular culture form the backdrop to 'No More (The Sub-Mariner)', a pulsating track powered by sonorous piano and needling stabs of synthesizer. Hammill's voice swoops demonically around the remnants of his childhood memories, raging at the loss of certainty and the approach of doubt that comes with adulthood. In a finely wrought middle section, choral vocals ascend from tolling piano and luminous washes of synth, adding to the sense of nervous hesitation that haunts the song.

'Tapeworm'

Something of a relief from the austere soundworld of most of the album, this gleeful cut sees Hammill rock out more brazenly than he had on any previous track bar 'Rock and Role' from *Chameleon*. Anticipating the strident proto-punk of his next album *Nadir's Big Chance*, Hammill has enormous fun even as he senses he's in the throes of 'devilish leanings' from which he's 'beginning to lose control.' An insistent piano riff ushers in blaring electric guitar and rasping, nihilistic vocals, while Evans' powerhouse drumming drives the song relentlessly forward. The goofy *a cappella* section in the middle represents a rare lapse into foolishness from the normally impeccably tasteful Hammill.

'Again'

A harsh and bitter dissection of a failed relationship, 'Again' is one of Hammill's saddest, most tragic love songs. A sense of abject defeat hangs over the song, limned by broken acoustic guitar chords and coils of lowering bass. Hammill's traumatised voice struggles for a glimmer of hope among the memory of a lover's picture and the lingering scent of her perfume; finding none, he is left with no choice but to lament the passing of 'what will never come again.' Hammill's concerts occasionally end with him singing this *a cappella*; if you're lucky enough to catch one of these and it leaves you unmoved, you might want to check that your heart's still beating.

'Faint-Heart and the Sermon'

Here's a kind of sequel to 'The Lie', with Hammill brooding darkly on the prospect of religious enlightenment when 'the end is nowhere in sight.' Characteristically, no definitive conclusion is drawn, except to acknowledge 'the conflict raging between my head and my brain.' This is weighty stuff, and the instrumentation is appropriately severe: synthesised cello gives way to wintry electronic tones and glacial Mellotron shifts, all of it held in check by the processional tempo of the song. Like a few other solo PH songs from this period, this song had an afterlife as a VdGG number, being regularly performed by the group during 1975.

'The Comet, the Course, the Tail'

In 1973, a comet called Kohoutek was visible in the night sky for the first time in 150,000 years. (If you missed it, don't worry; it'll be back in 75,000 years.) The appearance of Kohoutek inspired Hammill to write 'The Comet, the Course, the Tail', another song he has revisited many times over the years in different live settings. Hammill wasn't the only artist to have been inspired by Kohoutek – Kraftwerk, Sun Ra and Argent all recorded their own tributes to the visiting celestial body – but his was the only one to be conceived of as a guitar quartet, with acoustic, electric, twelve-string and bass all contributing to the sense of astral space that underpins the song. Hammill's text speculates vividly on what he calls 'the founding questions': whether belief in a social order is compatible with concepts of individual autonomy and free will, and whether the notion that 'I am my own direction' has value in the context of a world in which, as Hammill acidly points out, 'all corpses smell the same.'

'Gog'

In a crowded field, this gets my vote for Hammill's most oppressive and extreme song. Over seven-and-a-half minutes of blasted imagery, deathly shrieks and malicious incantations, the song conjures an atmosphere of pure evil: as Hammill writes on his website, this is 'wild, swirling, edge-of-control stuff.' In Christian eschatology, Gog and Magog are the tribes gathered together by Satan for the final battle with the forces of good (Revelation 20:8). In Hammill's fevered reimagining, Gog is recast as 'a God who just doesn't care': an infernal being whose evil presence stretches from ancient Rome to the bloody fields of World War I. The song is hewn from vast, looming slabs of harmonium from which Hammill's vocals descend into black-hearted chaos, while Evans adds drumbeats to chill the bones. Gog's wicked urgings and frenzied invocations echo that other great conjuring of the end times, Yeats' 'The Second Coming', in which 'the blood-dimmed tide is loosed, and everywhere the ceremony of innocence is drowned'.

'Magog (in Bromine Chambers)'
The album ends with ten minutes of *musique concrète*: a brief, unsettling song fragment, indistinct rumbles, lurching drones and nerve-jangling, skeletal percussion. In later years Hammill would release whole albums' worth of experimental music (*Loops and Reels*, *Sonix*, *Unsung*), all of which sit some distance apart from his main run of song-based albums. But in the more open times of the early 1970s, and with the backing of a fully supportive label in Charisma, there was no problem in Hammill devoting almost a quarter of *In Camera*'s running time to a track like 'Magog'. The piece is a dark and scary assemblage of sounds, clearly influenced by the likes of early innovators such as Pierre Schaeffer and Luc Ferrari but a long way from being derivative of their work. As Hammill writes in the sleeve notes, the piece is 'tensely structured ... shimmering tension is the main game.' The piece reaches a kind of climax at around the eight-minute mark, as a doomy bass drone cuts out and gives way to murky, irradiated static.

Bonus tracks
The 2006 reissue includes solo versions of 'Faint-Heart and the Sermon', 'No More (the Sub-Mariner)' and the VdGG track 'The Emperor in his War-Room', all taken from a 1974 Peel session.

Nadir's Big Chance (1975)

Personnel:
Peter Hammill: vocals, guitar, piano, keyboards, bass
Hugh Banton: bass, organ, piano
David Jackson: saxophones, flute
Guy Evans: drums
All songs by Peter Hammill, except where noted
Recorded at Rockfield Studios, Monmouth, 1–7 December 1974
Produced by Peter Hammill
UK release date: February 1975
Cover: Peter Hammill

By the time Hammill, Jackson, Banton and Evans got together at Rockfield to cut the songs that would form *Nadir's Big Chance*, they had already made the decision to reform VdGG. There was a kind of urgency about the sessions, a feeling of clearing the decks prior to launching into a new phase of group activity. Whereas it had taken Hammill two months to record *Silent Corner* and three to record *In Camera*, the follow-up was laid down in just a week – a sure indication of where Hammill's thinking lay at the time.

Of course, the material also lent itself easily to a quick turnaround since Hammill had never written a set of songs like this before. *Fool's Mate* had been an essentially retrospective collection of mostly lighter material, and songs like 'Rock and Role' and 'Tapeworm' had highlighted Hammill's desire to forego the strictures of progressive rock in favour of a more elemental approach. But here, from out of nowhere, was something new – an album's worth of what Hammill accurately described in his original sleeve notes as 'the beefy punk songs, the weepy ballads, the soul struts', all sung by his *alter ego*, the 'loud, aggressive perpetual sixteen-year-old', Rikki Nadir.

The story is by now well known of how John Lydon of the Sex Pistols appeared on a radio show at the height of punk in 1977 and played two songs from *Nadir*, hailing Hammill as 'great, a true original'. As a result, Hammill has gone down in history as one of the few progressive rock musicians to have escaped the opprobrium of punk, and *Nadir* itself has often been cited as an *ur*-text of punk rock. What is less often remarked upon is that *Nadir* has clear antecedents of its own. The insistent throb of Hawkwind looms large, as does the reckless abandon of the Stooges' *Raw Power* and MC5's *Back In The USA*. Nor can one readily dismiss the influence of Bowie, both in Hammill's adoption of the Nadir persona and in the smart, inventive hooks that litter the album.

It's also worth noting that *Nadir* was not alone in its adoption of proto-punk tendencies at this time. It's interesting to compare the album to Neu!'s *Neu! 75*, recorded and released at almost exactly the same time as *Nadir*. Side two of *Neu! 75* contains three long songs that radiate the same kind of stroppy energy as we find on *Nadir*. In particular, the classic 'Hero' sees

Klaus Dinger sing in very Hammillesque tones about someone who is 'just another hero riding through the night.' Dinger's anti-hero is a kindred spirit of Rikki Nadir, particularly when he shouts 'f*ck the press, f*ck the program, f*ck the company.'

As for *Nadir*'s supposed influence, Hammill said it best in the sleeve notes to the 2006 reissue: 'if any influence was passed on, it was in the area of 'Attitude' rather than music.' Certainly, of the album's eleven songs, only three have an overtly punky feel to them. Indeed this is probably Hammill's most soulful album, thick with sensitive guitar work and with Jackson's emotive sax a strong presence throughout. Lyrically, Hammill is at his most direct and communicative here, lending the album a wit and verve not often associated with the man. However, a note on the inner sleeve stated that there was no lyric sheet available on the grounds that 'de songs don' suit'. They were finally published in Hammill's second book of lyrics, *Mirrors, Dreams, and Miracles*, in 1982.

The reference to 'beefy punk songs' was remarkably prescient. The word had been used to describe a style of music as early as 1970, but only in the USA. The Oxford English Dictionary's first recorded use of the word as a musical term in the UK was in the 'New Musical Express' in February 1976, in a Sex Pistols live review ('a quartet of spiky teenage misfits ... playing '60s-styled white punk rock'). But *Nadir's Big Chance* was released in February 1975. Hammill had got there first.

'Nadir's Big Chance'

A rock-solid guitar intro, a chugging sax riff, an exuberant 'one, two, three, four' and we're off, pitched headfirst into the anarchic presence of Rikki Nadir. As he makes clear in the lyric, Nadir is no fan of glam rock and its 'jerks in their tinsel glitter suits', who were at the height of their popularity in late 1974. In their place, Nadir suggests an alternative: to 'bang your feet in a rage ... smash the system with the song.' The action proposed seems not only attractive but imperative, given the sheer gusto with which Hammill sings and thrashes out the chords to this nihilistic anthem. Yet there's a fierce musical intelligence at work here too, evident in the abrasive blasts of lap steel and in the way Jackson's sax lurks manically at every corner.

'The Institute of Mental Health, Burning' (Hammill, Smith)

The lyric to this song was penned by Hammill's VdGG co-founder Chris Judge Smith; according to the sleeve notes to the 2006 reissue, the duo used to play the song in the early days of the group at Manchester University. Like many of Smith's songs (*cf.* 'Imperial Zeppelin', 'Viking'), it's an oddity, especially when set against the deconstructive mood of most of the album. Its presence here feels unearned due to its footling text (apparently inspired by actual life events) and lumbering sense of rhythm. The scrappy instrumentation, including, for some reason, backmasked piano, doesn't exactly help matters either.

29

'Open Your Eyes'

Subtitled 'The Locarno Song' on the inner sleeve, this insanely catchy slice of reminiscence skips along on a bed of zany organ from Banton and a mesmerising saxophone outro by Jackson. Hammill sings in an unusual register for him, all wide-eyed bravado and wounded pride. The Locarno in question was a nightspot in Derby, a regular haunt of Hammill's in the mid-1960s and one deliciously evoked by the usherette's fishnet tights and knowing smile. In the sleeve notes to the 2006 reissue, Hammill explains that this is another resurrected old song, written on a Hammond organ belonging to the occultist Graham Bond. Thankfully, perhaps, little of Bond's eccentricity found its way into the song, which remains one of the most purely enjoyable Hammill ever wrote.

'Nobody's Business'

It's rare to find anything as conventional as a chorus in a Peter Hammill song, so it's hardly surprising that when he does drop one in, he puts his own particular spin on it. The chorus of this snotty cut is twice as long as the verses, adding to the deliriously lopsided vibe of the song. The lyric is a rather nasty tirade against a 'tired and forlorn' girl who 'used to care about her smile and not her face.' Jackson's jazzy, almost funky sax breaks and Evans' hyperefficient drumming steer the song into fairly choppy waters, while Hammill whoops it up in considerable style with his echo-drenched vocals and air of casual insouciance.

'Been Alone So Long' (Chris Judge Smith)

This time Chris Judge Smith plays it straight, and in doing so, gifts Hammill a perfect love song. When Nadir refers to 'weepy ballads' in the sleeve notes, it's presumably this and 'Shingle Song' that he has in mind. Ever the iconoclast, Nadir's offhand dismissal does a disservice to the beauty and intimacy of this song, and to the way it shines a hesitant light on the clumsy uncertainty of a relationship's early stages. The protagonist is touchingly reluctant, despite mounting evidence to the contrary, to believe that there really is a girl 'breathing peacefully' in bed next to him. There's a raw sensitivity to Hammill's voice, complemented beautifully by plangent acoustic guitar chords. But it's Jackson's closing sax solo, laced with empathy and sadness, that lifts the song into the realms of the unforgettable.

'Pompeii'

Here's a real curio: a musical setting of a poem Hammill wrote in his teens in memory of those who died and are preserved in the ruined city of Pompeii. We're a long way from the spirit of Nadir, but on the other hand, this is one of four examples on the LP of Hammill's habit of returning to old material that he had not previously recorded to his satisfaction – or, in this case, not recorded at all. The lyric bears a clear debt to the poetry of Thomas Hardy, but I love

Hardy, so that's OK. Hammill's grave tone is framed by some lovely chiming electric guitar and quicksilver sax, but the most lasting impression is left by Evans' wondrous percussion, all fluidity and elegance among the ruins.

'Shingle Song'

If 'Been Alone So Long' depicted the doubt and hesitancy of a nascent relationship, 'Shingle Song' takes up the story at the end of the romance, with all its early promise in tatters. Like the earlier 'Again', this song renders lost love in terms of utter helplessness, the deserted shoreline a stark metaphor for abandonment and rejection. Not for the first time or the last, Hammill shows an unerring eye for memorably filmic description: there's something Bergmanesque about the image of a man standing alone on a beach, his head bowed, looking for his lover but finding her 'forever out of reach'. Hammill's vocals wring every shred of emotion from the text, his guitar playing is a sober delight, and Jackson's elegiac sax adds to the lovelorn mood of the song.

'Airport'

A quirky little number, described by Hammill in the 2006 sleeve notes as 'pretty flippant ... a decent toon.' Structurally, this bears comparison to 'Nobody's Business' in that the chorus is twice as long as the verses, giving the song a plaintive tone boosted by Hammill's artless vocal and Jackson's unobtrusive sax. In 1974 there was still a certain novelty and even glamour attached to air travel, leaving Nadir powerless but to gaze sadly at 'the tail-smoke of the Boeing jet' that's taking the girl away from him. Fraught with dejection and loneliness, Nadir walks away alone, trailed by the song's downbeat melody and restrained guitar work.

'People You Were Going To'

Another old song revisited, this dates back to Manchester University in 1967. An earlier version was cut as the A-side of the first-ever VdGG single in 1969, but this version knocks it out of the park with sumptuous organ work by Banton, spirited sax by Jackson and a stunning vocal/instrumental outro that provides one of the album's most sublimely poppy moments. This is the third track in a row about lost or unrequited love, so if you're not feeling sorry for Nadir yet, you should probably start now.

'Birthday Special'

Nadir's proto-punk tendency reaches its apex here, with a rollicking blast of a tune that's cooking on gas mark 9. In many interviews over the years, Hammill has extolled the virtues of thrashing out three chords on an electric guitar, which is what always set him apart from other figures in the world of progressive rock. Certainly, I can't think of another artist who could have recorded two songs as far apart as 'Gog' and 'Birthday Special' within a year. Listen to the rowdy vigour with which Hammill sings and plays, and you can hear the elegance and refinement of prog being flung off with every impassioned power chord. By the way, the lyric quoted in *Mirrors, Dreams, and Miracles* renders a line in the second verse as the meaningless 'there's bloaters in the bathroom', whereas I'm fairly certain that what Nadir actually sings is 'there's floaters in the bathroom'. And if you don't know what a floater is, count yourself lucky.

'Two or Three Spectres'

A snatch of studio chatter from Banton kicks off the last song on the album: 'Oh, why didn't you say? More Stevie Wonder!' Bang on cue, the organist launches into a funky, burbling tune that sees a rare excursion into bass guitar territory from Hammill, who, according to the 2006 sleeve notes, wrote the song entirely on bass. Jackson lays down some pretty funky grooves himself on sax, and Evans joins in the fun with dashing syncopated rhythms. The lyric's a barely controlled rant against the more unsavoury aspects of the music industry, full of barbed humour and funny, clever putdowns. The closing line about 'ten thousand peace signs, but they're different from the back' is a trifle obscure, the idea being that a peace sign (two fingers raised), when viewed from behind, is a 'f**k off' gesture. And with that thought, Nadir leaves us, as anarchic and temperamental as when he began.

Over (1977)

Personnel:
Peter Hammill: vocals, guitar, piano, keyboards
Graham Smith: violin
Nic Potter: bass
Guy Evans: drums
All songs by Peter Hammill
Recorded at Foel Studio, Llanfair Caereinion and Rockfield Studios, Monmouth,
June-July 1976
Produced by Peter Hammill
UK release date: April 1977
Cover: Frank Sansom
Photography: Sebastian Keep

A lot happened in the world of Peter Hammill between the release of *Nadir's Big Chance* and that of its follow-up, *Over*. In the first place, Van der Graaf Generator reformed and released three albums: *Godbluff* (October 1975), *Still Life* (April 1976) and *World Record* (October 1976). But the classic line-up of the group was not to last, and both organist Hugh Banton and saxophonist David Jackson departed the band in quick succession. The new line-up, which would convene in May 1977 to record *The Quiet Zone/The Pleasure Dome*, included violinist Graham Smith and returning bassist Nic Potter alongside Hammill and drummer Guy Evans. This new incarnation of Van der Graaf should have come as no surprise since the same line-up had already cut *Over* at Foel Studio in June 1976. *Over*, then, was something of a dry run for Van der Graaf, even though the four musicians were never in a room together during the Foel sessions.

The other major turn of events was, of course, that Hammill broke up with his long-time girlfriend Alice, a traumatic split that inspired several songs on the album. To his credit Hammill has never sought to mystify or depersonalise *Over*, referring to it in the sleeve notes to the 2006 reissue as 'my 'break-up' album'. Indeed, as a break-up record, it stands alone with Dylan's *Blood on the Tracks*, the only other LP that depicts the end of a romance with such gravity, but which suffers in comparison with *Over* thanks to Dylan's habitual myth-making and obfuscation. For Hammill, by contrast, it was essential that the songs be truthful and honest accounts of the events that gave rise to them and the emotions they precipitated. As he writes in the sleeve notes, 'if I was to consider myself something of a songwriter, then I could hardly avoid documenting my feelings.' Having given full rein to his Gothic imagination on *Chameleon*, *Silent Corner* and *In Camera*, and created an entire persona on *Nadir*, it was time for Hammill to step out of the shadows and present his true face to the world.

Over is a key text for Hammill, and indeed it's always been my favourite of all his albums. It's essential listening, not only for its brutal emotional honesty but because it strikes the perfect balance between the different musical approaches he has adopted over the years. Progressive ambition, scarred balladry, stinging punk rawness – it's all here in *Over*, the harrowing pinnacle of Hammill's songwriting genius.

The evocative cover photo by Sebastian Keep shows a calm, autumnally lit Hammill with only a guitar and a roll-up for company. The guitar, incidentally, is Hammill's black Guild, the subject of the VdGG song 'Meurglys III, The Songwriter's Guild'.

'Crying Wolf'

Hammill had a very clear idea of how he wanted to structure *Over* for maximum impact and truthfulness. The bleakest of the songs – those 'written from within the eye of the storm', as he puts it in the sleeve notes – were to form the core of the record, bookended on either side by other cuts that would provide a certain amount of context and even a touch of optimism. 'Crying Wolf' is the first of these, a livid rush of a song with furious drumming by Evans and incendiary vocals from Hammill. The song's a stern caution against taking the railing to come at face value, noting that 'when you've raised your last howl … you'll be left a lonely man.' But it's also a fantastic opening number, driven by a thermonuclear riff, an anthemic chorus and stylish harmony vocals that effortlessly evoke the spirit of Rikki Nadir.

'Autumn'

This is a desperately sad song, Ozu's *Tokyo Story* set to music. The characters are parents whose grown-up children have left home and are 'living their own lives', leaving the parents feeling 'discarded, of no further use.' This bleak scenario is played out with great sensitivity by Hammill and Smith, whose violin hovers and descends oppressively around Hammill's sorrowful vocals. Parenthood is a subject Hammill has addressed a few times (*cf*. 'Wilhelmina', 'Sleep Now', 'Once You Called Me'), but here, in the context of *Over*, it represents what Hammill describes in the sleeve notes as 'an alternative future … lacking in unbounded joy and celebration'.

'Time Heals'

Here's another example of Hammill reaching back into the past and bringing old material back to life. Although the lyric seems to fit the autobiographical nature of the album, the bulk of it was actually written at Worth in 1972 and had been published in Hammill's first book *Killers, Angels, Refugees*. The longest track on the album, it seems to anticipate the resolution of 'Lost and Found', finding some consolation in 'thinking back' and realizing that 'it's all just song lines'. Still, there's an inner turmoil here that's reflected in the song's ragged structure, shifting time signatures and sharp, fizzing synth tones.

'Alice (Letting Go)'

The only point on the record where Hammill's lost love is mentioned by name, this is a strung-out *tour de force* of bare-wired emotion. Structured around a merciless acoustic guitar riff, it seems to portray the relationship as an addiction from which Hammill is painfully withdrawing, every struck note a knot of agonised nerve-endings. The song remorselessly tracks every flicker of emotional anguish, leading Hammill to question his very *raison d'être* as a songwriter: 'What's the good of songs anyway? They're just exercises in solitude.' Crushed by self-doubt, still clutching at what little hope remains, by the song's end Hammill's voice has ebbed away in tremors of weakness and loss.

'This Side of the Looking-Glass'

Described by Hammill in the 2006 sleeve notes as 'the centrepiece song', this swooning orchestral piece provides a sombre counterpoint to the brimming anger and jealousy of the preceding and following songs. Drawing on the 19th-century Romantic tradition, the lyric places Hammill alone against the vastness of the night sky, the tragic hero lost in contemplation of his break-up. This turn towards the infinite, in stark contrast to the extreme solipsism of the narrator, is depicted in gorgeous strains of brass, strings and woodwind, arranged for orchestra by the composer and conductor Michael Brand. This is one of the great Hammill vocal performances, his rich baritone occasionally modulating into a higher register and investing every syllable with tragic intensity.

'Betrayed'

The blackest of the album's songs, 'Betrayed' illustrates the paradox of *Over*: that although events have led Hammill to declare in nihilistic terms that 'I don't believe in anything anywhere in the world', he does so in bursts of righteous anger and self-belief. From the way he sings here, every sinew and fibre stretched and taut, it certainly sounds like he believes in *something*. It's an impression reinforced in the text by Hammill's obsessive focus on a particularly virulent set of terms – revenge, spite, bitterness, worthlessness, contempt. Smith's wild, disturbed violin slashes its way through Hammill's guitar, its vertiginous presence crucial to the draining impact of the song.

'(On Tuesdays She Used To Do) Yoga'

After the harrowing 'Betrayed', it's almost a relief to step into a seemingly tranquil domestic set-up, with one partner slumped in front of the TV while the other is out at her yoga class. But of course, things don't turn out too well, with hints of infidelity ('though I'd cheat, I never lied'), bitter remorse ('too late now to say that I'm so sorry') and the eventual departure of Hammill's lover. That said, there's a perceptible lightening of the mood here, as Hammill recognises his own self-pity and humorously imagines himself in yogic contortions. This Pinteresque mini-drama is played out against a muted soundtrack of echoing vox, silvery lute (an instrument given to Hammill by the late Tony Stratton Smith, founder of the Charisma label) and dark washes of synthesizer.

'Lost and Found'

This epic of recovery and resolution acts as a kind of catharsis, as defined by Aristotle: a release of emotional tension after an overwhelming vicarious experience. There's certainly a sense of relief here, as Hammill is finally able to take a step back from the trauma of the break-up and look forward to a future in which he is 'free at last.' The music resolves into gentler tones for the first time, underpinned by Potter's fluent bass and Evans' prodigious drumming. A choppy middle section sees La Rossa, the siren beauty of the VdGG song from *Still Life*, make a guest appearance before Hammill lays down what is probably his best ever guitar solo. Hammill has never claimed to be more than a technically proficient guitarist, but here the solo fits the song perfectly, its notes wreathed in delay and sustain. The lengthy outro is an emotive end to the album, with pulsing currents of guitar framing dreamy falsetto vocals. The surprising reference to Tommy Tucker's 1964 hit 'Hi-Heel Sneakers' glows with promise and sex appeal, a hopeful glimpse of the future that is only partly undermined by the question mark at the end of the last line: 'everything's going to be ... all right?'

Bonus tracks

The 2006 reissue includes Peel session versions of 'Betrayed' and 'Autumn' with Graham Smith from 1977, plus a 1978 live solo recording of 'This Side of the Looking-Glass' taken from the essential *Skeletons of Songs* bootleg.

The Future Now (1978)

Personnel:
Peter Hammill: vocals, guitar, piano, keyboards, synthesizer, harmonica
Graham Smith: violin
David Jackson: saxophone
All songs by Peter Hammill
Recorded at Sofa Sound, Byfleet, Surrey, March-April 1978
Produced by Peter Hammill
UK release date: September 1978
Cover: Barney Bubbles
Photography: Brian Griffin

What a strange, brave record this is – aside from his run of purely experimental albums (*Loops and Reels*, *Sonix*, *Unsung*), probably the most unconventional-sounding album Hammill has ever made. By the spring of 1978, when *The Future Now* was recorded, Van der Graaf were on the verge of breaking up again; unsurprisingly, therefore, Hammill began to rethink his strategy as a solo artist. As he writes in the notes to the album on his website, he 'began to map out an alternative, solo, way of working which, while 'serious', did not bow to or, indeed, make any reference to, the work and style of the group.'

In other words, there is little here to mark out Hammill as a progressive rock artist. Instead, I prefer to view *The Future Now* in the context of the first wave of British post-punk that emerged in 1978, alongside such albums as Wire's *Chairs Missing*, Magazine's *Real Life* and Public Image Ltd's self-titled début. Like those records, *The Future Now* took its cue from punk and went beyond, incorporating elements of noise, electronic music, an emphasis on rhythm and unconventional production techniques, to say nothing of brevity (nothing here goes over the five-minute mark) and a heightened sense of social awareness and injustice on several songs.

The range of approaches adopted by Hammill on *The Future Now* is remarkable, from full-on rock songs to anguished ballads via agitated chants and tape loop experiments. Back in 1974, as we saw in the chapter on *In Camera*, Hammill was already producing work with what he would later describe as an 'extreme stretch of style and subject matter'. However, the different styles were still by and large being separated on a track-by-track basis. In 1978 the diversity of approaches remained, but the *concrète* elements were being folded into what could accurately be described as songs. As Hammill wrote in the sleeve notes to the 2006 reissue, the trio of experimental songs on side two 'broke through some kind of mental barrier I'd previously maintained, which separated concrete music from songs. From this point on, I was happy to mix them up together.'

The Future Now was recorded in a cold rented house in Byfleet, Surrey in the space of just over a month. Hammill worked alone for the most part, with only Graham Smith and David Jackson for company on several tracks. He had various instruments at his disposal, ranging from a grand piano to guitars, a synthesizer and a drum machine. The album was recorded to eight-track analogue, described by Hammill as 'noisy and chunky, but pretty reliable'. No studio overdubs this time, which may help to account for the wonky, unvarnished soundworld of the album, much of which still sounds as though it was beamed down from another planet.

'Pushing Thirty'
Rikki Nadir lives! This barnstorming opener is a kind of sequel to 'Two or Three Spectres', with the line in the earlier song about 'groupies offer their bodies, the hangers-on their coke' brought up-to-date: the one-liners are 'the kind that get up everyone's nose', while Nadir himself is now 'pulling sixteen'. Elsewhere the down-to-earth British musician Nick Lowe, who had been in the VdGG orbit in the early 1970s and was, like Hammill himself, pushing thirty at the time of the album's release, is playfully contrasted with the actor and icon of pop-cultural cool, David Hemmings. And since Hemmings' name conveniently rhymes with 'lemmings', the title of a classic VdGG song, the reference was obviously too hard to resist. Hammill's barrelhouse piano and Jackson's wailing sax lend the song a hard, almost Stonesy feel.

'The Second Hand'
The angular, post-punk vibe of the album really starts to kick in here, with this arid number on the subject of time. Hammill's subject is an 'old man acting like a fool' whose life seems to have gone on longer than he had bargained for. Faced with gradual physical and mental deterioration, there's nothing for it but to await the inevitable. Mythological and speculative references litter the text – King Canute, Excalibur, Count Dracula – yet Hammill's vocal remains resolutely calm and controlled, while the steady pulse of the drum machine is disrupted by Jackson's gritty saxophone.

'Trappings'
'Fill in whatever superstar takes your fancy here', writes Hammill on his website. Indeed the subject of the song is a generic celebrity, probably a rock star or actor, who finds himself 'a prisoner in a gilded cage', on his own, with no home or friends. A year or so later, Pink Floyd's *The Wall* would tackle similar themes in a more expansive and justly celebrated fashion. For Hammill, the problem boils down to the question of why the subject 'still said yes ... to the trappings of success' when 'he could have had it all'. Taking its cue from Van der Graaf's guitar-heavy *The Quiet Zone/The Pleasure Dome*, the guitar looms large here, with deft acoustic buttressed by ebow electric (its first appearance of several on this album). There's also a good deal of layered backing vocals, a technique that Hammill was to make ever more frequent use of as time wore on.

'The Mousetrap (Caught In)'

The Mousetrap is the longest-running play in the history of London's West End, running continuously from 1952 until 2020. Small wonder, then, that Hammill invokes it in the title of this perfectly judged song depicting the *ennui* of a stage actor doomed to repeat his lines over and over again. But as Hammill writes on his website, 'evidently I was talking about a singer as much as an actor', a parallel made explicit by the line 'in the third act of this twenty-ninth year of the show'. Hammill was, of course, in his 29th year when he recorded the song, and he changes the number to reflect his current age when he sings the song live. The lyric is one of Hammill's most moving and poetic, and he brings great empathy to the role, his solemn voice accompanied only by distant piano and vibrant synthesizer.

'Energy Vampires'

The first of a couple of PH songs taking aim at a certain type of over-zealous fan (see also VdGG's 'Nutter Alert' and the story 'Audi' in *Killers, Angels, Refugees*), this nervous, fidgety tune skates around on a surface of inflamed guitar and Graham Smith's lurching violin. Hammill is at pains to point out on his website that the phrase 'energy vampires' does not refer to fans in general, but to a particular kind of follower, those who 'want to steal my vitality ... want to drink it all'. Tautly experimental in tone, constructed from a succession of multi-track tape edits, 'Energy Vampires' is the sound of Hammill warping the pop song out of all recognition.

'If I Could'

Has any songwriter ever written more poignantly about the end of love than Hammill? Having anatomised heartbreak so affectingly on 'Again' and 'Shingle Song', not to mention the entire *Over* album, here Hammill captures the stomach-churning moment when a relationship begins to falter and fail. There are no sadder lines in all of Hammill's work than 'may my voice fall into silence if my words turn out to be lies', but the whole song is a grim litany of silence and lost connections. Smith's mournful violin tracks Hammill's grave lead vocal through the bleak terrain of the song.

'The Future Now'

This masterful song packs an enormous amount of fire and incident into just over four minutes. Along with 'Mediaevil' and 'A Motor-Bike in Afrika', it marked the first time Hammill had taken an overtly political position in song, another indication of the way his work at this time fitted squarely within the context of post-punk. The song shows Hammill as a visionary, an idealist, but one whose dreams are firmly grounded in reality: *prenez vos désirs pour la réalité*, as the French agitators of May 1968 had put it. The catalogue of injustice – 'oppression and torture, apartheid, corruption and plague' – is, sadly, just as relevant and pressing now as it was in 1978. Stung by haunted piano and menacing ebow guitar, there's a coiled tension to the song that escapes from every syllable of Hammill's damning, outraged vocal.

'Still in the Dark'

'The more that we know, the greater confusion grows', Hammill had written on 'Red Shift' from 1973's *The Silent Corner and the Empty Stage*. Five years later, he was still tracing the limitations of the scientific method on this knotty little piece animated by buzzing ebow and frozen synth tones. This is one of those quietly reflective songs that Hammill does so well, steeped in philosophical speculation yet lyrically accessible and profoundly tuneful.

'Mediaevil'

This and the next two songs form a 'truly experimental triad', according to Hammill's website notes on the album. The odd title is not, of course, a typo for 'mediaeval', although it was treated as such and wrongly 'corrected' by some craven proofreader at Virgin for the 2006 reissue. It's actually a portmanteau word combining 'media' and 'evil'; 'a different power now holds sway ... now we follow the pundits on TV', as the lyric puts it. Hammill also takes caustic aim at organised religion and its complicity in a world where 'those who are rich are still getting richer/and those who are poor still foot the bill'. This is trenchant stuff, sculpted out of magisterial lead vox, choral backing vocals and stabbing shards of synth.

'A Motor-Bike in Afrika'

Hammill's friend and occasional collaborator Peter Gabriel came to global attention in 1980 with 'Biko', a eulogy for the murdered South African anti-apartheid activist Steve Biko. It brings no satisfaction, but is still worthy of note to point out that Hammill had referenced Biko and apartheid two years earlier in this angry collage of tape edits, dense rhythms and synthesized noise. Hammill is not in the mood to mince words, raging against 'racial war in Africa today' as the music casts long shadows evoking slow torture and death.

'The Cut'

This one is a real enigma: one of Hammill's most opaque and puzzling lyrics, delivered in a half-spoken, half-sung voice that we've never heard from him before. The cryptic text, seeming to play on different meanings of the word 'cut', drifts along on a bed of hammering acoustic guitar, backmasked tapes and spectral ebow lines. The last minute and a half are given over to an astonishing chorale of discordant, juddering noise, dissolving into woozy synth sounds and then to silence.

'Palinurus (Castaway)'

In Roman mythology, Palinurus is a navigator and the helmsman of Aeneas' ship. Hammill focuses on the part of the myth in which Palinurus, who is to be sacrificed to the gods, falls overboard and spends four days at sea before being washed ashore and killed. The song forms a sober, meditative finale to the album, with ghostly piano and synthesizer shadowing Hammill's darkly expressive voice. There's even a touch of harmonica, the only time Hammill has ever played it on record.

Bonus tracks

The 2006 reissue includes live solo recordings of 'If I Could' and 'The Mousetrap (Caught In)', both taken from the *Skeletons of Songs* bootleg.

pH7 (1979)

Personnel:
Peter Hammill: vocals, guitar, piano, keyboards, bass, drums, drum machine
Graham Smith: violin
David Jackson: saxophone, flute
All songs by Peter Hammill, except where noted
Recorded at Sofa Sound, Wiltshire, spring 1979
Produced by Peter Hammill
UK release date: September 1979
Cover: Rocking Russian
Photography: Daniel Kirk

Between the recording and release of *The Future Now*, Van der Graaf finally disintegrated. The split was amicable, being mainly due to financial difficulties rather than interpersonal conflicts. It also left Hammill in no doubt that the way forward for him was as a solo artist, in which capacity he was in any event still signed to Charisma. Having laid the groundwork for a new approach to solo work on *The Future Now*, Hammill sought to consolidate his position on *pH7*.

This was the eighth, not seventh, PH album, so the title *pH7* may have been one of those jokes for which Hammill is so famous. More to the point, in chemistry, a solution with a pH value of seven is perfectly balanced between acidity and alkalinity, a balance reflected in the songs contained herein. As Hammill writes in the notes to the album on his website, 'the album divides more or less evenly between traditional and radical work'.

By this time, Hammill had moved to Westbury in Wiltshire, and his home studio was at its most well equipped yet. The recording set-up was still eight-track analogue (a grid showing the tracks and the instruments occupying them was printed on the inner sleeve), but Hammill had accumulated additional instruments and even a drum kit. The set-up allowed for a wider range of sounds than had been the case on *The Future Now*, the politically and socially conscious songs were still in evidence, and there was a neo-epic to end the album in 'Mr X (Gets Tense)'/'Faculty X'. Hammill played all the instruments himself, joined on several tracks by David Jackson on sax and Graham Smith on violin. If you're looking for music that grabs you by the shoulders and hurtles you around, music that takes all the best parts of progressive rock, punk and art rock and makes of them something new, dangerous and thrilling, you could do worse than to start here.

This was evidently too much for Charisma, who dropped Hammill after this album. Clearly, he could have come up with a more palatable set of songs which might have bought him time with the record company. But artistic compromise has never been an option for Hammill, who made the album he wanted to make and saw the support of the record company evaporate as a result. He knew what he was doing, though. As we have seen going back to

Chameleon in 1973, self-sufficiency has formed part of his strategy since the early days, and the progressive development of Sofa Sound was to stand him in good stead in the years to come.

The cover photo was taken by photographer Daniel Kirk at his home in New York City. Hammill alludes to the sense of fear and panic it evokes in a note on his website: 'As we left Dan's place in search of a cab, Graham and I ran into some trouble from which, frankly, we were lucky to escape.' Writing on an internet discussion group years later, Kirk takes up the story: 'a couple of 'heavy dudes' ... made an effort to either grab the cab from them, or rob them ... they managed to get the cab door shut and sped away from possible danger.'

'My Favourite'

Ironically for an album that led to Hammill being dropped from his label, it opens with one of his simplest and most accessible love songs. Indeed one might say that it's a little *too* simple, since it lacks the grit in the oyster that usually makes Hammill's love songs so compelling. The horse-racing metaphor is rather laboured and the sentiments expressed somewhat cloying. On the other hand, the guitar is beautifully played, there's elegant violin from Graham Smith, and Hammill's vocal is romantic enough to melt the hardest of hearts.

'Careering (Don't Ask Me)'

In the 1970s, there was a famous piece of graffiti alongside a stretch of the Underground in west London. Attributed to the radical post-Situationist group King Mob, it went 'SAME THING DAY AFTER DAY – TUBE – WORK – DINER [sic] – WORK – TUBE – ARMCHAIR – TV – SLEEP – TUBE – WORK – HOW MUCH MORE CAN YOU TAKE – ONE IN TEN GO MAD – ONE IN FIVE CRACKS UP.' If the middle-aged protagonist of 'Careering' had seen this graffito, it might well have made him stop and think, troubled as he is by the thought that he is 'careering, simply day to day/careering for the work and the pay.' There's a punky snarl to Hammill's voice, the bass and electric guitar swirl aggressively, and David Jackson's searing sax solo approaches free jazz territory.

'Porton Down'

In the notes to the album on his website, Hammill describes how he 'used to drive past the turn-off for Porton Down whenever I went up to London.' Strangely enough, as a teenager growing up in Salisbury in the late 1970s, I used to pass Porton Down every day on the bus to school. This is a menacing hulk of a song, driven by forceful guitar and possessed of an overwhelming sense of moral outrage. The twin dangers of Jackson's sax and Smith's violin take the song to the brink of 'the ultimate madness', baited by Hammill's horrorstruck vocal performance. The German theorist Adorno wrote that 'the depiction of fear lies at the centre' of expressionist music. With terror inscribed in every note and syllable, 'Porton Down' amply fulfils Adorno's criteria.

'Mirror Images'

Here's another song that began life as a Van der Graaf number and was then refashioned into a solo tune. In the case of 'Mirror Images', it was released on the chaotic VdG live album *Vital* but was never recorded by the group. The solo version is a good deal more structured, with Hammill's multi-layered vocals contoured around doomy, pulsating synth drones. The narrator of the song seems to be going through a mental breakdown; looking at himself in the mirror, he sees only a 'nervous wreck' who 'can surely tell that he's not yet free.' Lashing out at 'your infant pique and your angst pretensions', he concludes that 'these mirror images won't stay, go away, are no help.' The interplay between the lead and backing vocals dramatises this duality of selves to powerful effect.

'Handicap and Equality'

As close as Hammill ever got to writing a folk song, this earnest little number floats by on softly strummed acoustic guitar, piano and some decidedly underpowered organ. The lyric is a plea for understanding towards disabled people on the unarguable basis that 'they're people just the same.' Although the sentiments are irreproachable, the song still represents a rare lapse of taste on the part of Hammill. The references to 'the crippled human frame' and 'their grunts, their stumps, their tumours' are gratuitous; these days, we do not draw unnecessary attention to a person's physical disability, any more than we would draw unnecessary attention to the colour of their skin. The aim today is to encourage positive images of disabled people, not to reinforce negative stereotypes – to portray what disabled people can do, not what they can't – and to avoid words like 'crippled' and 'defective', which are now widely regarded as offensive. Whether the values and sensitivities of today were or were not in place in 1979 is beside the point; the song remains a period piece.

'Not For Keith'

Keith Ellis was the bass player in the first incarnation of Van der Graaf Generator, playing with them between 1968 and 1969. He died at the tragically young age of 32, of a drug overdose while on tour in Germany with the group Iron Butterfly. Hammill has often spoken of his debt to Ellis, who was the first working musician Hammill had ever worked with. Ellis taught the younger man the importance of commitment and dedication as a musician: to do the gig and to give it everything. 'Not For Keith' is Hammill's finely judged elegy for his departed bandmate, a stark piano ballad played and sung with great tenderness. The lines 'I never thanked him at all for his friendship, and now I never will' are especially moving.

'The Old School Tie'

1979 was a tempestuous year in British politics. The Labour Party, which had ruled the country for eleven of the previous fifteen years, was defeated by the

Conservative Party under Margaret Thatcher. 'The Old School Tie' is a tirade against the 'bright young men in their tight-buttoned suits' whose overriding interest is in securing for themselves 'a cushy job in politics'. The title refers to the 'old boy network' whereby political advancement is facilitated by having attended a particular school or university. It was egregious enough at the time, but, as Hammill writes in the sleeve notes to the 2006 reissue, 'this kind of stuff has become all-pervasive in the intervening years.' A flinty piano riff runs through the song, bolstered by simmering synth and coils of electric guitar.

'Time For A Change' (Chris Judge Smith)

It's back to the acoustic guitar for this enigmatic cut from the pen of Chris Judge Smith. The lyric seems to refer to the transition between childhood or adolescence and adulthood – a key time of life, for sure, and one where you certainly do get the feeling that 'something big has got to happen soon.' As on 'Mirror Images', there's a marvellous interplay between lead and backing vocals, the baritone and falsetto voices warily stalking each other. Frequently performed live, this is one of Hammill's most accomplished performances on acoustic, elegance and flourish tempered by raw discipline.

'Imperial Walls' (words: anonymous 8th century Saxon, music: Hammill)

The story goes that Hammill had worked up this track as an instrumental, and was still searching for a lyric as the recording of the album was drawing to a close. On a visit to the Roman baths in Bath, he saw the text inscribed on a wall and found that it fitted the music perfectly. In terms of both lyric and music, this is one of the most striking songs on the album, the text drunk on imagery of decay and collapse, the music a crucible of feverish rhythms and harmonies. The ominous stickwork is by Hammill himself; as he writes in the 2006 sleeve notes, 'this was the time when I felt that I really had to begin to understand what happens with drums.' He also contributes excellent lead guitar lines and, of course, sings with blistering power.

'Mr X (Gets Tense)'

X is tense, geddit? There's more than a touch of Sartrean existentialism here, as Hammill grapples with the founding questions: 'what's the drive of each individual? And what's the way that the story ends?' The song proposes two alternative responses to the second question, 'under ice' or 'under fire'. Neither seems particularly attractive, but the dilemma plays out in exuberant blasts of guitar, manic drumming, head-spinning synth and swirling vortices of violin. Segueing from one to the other, this song and 'Faculty X' naturally form a pair; as Hammill writes in the sleeve notes, they also form an epic, 'the kind of thing which once I might have presented to VdGG.' Which brings us neatly to:

'Faculty X'

If there was ever a British equivalent to Sartre, it was the author Colin Wilson, who did much to popularise existentialism with his 1956 book *The Outsider*. Fifteen years later, Wilson published *The Occult: A History*, in which he introduced the notion of what he called 'Faculty X'. For Wilson, Faculty X is 'a sense of the purpose of life, quite direct and un-inferred ... we already possess it to a large degree, but are unconscious of possessing it.' Hammill sees this paradox in terms of a path through the unknown: 'it's all that I fear, it's all I suspect, and I'll disappear in Faculty X.' Yet it's good to see Hammill, a cricket fan like me, ultimately resort to a cricketing metaphor as the key to existential self-awareness: 'looking for a method, I play a straight bat, throw away the chances to slip.' This is another song that Hammill has frequently performed live – unsurprisingly, given its persuasive melodic touches and catchy lyrical hooks.

'The Polaroid'

Included on the US release of *pH7* was this bizarre track which, for reasons best known to himself, Hammill had previously released as a single under the Rikki Nadir alias. Sung in a dire faux-Cockney accent, it tells the cautionary tale of a man who is approached by an attractive young woman on the beach. She asks him to photograph her topless, which he gladly does with his instant camera. He's clearly been the victim of a set-up, for by the time the photo has developed, the girl has scarpered, but a policeman has arrived. Taking one look at the photo, the cop arrests the man for indecency and, in the only believable part of the story, keeps the photo for himself. Wisely, perhaps, this song has never been reissued.

Bonus tracks

The 2006 reissue adds solo piano versions of 'Mr X (Gets Tense)' and 'Faculty X', recorded for a 1979 Peel session.

A Black Box (1980)

Personnel:
Peter Hammill: vocals, guitar, piano, keyboards, bass, drums
David Jackson: saxophone, flute
David Ferguson: synthesizer, tambourine
All songs by Peter Hammill, except where noted
Recorded at Sofa Sound, Wiltshire, November 1979-April 1980
Produced by Peter Hammill
UK release date: October 1980

What's in *A Black Box*? The title refers, of course, to a flight recorder, in reference to the epic suite 'Flight' that takes up the whole of side two of this album. But in systems theory, a black box is any device where only the inputs and outputs are known, the inner workings of the device remaining a mystery. You could say the same about Hammill's music, where the inputs (vocals, lyrics, instrumentation, recording, production) and outputs (the finished product) are apparent, but the process by which such mercurial music is produced remains opaque – as opaque, in fact, as the slab of black marble on the cover of this album, out of which the name of the artist and the title have been scratched defiantly in white.

Hammill's deal with Charisma having expired, he decided to self-release the album in partnership with his manager Gail Colson. The LP was the first and, as it turned out, the only release on S-Type Records, a short-lived entity indeed. Subsequent reissues were on Virgin, as would be the case with the rest of Hammill's 1970s and some of his 1980s output.

As with *The Future Now* and *pH7*, the album was recorded at Hammill's home studio, with him playing most of the parts himself. David Jackson contributed sax and flute on 'Fogwalking' and 'Flight', and Hammill was also joined by David Ferguson on synth on 'Fogwalking', 'In Slow Time' and 'The Wipe'. Ferguson was the co-founder of British post-punk group Random Hold, whose début album *The View From Here* Hammill was producing as *A Black Box* was being recorded. He sadly died in 2009.

If *The Future Now* and *pH7* are two sides of the same coin, *A Black Box* is a different kind of record. The politically and socially conscious songs were to take a back seat this time, and there were none of the passionate love songs that had been a feature of most Hammill albums until then. It's an intense, claustrophobic, at times downright scary listen, full of forbidding and *unheimlich* atmospheres, and as such has always been one of my favourite Hammill albums. Plus, of course, it contains 'Flight', which I regard as Hammill's single greatest achievement.

'Golden Promises'

This spectacular opening track sets the blueprint for the album with heavy rock guitar, crashing drums and a towering lead vocal. The song's an urgent caution

47

against being taken in by 'golden promises' –those of organised religion, perhaps, or any kind of fanaticism and zealotry. The drums, by the way, are all played by Hammill himself. In the sleeve notes to the 2006 reissue, Hammill describes his drumming style on this album as 'genuinely mad', which seems to sum it up nicely. He's no Guy Evans, that's for sure, but there's an intent, ever so slightly deranged quality to Hammill's drumming that's completely suited to the material here.

'Losing Faith In Words'
The French philosopher Derrida, who originated the theory of deconstruction, wrote: 'I only speak one language, and it is not my own.' It's not known whether Derrida was a Peter Hammill fan, but he would certainly have sympathised with the way this song struggles to articulate meaning even as it acknowledges the impossibility of doing so. For my money, this is one of Hammill's greatest songs, a song about the difficulty of communication that, paradoxically, comes out in a frenetic torrent of words. There's a stunning energy here; an attack-dog urgency etched in nerve-shredding piano, primitivist drumming and the compulsive shriek of Hammill's voice.

'The Jargon King'
If 'Losing Faith In Words' is about the 'sheer frustration' of not being able to get one's meaning across, the next song focuses on another aspect of the problem of language. The Jargon King deliberately obscures the paucity of his thought by imposing 'pigeon-holed allusions' and 'minion code words', a strategy designed to ensure that 'we don't understand/he must be clever/he must be right'. This taut little piece is constructed on treacherously shifting sands of synthesizer, reminiscent of Cabaret Voltaire at their most industrial, over which Hammill intones darkly about 'ju-ju speak' and 'quantifying chaos'.

'Fogwalking'
And speaking of dark, here's one of Hammill's scariest and most cinematic set-pieces. Grimly pathological in its night-time imagery, the song paces the streets of London in fog after dark, hinting at an authoritarian clampdown in the midst of societal breakdown. As the horror accumulates, homelessness, disease and madness are rife. The setting is 'what used to be Whitechapel', formerly one of the most deprived areas of the capital and the location of the Jack the Ripper murders in the late 1880s.

In recent years writers such as Iain Sinclair and Peter Ackroyd have carried out significant research into the psychogeography of London, much of it focused on Whitechapel and neighbouring areas of the East End. 'Fogwalking' could almost be the soundtrack to these explorations. Looming walls of electric guitar are fractured by the spectral dance of Ferguson's synthesizer, while Jackson blows virulent sax into the fissures of Hammill's sinister voice. In an album loaded with highlights, this is a key track, every second of it stricken by panic and fear.

'The Spirit'

There's not a whole lot of acoustic guitar on *A Black Box*, but 'The Spirit' is constructed from a gorgeous chord progression that brings a welcome shaft of colour to an otherwise decidedly monochrome album. In the sleeve notes to the 2006 reissue, Hammill says that the tune (which he had had since his teens!) was originally a setting for a poem by the British poet John Betjeman. Urbane, unfailingly polite and wryly comic, Betjeman would have made a strange bedfellow for Hammill, so it's probably a good thing that PH ultimately wrote his own text to go with this cracking tune. The lyric's a stirring statement of intent, a vow to keep living to the max even though 'the body grows seemingly weaker.' An awesome electric riff and more of that 'genuinely mad drumming' keep the song storming forward.

'In Slow Time' (Hammill/Ferguson)

Another eerie, synth-driven mood piece, this time fused with ominous ebow guitar and haunted vocals. The song seems to have some kinship with the short-lived New Romantic movement that briefly flourished in Britain around this time, with its ambiguous portrayal of nightlife as an escape from domestic tedium, which nevertheless brings its own form of existential *ennui*. The New Romantic groups made extensive use of synthesizers, of course, but Ferguson's synth treatments here (for which he earned a co-writing credit) have more in common with the glacial forms of side two of Bowie's *Low* than with anything the New Romantics ever came up with. A different version of this song was later used as the backing track for a dance performance broadcast on BBC TV and was released on the *Loops and Reels* album.

'The Wipe'

A short, assaultive noisescrape defined by hellish loops, intimidating siren blasts, grinding vectors of percussion and waves of vicious guitar. It's less than two minutes long but says all that it needs to say in that time – severe, oppressive and awash with dread and foreboding.

'Flight'

This is the one. I hesitate to describe 'Flight' as a song, but if song it be, then by my reckoning, it is Hammill's greatest ever, a phantasmagoric dream narrative drawn in seven tense scenes of fear, escape and doom. Hammill's second longform composition after VdGG's 'A Plague of Lighthouse-Keepers', it had a long gestation period. He had begun writing it after *The Future Now*, but it was still unfinished when the time came to record the follow-up *pH7*, so was put on the back burner for a while. Clearly, it was worth the wait, since the piece forms the dramatic core of *A Black Box*. Conceptually impeccable, lyrically acute and sonically seductive, 'Flight' is every inch a masterpiece.

There is also, perhaps, an element of personal history to the piece. It's not generally known that Hammill's father was an airman with the Royal Air

49

Force during World War II. On the night of 13 May 1943, he was in an Allied bomber with five other men when the aircraft was shot down off the coast of the Netherlands. Three of the six airmen were killed, but Hammill's father and two others survived by parachuting to safety. Listening to the 'Silk Worm Wings' section, in particular, it's hard not to hear an acknowledgement of these men's wartime courage and heroism.

Like much of Hammill's work, 'Flight' is intensely cinematic. For one whose lyrics are often vaguely described as 'philosophical', what's less often remarked upon is how *visual* a writer Hammill is, his texts full of striking images and filmic turns of phrase. These images, however, tend to be of a glancing and allusive nature, and are rarely deployed in the service of a coherent narrative. 'Flight' is no exception; there's some kind of story going on here, but trying to follow it is really not so important. Just strap yourself into your seat, sit back, and enjoy the ride.

(i) 'Flying Blind'

This desolate opening section is ushered in by half-distant piano and pensive, almost distracted vocals. Drifting hazily in and out of consciousness, the narrator struggles to reach an understanding of 'what constitutes a conscious mind'. As he begins to clarify matters in his head, the music bursts into life in lightning bolts of electric guitar and salvos of forceful drumbeats. Since it appears that 'the Fortress [a type of World War II bomber] was flying blind' (i.e. relying on the instrument panel alone), it's little wonder that 'nothing was quite what it seemed'.

(ii) 'White Cane Fandango'

The piece makes a sudden detour into the world of high finance here – bizarre, yet not entirely unexpected for those familiar with the Van der Graaf song 'Sci-Finance' from a couple of years earlier. 'Contango' and 'backwardation' are technical terms related to the price of futures contracts, here deployed amid speculation that 'if we survive the flight, the future will work out'. The white cane and Braille, meanwhile, seem to hark back to the pilot's 'flying blind'. This is esoteric stuff, hammered out in a furious piano figure and with Hammill's voice rising to full-throated chaos.

(iii) 'Control'

After the break-up of Van der Graaf in 1978, Hammill was very much a solo artist, yet every so often, traces of his old group would resurface in his work. 'Control' is one such, a sweeping chorale for piano and voice that recalls VdGG at their most expansive. Jackson's radiant flute and sax cast shafts of light around the room while an air traffic controller, stuck in his control tower, waits for a phone call 'to release him from responsibility'. But the call never comes, and the controller is left staring at the radar screen, faced with the gradually dawning realisation that something has gone badly wrong.

(iv) 'Cockpit'

The VdGG vibe extends into this full-on rock section, with Jackson taking a heady sax solo at altitude over thunderous drums and Hammill's crushed-glass vocals. The scene seems to have shifted to a passenger aircraft, perhaps one operated by British Caledonian, a now-defunct British airline of the 1970s whose female cabin crew wore tartan uniforms. Some poor girl's clothes are under attack, and her tights are ruined: 'beneath the tartan two-piece something rips undone ... wait for the ladder to run'. This part is also notable for containing the only reference in rock music to *Wisden Cricketers' Almanack*, the Bible of cricket.

(v) 'Silk Worm Wings'

A brief vocal-driven overture to the next part of the suite. The silk worm wings of the title are, of course, the pilot's parachute, which he opens having ejected from the aircraft. Hammill kicks up a storm on electric guitar, which carries over into:

(vi) 'Nothing is Nothing'

This turbulent section sees Hammill issue thick flurries of piano in the midst of some of the most incendiary guitar he has ever committed to tape. The mad onrush of helter-skelter sound dials up the tension incrementally, culminating in a jaw-dropping moment where the piano drops out and a mighty guitar riff takes us into the final section.

(vii) 'A Black Box'

The finale of the piece is, in my view, the most emotionally devastating three minutes in the whole of Hammill's work. Soft keyboard notes pick out a placid, beautiful melody to which Hammill sings one of his most eloquently moving lyrics. The piano enters and the music lifts heavenward as if raking the sky for the missing airman. Hammill's multi-tracked vocals are vast, distant and chilling, and the title of the album reveals itself for the first time: 'Is the empire of sensation, locked in a black box deep in me, encoded there somehow?' We're left with a message, or perhaps a warning: 'better think on today.'

Sitting Targets (1981)

Personnel:
Peter Hammill: vocals, guitar, keyboards
David Jackson: saxophone, flute
Guy Evans: drums
Morris Pert: percussion
Phil Harrison: synthesizer
All songs by Peter Hammill
Recorded at Sofa Sound, Wiltshire and Crescent Studios, Bath, November
1980-March 1981
Produced by Peter Hammill
UK release date: 15 June 1981
Cover: Rocking Russian

Sitting Targets was something of a back-to-basics album for Hammill after the
increasingly complex arrangements of the last three LPs, culminating in the
majesty and mystery of *A Black Box*. As he wrote in the sleeve notes to the 2007
reissue: 'I made the conscious decision that the next recording would be more
direct and concise.' This directness manifested itself in a simplicity of writing
and instrumentation, with the record consisting of eleven short tracks that
eschew too much elaboration in favour of a no-nonsense beat-driven agenda.

The basic tracks for the album were laid down at Hammill's home studio,
with the other musicians adding their parts at Crescent Studios in Bath (a
facility owned by David Lord, later to work with Hammill as his co-producer).
Hammill was joined by regular collaborators Guy Evans on drums and David
Jackson on saxophone, plus a couple of new faces. Percussionist Morris Pert
was a well-known session musician and composer who had been a member of
jazz fusion outfit Brand X when Hammill supported them on tour in 1978. He
sadly died in 2010. Synth player Phil Harrison had been a member of quirky
pop group the Korgis, and had played on their 1980 hit 'Everybody's Got to
Learn Sometime'. Like Hammill, the Korgis were clients of Lord's at Crescent.
Another ex-Korgi, violinist Stuart Gordon, would later record and tour
extensively with Hammill.

This was an important album for Hammill for at least two reasons. Firstly, it
laid the foundations for the K Group, the neo-beat group with whom he was
to record and tour for the next several years. *Sitting Targets* was not a K Group
album, but its punchy, new wave style would certainly influence the genesis
and future direction of the group, and several of its songs were to become live
K Group favourites. Secondly, several of the album's songs have become staples
of Hammill's live sets over the years, in solo and duo as well as group formats.
For Hammill, this is because (as he wrote in the 2007 sleeve notes) 'there's a
real open architecture about many of these songs.' Songs like 'Stranger Still',
'Ophelia' and 'Central Hotel' often crop up in Hammill's setlists to this day, a
testament to the lasting appeal of the album.

As so often with Hammill's work, one struggles here with issues of genre: is *Sitting Targets* progressive rock, art rock, post-punk, new wave, synth pop or what? I'm not one of those writers who denies the importance of genre: to deepen our understanding of and enjoyment of music, we need contexts and categories. In this case, I would say that there's a definite post-punk feel to the album, filtered through an art rock sensibility and exhibiting a distinctly contemporary awareness of electronic music in the early 1980s. Hammill was never likely to trouble the singles charts (even though 'My Experience' was released as a single), but he cannot have been unaware of the rise of synth pop or the importance of Kraftwerk to the music of the time. In any event, there's a real emphasis on synthesizers here, particularly in the contributions of Harrison (who played the Synclavier, an early digital synth, on the album at a time when few other artists had recourse to one).

'Breakthrough'

As noted in the previous chapter, Hammill is a master at writing lyrics that are loaded with arresting images but which stubbornly refuse to resolve into conventional narratives. 'Breakthrough' is a fine example, its text hinting at some kind of disturbance (who are the visitors, and is there a school shooting threatened?) without ever revealing the full circumstances behind it. The song's a nagging bass-driven piece, with looming synth tones adding to the sense of disquiet that infects Hammill's nervy vocal. Some chunky rhythm guitar work from Hammill and inspired drumming by Evans add to what Hammill describes as a 'band-not-band' sound, the various sonic elements combining in a tetchy, not quite organic way.

'My Experience'

Here's a storming number that was to become a live K Group staple – unsurprisingly so, since its vigorous in-your-face presence was perfectly suited to the heads-down guitar/bass/drums approach of that outfit. The song's a pure, unadulterated rush of guitar-fuelled energy; the spirit of Rikki Nadir hovers over the enterprise, while not since 1977's 'Crying Wolf' had Hammill cut something so frenetically enjoyable. Lyrically it's another elusive mini-drama, with hints of domestic violence and paranoia cutting through the casual remarks. Intriguingly, when the K Group played this live, Hammill would substitute the word 'Marilyn...' for 'I just can't stop it...' in the chorus. If, as seems likely, the Marilyn referred to is Monroe, then another layer of rumour and conspiracy is added.

'Ophelia'

The temperature gets taken down several notches on this haunting ballad, 'two parts the Lady of Shalott to one part Ophelia' as Hammill wrote in the sleeve notes to the *Calm (After The Storm)* compilation. Clearly, Hammill had those twin Pre-Raphaelite masterpieces by Waterhouse and Millais in mind, their swooning and tragic imagery encoded in the wistful fatalism of the song. Dreamlike wisps of synthesizer thread their way through the delicate tracery of Hammill's acoustic guitar while his voice hangs in the air, stricken by absence and loss. 'Ophelia' is not so much a love song as a song of departure, with the shadowy presence of a stranger coming too late to save the doomed heroine.

'Empress's Clothes'

This is another one of those edgy, truculent numbers that Hammill likes to throw in from time to time. Bass-heavy and emphasising rhythm at the expense of melody, the song presents a man and woman who are never going to see eye to eye, and who end up trying to stand their ground in a 'strangleholding scene.' There's deft, skittering percussion from Pert and warped fanfares of sax from Jackson, but it's Hammill's tentacular bass that dominates, throwing his cruelly authoritative vocal into sharp relief.

'Glue'

This is a sticky little saga built on overlapping sheets of guitar and a blurred, flickering vocal. Ripples of synthesised percussion dart through the song, underscored by tense fragments of piano. As with much of the album, the song shows Hammill in a new lyrical mode; terse and aphoristic, these texts derive much of their force from what's unsaid rather than what's said. Plus, like more than half the songs on the album, 'Glue' addresses the character 'you'. There's something oblique and unsettling about this lyrical strategy, as though some half-unseen presence is being repeatedly invoked.

'Hesitation'

If you're one of those people who believes that Hammill never bettered the work he did in the early to mid-1970s, and who bemoans his repudiation of progressive rock in the late 1970s and early 1980s, 'Hesitation' might be the song for you. Admittedly it's only four minutes long, but it has three-quarters of VdGG on it; its lyric is a thorny speculation on the nature of time, and it crams plenty of melodic invention and virtuoso playing into those four minutes. Hammill sings with a manic intensity that wouldn't have sounded out of place on VdGG's *Godbluff*, there's masterly sax from Jackson, and Evans' propulsive drumming keeps the whole thing on the boil. Yet it's the wild refrain 'this is no time for hesitation' and the repeated cry of 'oh no' towards the end that give this song its frantic urgency, making it the perfect closer to side one of the album.

'Sitting Targets'

And what better way to kick off side two than with this scintillating post-punk workout. As Hammill points out in the notes to the *Storm (Before The Calm)* compilation, 'the car's always a good place for serious conversation – no eye contact.' Taking full advantage of the situation, the hero of the song urges his co-driver to 'keep your eyes on the road up ahead, while I try to forget what's been going wrong.' The reference to CB radio sounds dated now, but would have seemed rather modish in 1981, in keeping with the slick, restless motion that pervades the song. Evans sets down an almost *motorik* beat to emphasise that sense of movement, while Jackson plays relentlessly kinetic sax and Hammill alternates tensile rhythm guitar with abrasive lead lines.

Hammill is not often mentioned in the same breath as Bruce Springsteen, but this is his most Springsteen-like song. For Springsteen, the car and the open road are the keys to escape and salvation from the drudgery of life in small-town America. For Hammill, too, there's an urgent imperative to get on the road and keep moving since staying in the same place is 'surely no better than living a dream.' On the other hand, Springsteen, for whom the highway stretches into infinity, would probably be aghast to find himself on the British road network, whereas Hammill takes comfort in the fact that his destination, wherever it may be, is 'not too far to drive.'

'Stranger Still'

Apparently written over lunch in a Parisian restaurant and addressing pre-show nerves, this for me is another of Hammill's greatest songs. There's something profoundly moving about its main melody, picked out first on piano and then restated on frosty synth with sad choral undertones. Hammill sounds defiant, almost but not quite defeated, in some liminal state between composure and panic. His scientific education comes into play again, as he characterises his state of mind in terms of entropy, the amount of disorder present in a system.

Although the studio version does not want for emotion, the song has taken on immense power and passion when it has been performed on stage over the years, initially with the K Group and later as a solo piano song. Live, Hammill presents 'Stranger Still' as a volcanic expressionist drama devoid of empathy and wracked with existential anguish. Those who have heard him perform the song, and in particular, heard him repeat the last line 'a stranger, a worldly man' over and over as if possessed, every syllable stretched to the point of obliteration, will not forget the experience in a hurry.

'Sign'

This could almost be another song about obsessive fandom *à la* 'Energy Vampires', although the narrative remains tantalisingly out of reach. Like the Van der Graaf song 'Last Frame', the song focuses (no pun intended) on the way the camera captures a fleeting moment and makes it last forever. The French theorist Barthes wrote that 'what the Photograph reproduces to infinity has occurred only once: the Photograph mechanically repeats what could never be repeated existentially.' Hammill makes the point more succinctly: you can 'throw the picture away ... although it's going to come back.' Powered by a rippling acoustic guitar riff, the song makes an immediately favourable impression with strong stickwork from Evans and persuasive, almost poppy layered vocals from Hammill.

'What I Did'

In the sleeve notes to the 2007 reissue, Hammill describes this song (along with 'Sign' and 'Hesitation') as one that is 'rooted in direct/observed experience'. The line about an 'overdue debt to the taxman' certainly has the ring of truth to it; that apart, the song is fairly non-specific in its catalogue of regrets and frustrations. There's zippy electric guitar from Hammill, but Jackson's honking sax feels arbitrary, and the refrain of 'I must have been crazy, crazy, crazy' outstays its welcome. Quite fun, but probably the least essential tune on the album.

'Central Hotel'

A brilliantly effective closer to the album and another live favourite to this day, 'Central Hotel' is a perfect fusion of art-rock ambition, post-punk discipline and sheer bloody-minded racket. The song's a vortex of neurotic activity; Hammill's stormy guitar and piledriving drums form dark clouds around his corrosive vocals, while Jackson takes a ferocious solo. The hotel in question was in Brussels; according to the notes in the *Storm (Before The Calm)* compilation, Hammill 'found myself on the balcony, looking down on the road works which went on year after year.'

Although the song takes its cue from the repetition and *ennui* of life on the road, there's a good deal more lurking beneath the surface: 'stripling terror, naked to the bone.' I think of Kubrick's *The Shining*, its hotel setting a site of unimaginable horror, not to mention our old friend Sartre (see the chapter on *pH7*), whose 1944 play *No Exit* posits hell as a comfortable hotel from which there is no escape. One should probably also note the Eagles' 'Hotel California', and in particular, the way its famous payoff line 'you can check out any time you like, but you can never leave' is echoed in the last lines of this song. For Hammill, too, leaving the Central Hotel is a matter of existential struggle. At first resolving that 'I'm not going back', as the song progresses, he begins to have doubts: 'I won't be going back, not if I can help it.' Finally, faced with the dawning realisation that 'I can't help it if I still am what I was', he becomes resigned to staying: 'I know I'd better check out, but anyone here can tell I'll be coming back.'

Enter K (1982)

Personnel:
Peter Hammill: vocals, electric guitar, piano, organ, synthesizer
John Ellis: electric and acoustic guitar
Nic Potter: bass
Guy Evans: drums
David Jackson: saxophone
All songs by Peter Hammill
Recorded at Sofa Sound, Avon and Crescent Studios, Bath, 1982
Produced by Peter Hammill
UK release date: October 1982
Cover artwork: Steve Byrne and Valerie Hawthorne
Photography: Jo Swan

Enter K was the first of two albums Hammill recorded with the K Group, consisting of VdGG alumni Nic Potter on bass and Guy Evans on drums, and ex-Vibrators man John Ellis on lead guitar. The group had been formed back in 1981 as a touring outfit, largely playing songs from the last few Hammill albums along with a smattering of PH and VdGG classics. By 1982, things were going so well that Hammill felt the time was right to take the group into the studio. In fact, over half the songs ('The Unconscious Life', 'Accidents', 'Don't Tell Me' and 'She Wraps it Up') were initially worked up solo by Hammill at his eight-track home studio, with overdubs added later at Crescent. The remainder were rehearsed and recorded with the full band at Crescent in just a month. Along with the K Group proper, additional contributions on two tracks came from the ubiquitous David Jackson on saxophone. As Hammill writes in the notes to the album on his website, 'the freshness of performance was fuelled by the just-learned as well as by innate energy.'

Hammill has often referred to the K Group as a 'beat group', and with good reason. As we saw in the previous chapter, *Sitting Targets* had been a more concise and direct album than its three predecessors and occupied a curious space between solo and group recording. Given the nature of the material, it was natural that the group Hammill formed to tour around that album, and subsequently to record *Enter K* and its follow-up *Patience*, should be a more out-and-out rock band than any Hammill had previously put together.

The secret ingredient was, of course, the second guitar. Discounting Robert Fripp's fleeting guest appearances on a few early PH/VdGG tunes, Hammill had never before worked with a lead guitarist. He had played lead guitar himself on many occasions, but by his own admission, was more of a rhythm than a lead player. The arrival of Ellis, who had toured with Hammill's friend and contemporary Peter Gabriel, allowed Hammill to focus on rhythm guitar and piano in the studio. Ellis was a fine lead guitarist, his tough and economical soloing the perfect counterweight to Hammill's fierce rhythmic attack. Potter and Evans, meanwhile, formed their usual formidable rhythm section. Together, the K Group were an outfit more than capable of giving structure and weight to the acute and artful new songs that Hammill was writing.

A new group called for a new set of identities. In the credits of this and other K Group albums, and occasionally on later releases, the members of the group assumed nicknames to go alongside their real names: Ellis was Fury, Potter was Mozart, Evans was Brain and Hammill was, of course, K, which at least settled the issue of what the K Group's début album should be called. The origins of the other three names are lost in the mists of time, but as for K, Hammill writes in the notes to the album on his website that '[Van der Graaf violinist] Graham Smith gave me the name ... the prophet of unlikely ventures; the constant unknown.' To which it might be added that the letter carries echoes of the work of Franz Kafka, who named one of his characters Josef K and another one simply K. Both K in *The Castle* and Josef K in *The Trial* are everyday people who find themselves at the mercy of remote, mysterious authorities that exert control over their lives. Not that there's anything particularly Kafkaesque about the songs on *Enter K*, but the album certainly explores states of unconsciousness that approximate to the fractured logic of Kafka's dream worlds.

'Paradox Drive'

A lean, insidious riff ushers in the recorded works of the K Group, and we're off to Paradox Drive. This massively enjoyable opener sets a trap with its slick verses before falling headlong into a crunchy, highly addictive chorus. The song also provides an excellent example of the fine interplay between Ellis' lead and Hammill's rhythm guitar, as Ellis' shimmering ebow lines surge and retreat around Hammill's muscular riffing. Lyrically the song seems to form a pair with 'The Unconscious Life', evoking the liminal zone between waking hours and night, and the longing for 'the sweet comfort of a life on my own, asleep.' An edited version of this song was even released as a single, but needless to say, the call from *Top of the Pops* never came.

'The Unconscious Life'

'Our aim is wakefulness,' went an old Temple ov Psychick Youth slogan, 'our enemy is dreamless sleep.' TOPY was a loose network of magic practitioners that first came together in the early 1980s, influenced by the occultist Austin Osman Spare's writings on what would later come to be known as chaos magic. Spare believed that the unconscious mind could be accessed through the use of symbolic diagrams, known as sigils, which could bypass consciousness and bring about a desired outcome. I'm not suggesting that Hammill was ever influenced by magic, despite the early VdGG track 'Necromancer' and his association with the occultist Graham Bond. But 'The Unconscious Life', like 'Paradox Drive' before it, is an oblique commentary on the latent potential of the human mind to influence external events: 'someone that I barely know must unpick the stitch/

to unravel the unconscious life.' The song starts off with dreamy piano and vocals, before snarling into overdrive thanks to Evans' white-hot drumming and Jackson's flamboyant sax work.

'Accidents'

This one's an outlier; on an album of wonky ballads and left-field rock workouts, it demonstrates Hammill's continued commitment to the awkward and the speculative. The track represents an incursion into experimental song form that, as Hammill writes in the notes to the album on his website, 'in construction and execution owes a passing debt to the experimentation of *The Future Now/pH7* era.' But this is no dry avant-garde exercise; it combines biting vocal hooks with hectic flourishes of synth and busy percussion amongst the dissonance. Although Hammill has never been one to implement Cageian chance procedures in his music, the lyric celebrates the range of possible outcomes where chance is permitted to thrive. And there's a surprise buried in there: the quiet section in the middle contains a snatch of the piano melody from 'The Unconscious Life', played backwards.

'The Great Experiment'

Who else would kick off a song with a supremely catchy piano motif, add foot-tapping percussion and crackling guitar, and then launch into a lyric like "Is that all there is to it,' he asks, 'no more conjecture or controversy?" Hammill can write a killer pop song when he feels like it, and 'The Great Experiment' is a fine example. The lyric is enigmatic but seems to tell the tale of a man who finds himself, whether by accident or design, on the verge of some major discovery. As so often in Hammill's world, the scenario is framed as a screenplay: we're 'near the end of the reel now', and time is short. The K Group shape this urgency in breakneck fashion, with Evans firing on all cylinders, Ellis soloing with brutal efficiency and Hammill delivering a vocal performance that burns with conviction.

'Don't Tell Me'

This gutsy piano ballad is another regularly performed number at solo concerts. Indeed Hammill has often begun live performances with this song, the idea being that its dizzying dynamic shifts allow him to stretch his voice and gauge the acoustics in the room. The song's another take on the territory mapped out by 'If I Could'; traumatised by the suspicion that his girl is about to leave him, the narrator falls back on jealousy and recrimination. In this wasteland of lost communication, the most troubling aspect is left until the last line, 'you don't even tell me the bell won't ring'; the man still clings to a scrap of hope for comfort, however tiny it may be. Jackson's sparkling sax solo adds a vivid extra dimension to the steely piano figures that stalk the song.

'She Wraps It Up'

Hot on the heels of 'The Great Experiment', here comes another cut from the poppier end of the Hammill spectrum – indeed, he claims on his website that 'the organ part in particular nods towards the 'bop shoo-wop de bop shoo-wop's of the 1960s.' I'm not sure I would ever describe anything by Hammill as 'bop shoo-wop de bop shoo-wop', but this is certainly a rollicking good tune, driven by ritzy organ work. Lyrically, 'She Wraps It Up' is the obverse of 'Energy Vampires'; instead of sucking energy out of you, this girl is an 'energy donor': 'It'll be hard to stay so close, when all that special emptiness floods out.' The song's breezy tone is punctuated by a gorgeous, soaring middle eight.

'Happy Hour'

Clocking in at over nine minutes, 'Happy Hour' was Hammill's longest song ('Magog' and 'Flight' excepted) since 'A Louse Is Not A Home'. It's tempting, therefore, to see it as, in some sense, a return to the expansive terrain of Hammill's early and mid-1970s work, both solo and with VdGG. For sure, there's an epic feel to the song, its shifting time signatures and heavy dynamics inevitably evoking former glories. Yet it's also one of the K Group's finest rock songs, with all four members at full strength and more or less solo passages giving way to stormy ensemble sections.

The song was apparently inspired by a night Hammill spent in a bar in Hamburg, and it certainly has that brooding, end-of-the-evening, staring-into-the-bottom-of-your-glass quality to it. Happy hour, though, normally takes place in the early evening, and is a promotional gambit to get people into the bar early by selling drinks at a discount. Our narrator is clearly in the mood to take full advantage of such an offer, with predictable results: the shaky hand, another round in, the inevitable fall towards the floor. But as the killer last line 'put on the greasepaint' suggests, referring back to the earlier line 'I've rehearsed it, so I'll carry on,' the whole scenario is essentially theatrical in nature. The fellow drinkers in the bar are the audience or perhaps have walk-on parts in the narrator's private psychodrama.

The soundtrack to this drama is provided by the K Group at their most thrilling, with Potter setting off depth charges around Evans' galvanic drumming and Ellis' fiery lead guitar. There's even a touch of flamenco in the instrumental break, while the last third of the song sees Hammill state and restate the final lines with ever-growing ferocity. It's a bold ending to this diverse, highly listenable album.

Bonus tracks
'Seven Wonders'

This cut was included as a bonus track on the remastered CD of *Enter K*, which Hammill released on his own Fie! label in 2003, although it was originally released in 1983 as the B-side to 'Film Noir', a track from Hammill's next album *Patience*. Why it was appended to the reissued *Enter K* rather than

Patience is unclear. Whatever the truth of the matter, 'Seven Wonders' is a delirious burst of K Group energy that was too good to be left on the shelf. There's a touch of the gamelan sound that the 1980s incarnation of King Crimson was perfecting around this time, with Ellis soloing nervily over Hammill's forceful insistence that 'nothing is permanent here.'

Patience (1983)

Personnel:
Peter Hammill: vocals, guitar, keyboards
John Ellis: guitar
Nic Potter: bass
Guy Evans: drums
David Jackson: saxophone, panpipes
Stuart Gordon: violin
David Lord: Prophet V
All songs by Peter Hammill
Recorded at Sofa Sound, Avon and Crescent Studios, Bath, December 1982
Produced by Peter Hammill
UK release date: August 1983
Cover photograph and design: John Ellis

The second and final K Group album was a considerable advance on its predecessor. Having toured Europe in the autumn of 1982, the K Group were by now a razor-sharp and intuitive unit, as disc two of the *Margin+* live album bears testimony. Honed to perfection by the demands of the road, the band regrouped at Crescent in December to record the follow-up to *Enter K*. The group's increasing confidence was reflected in the method of the album's recording. Four of the seven tracks on *Enter K* had been laid down as backing tracks in Hammill's home studio, with overdubs added later at Crescent. For *Patience*, this method was used for only two of the album's eight cuts, namely 'Labour of Love' and 'Comfortable?' The rest was recorded, dubbed and mixed at Crescent in the space of a month, an approach reflected in the fresh, organic sound of the album. What's more, five of the eight tracks – 'Labour of Love', 'Just Good Friends', 'Traintime', 'Comfortable?' and 'Patient' – have frequently been performed live over the years, giving *Patience* a higher hit rate than any other Hammill album (*Sitting Targets* is second).

Where does *Patience*, and indeed where does Hammill as an artist, stand in the context of early 1980s music? There is very little about this album that could accurately be described as progressive rock, but then again, the same could be said of most of the music being put out at the time by Hammill's contemporaries. Genesis and Yes went down the pop route, while Pink Floyd released *The Final Cut*, a record I love dearly but one that occupies a very particular place in space and time. King Crimson provide a more interesting comparison. As briefly mentioned in the last chapter, the early '80s incarnation of Crimson released three albums that saw them strike out in a new direction influenced by funk, world music and minimalism. Yet for all the creativity on show, there was something cold, precise and cerebral about '80s Crimson that made them a rather joyless proposition.

As for *Patience*, it's everything that the '80s King Crimson wasn't – barbed, aggressive and psychologically acute. Indeed, it seems to me that the record bears more relation to the art-punk of Talking Heads and Pere Ubu than to anything else being made at the time. Like those artists, the K Group combined avant-garde tendencies with a disruptive fondness for noise and repetition. Ultimately, however, the music of the K Group remains unique – and important in the way it presents Hammill's highly literate and visual imagination as part of a strong collective consciousness.

'Labour of Love'

A sincere, emotive song to open the album, this strikes me as nothing more or less than a dedication to the listener: 'it's a labour of love I offer to you.' Once a record is released, it has to make its own way in the world, the artist now unable to intervene in its journey; if you need to 'hold its stories', they will find their way to you. And as the text goes on to say, a song only begins to take on meaning when it's heard by the listener. By insisting that 'receipt will give it value', Hammill echoes the German literary theory of *Rezeptionsästhetik*. As the theorist Wolfgang Iser wrote in *The Reading Process: A Phenomenological Approach*, 'the text only takes on life when it is realised ... the convergence of text and reader brings the literary work into existence.' None of which gets us very far in accounting for the stark beauty of this song, nor for the way Hammill's gently insistent voice ebbs and flows around Jackson's caustic sax solo and Evans' warm, sympathetic stickwork.

'Film Noir'

The songs on *Patience* can be more or less divided into three categories: heartfelt ballads, mini-epics and punchy rock songs. 'Film Noir' falls into the third category, a classic example of a Hammill song framed as a little audio screenplay. The song's an absorbing tale of a jealous actress who decides to take revenge on her co-star in a *crime passionnel*. As film and reality blur into one, the actress takes the idea of method acting to an extreme by giving the leading man his final scene. This violent little drama is soundtracked by bracing lead guitar from Ellis, edgy riffing by Hammill and the usual peerless work by the Potter/Evans rhythm section.

'Just Good Friends'

Here's another one for fans of *Rezeptionsästhetik*. Although 'Just Good Friends' is one of Hammill's best-known love songs and would go on to be the lead track on the 1984 *Love Songs* project, it wasn't actually written as a love song at all. In various interviews, Hammill has told of how the song was written as a response to the straitened financial circumstances of the K Group, and he writes as much in the sleeve notes to the *Margin+* live album: 'part of the inspiration sprang from learning that the budgets for the next tour didn't seem to add up.' Clearly, Hammill was questioning his future within the music industry; equally clearly, he would have been alive to the ambiguities in the text, which are what make 'Just Good Friends' such a perfect love song.

This is not some youthful fling but a serious, adult relationship, unsparingly laid bare in all its pain and complexity. Wounded by his lover's departure, Hammill's character sings in a voice laced with bitterness and regret; the chorus approaches sublime harmonic beauty; and there's fleeting violin work by the late Stuart Gordon, making the first of his many appearances alongside Hammill.

'Jeunesse Dorée'

The title of this energetic cut was unfortunately misspelt as 'Jeunesse d'Orée' on the original LP cover and inner sleeve. There is no apostrophe in 'dorée', which means 'gilded'; Hammill was probably getting mixed up with 'd'or', meaning 'made of gold'. The original *jeunesse dorée* were gangs of well-dressed young men who fought against the French Revolution on the streets of Paris; here, they seem to function as fickle avatars of style, their shallow adherence to the dictates of fashion 'gilding the lily of pleasure.' One is tempted to shrug and reply, 'so what?', since the issue is not one of pressing concern. That said, there's much to enjoy here, from the raw energy of Ellis' guitar to Hammill's full-throated vocal.

'Traintime'

This luminous masterpiece, always a highlight of live concerts, is fully entitled to take its place in the pantheon of essential Hammill songs. Indeed for my money, this is the greatest of all the K Group's songs, its relentless forward motion taking the listener on a dangerous journey through inner psychological space. Ellis, Potter and Evans lay down an increasingly tense rhythm track over which Hammill declaims his text with astounding vehemence. The song is like a ritualised circuit diagram of discovery, the way ahead lit by nightmarish visions and bolts of electric current flashing in the darkness.

'Now More Than Ever'

As noted in the introduction to this chapter, the key to the K Group was their aggression, and John Ellis can take a lot of the credit for that. He had been there at the dawn of punk with the Vibrators, and was later associated with the Stranglers; indeed, it was when they both played at a 1980 Stranglers concert (when Hugh Cornwell was banged up for possession) that Ellis and Hammill had first met. Yet Ellis was no basic three-chord merchant – he could solo with practised ease. It's that tightly controlled, post-punk attack in his playing, reminiscent of Andy Gill's work with Gang of Four, that made him the perfect lead guitarist for the K Group. Nowhere is Ellis' prickly style heard to better effect than on this naggingly powerful track, tracked by a burbling bass line from Potter. The song marks a return to the dream world of *Enter K*'s 'Paradox Drive' and 'The Unconscious Life', that 'one field of life where free will won't cut through.' As noted in the previous chapter, this was a re-recording of a song previously released as the B-side of the 'Paradox Drive' single.

'Comfortable?'

Here's a return to the sentiments expressed in 'The Lie' and 'Faint-Heart and the Sermon': a spirited broadside against organised religion, seen through the eyes of a woman who 'just wants to feel comfortable.' But the song goes further, widening its scorn to include all those who 'wait for the mortal wound to heal when the abyss is adjacent.' This is angry, fearless stuff, expressed in a barrage of anti-folk acoustic guitar hammering. It's a frequently performed number at solo concerts, where its unforgiving message is matched by a full-tilt vocal delivery. The studio version, on the other hand, opens with acerbic blasts of sax from Jackson, who pops up again later on the panpipes – their only appearance in a Hammill song.

'Patient'

The album ends on a high with this finely wrought epic – six minutes of nerve-shattering menace, slashing guitar, ominously worded utterances and scathing percussive interventions. Hammill is an expert at composing seductive, masterfully arranged songs that burrow their way into your skull and set up home there. 'Patient' is one such, a dark and forbidding pathology of rage. The song draws the listener in with a deceptive calm, a quietness that explodes into convulsive distortions of guitar and dense thickets of percussion. Returning to a familiar Hammill theme, the lyric seems to speculate on the possibility of free will and agency in a world governed by 'the loaded dice of chance.' You may be 'waiting for the doctor to come', but you're in for a nasty shock when you realise that 'there isn't any cure.' Hammill's voice is at its savage best here; the line 'rattling in the throat' is particularly chilling, but the whole song sounds like an invocation of some hostile presence.

Loops and Reels (1983)

Personnel:
Peter Hammill: vocals, guitar, keyboards, percussion, kora
All songs by Peter Hammill, except where noted
Recorded at Sofa Sound, Wiltshire
Produced by Peter Hammill
UK release date: June 1983
Cover (CD reissue): Paul Ridout

Loops and Reels was originally self-released by Hammill on cassette in 1983, and was reissued on CD a decade later on his own Fie! label. It was the first of three albums (the others being *Sonix* and *Unsung*) in which Hammill showcased the more experimental side of his muse – largely (but not exclusively) instrumental pieces, with drones, ambient textures, manipulations and unconventional sounds to the fore. As such, this run of work might be described as being of interest mainly to the committed Hammill fan, although *Loops and Reels*, in particular, has much to recommend the more casual listener as well.

As early as 1974, Hammill had released 'Magog (in Bromine Chambers)' on the *In Camera* album, his first excursion into experimental realms. Subsequent albums *The Future Now* (1978), *pH7* (1979), *A Black Box* (1980) and *Enter K* (1982) had all contained radical musical elements folded into song form. Clearly, Hammill had long been committed to the idea that popular music could encompass *avant-garde* compositional practice. By 1983, it was time to put together a whole album that demonstrated that commitment.

The title *Loops and Reels* is a clear indication of the way in which many of these pieces were produced. The reissue is subtitled *Analogue Experiments 1980-1983*, and the process was a painstaking one: record, cut, edit, loop. As Hammill writes in the sleeve notes to the reissue, the context of the loops was 'physicality: the tape snaked out, often room-wide, from the focus of record replay heads.'

'A Ritual Mask'

Masks are an important element of ritual and ceremonial practice in many parts of sub-Saharan Africa. There is a persistent belief that such masks should not be removed from their owners, and that those who do so may be cursed. This is the fate that has befallen the man in 'A Ritual Mask', who proudly displays one on his living-room wall and is about to suffer the consequences: 'it won't take long before he finds out the bargain has turned out dreadfully wrong.'

The song had originally appeared on a WOMAD compilation album in 1982 and was given its only live outing at the inaugural WOMAD festival that year. It features Hammill playing the kora, a West African stringed instrument which he had been given as a gift while on tour in Switzerland. He hung the kora on the wall of his music room at home, where (to quote the sleeve notes of the 1993 reissue) 'it sat as an object stripped of purpose and identity ... this did not feel remotely positive.' The use of the kora thus forms an ironic commentary on the song's theme of cultural appropriation. Hammill also uses bodhran, Chinese drum and shaker, creating a heavily percussive vibe that adds to the jittery mood of the song.

'Critical Mass'
An eight-minute ambient drift constructed from looped piano and guitar. Inevitably there's more than a hint of Fripp & Eno's '70s work here, yet the textures retain a grit and hardness that give the piece a startlingly contemporary feel. Indeed the track can also be compared to the dark ambient music of industrial pioneers :zoviet*france:, with the same rough edges and careful accumulation of sonic detail.

'The Moebius Loop'
The inner sleeve of Hammill's 1979 album *pH7* contained a grid of the songs and the instruments on each track of the recording. One of the songs listed was 'The Moebius Jigsaw', although there was no song by that name on the album. It's possible, therefore, that 'The Moebius Loop' is related in some way to the earlier unreleased track. Whatever the truth of the matter, the song's an uneasy chorale for looped piano and voice, which makes a considerable impact with its layered vocals and woozy repetitions. The artist M. C. Escher is not mentioned by name, but his visions of 'indecision and uncertainty' inhabit the piece. Works by Escher (*Moebius Strip II*, *Metamorphosis II*, *Relativity*) are indirectly referenced in the text, contributing to the sense of bewilderment that haunts the song.

'An Endless Breath'
An unsettling instrumental piece that takes organ-generated sounds as a basis and subjects them to all manner of loops and manipulations. There's something almost infernal about the repeated patterns and sub-bass drones that emerge from this process, as though the endless breath of the title is a threat rather than any kind of relief. Again, industrial and dark ambient music is strongly evoked.

'In Slow Time' (Hammill/Ferguson)
A different version of the track from *A Black Box* (q.v.), this was used as the backing track for a dance performance choreographed by Nicolas Dixon and broadcast on BBC TV's *Riverside* arts programme.

'My Pulse'
By far the longest track on the album at just under sixteen minutes, 'My Pulse' was also the music for a ballet choreographed by Nicolas Dixon. It's a heady

mix of processed piano and electric guitar, with brief snatches of melody and chordal voicings manipulated and warped out of all recognition. The effect is mesmerising, not least when a churning piano motif emerges at around the halfway mark. This is instantly recognisable as the melody of the 'Dreaming' section from Act III of Hammill's opera *The Fall of the House of Usher*, which was not released until 1991.

'The Bells! The Bells!'

A more subdued instrumental piece to close out the album. The credits list the instrumentation as 'rhythm box'; this is the only track of the seven not to include either voice, guitar or a keyboard of some sort (piano, organ or synthesizer). It's as though this last track represents a progressive subtraction of possibilities until we're left with nothing but a skeletal structure, faint traces of beats and hollow, fragmented drones.

Skin (1986)

Personnel:
Peter Hammill: vocals, guitar, keyboards
David Jackson: saxophone
Hugh Banton: keyboards
Guy Evans: drums, percussion
Stuart Gordon: violin
David Coulter: didgeridoo
David Luckhurst: backing vocals
All songs by Peter Hammill, except where noted
Recorded at Sofa Sound, Avon and Wool Hall Studio, Bath, 1985
Produced by Peter Hammill
UK release date: March 1986
Cover design: Peter Hammill and Paul Ridout

Skin marked the beginning of a new way of working for Hammill – and also, in part, a return to old ways. It had been three years since his last 'proper' album, *Patience*, although he had been far from idle in the meantime. Extensive touring with the K Group, the release of the *Margin* live album and the hybrid *Love Songs* project had all kept him busy. By 1985, though, it was clear that the K Group was no longer viable as a working unit and that different ways of collaboration were called for. In addition, playing and recording technology had advanced to such an extent that Hammill was now able to record and mix almost the whole album at his (now sixteen-track) home studio, rather than laying down backing tracks at home and overdubbing the remainder at an outside studio, with its attendant time constraints, as he had largely been doing up until then.

On the performance side, Hammill's new kit included a Yamaha DX7 synthesizer and a Drumulator drum machine. The DX7 was both boon and curse; by far the most commercially successful digital synth of the 1980s, it made FM synthesis affordable to musicians for the first time but was so complex and difficult to program that most users (including Hammill) were content to rely on its 32 factory presets rather than attempting to generate their own patches. As a result, much pop music of the '80s came to be defined by the glassy sound of the DX7, in contrast to the fizzing analogue synth tones that had dominated the airwaves in the late '70s.

Hammill was not immune to the charms of the DX7, and *Skin* is very much a product of its time. Its sequenced keyboards may sound dated now, but they brought out a more pop-wise side to Hammill that was, and remains, highly refreshing. As he writes in the sleeve notes to the 2007 reissue, 'with a different voice on top of them, some [of these songs] might even be viewed as commercial.' You can even, gasp, *dance* to some of this stuff. It's one of Hammill's most appealing and accessible albums, with not a weak song on it, from uptempo synth-driven numbers to the three reflective ballads which remain live staples to this day. The album culminates with 'Now Lover', a ten-minute epic that effortlessly channels the spirit of VdGG. And speaking of that outfit, there are some familiar names listed in the credits: not only the ubiquitous Jackson and Evans, but also Hugh Banton, making his first appearance on a Hammill album since *Nadir's Big Chance*.

'Skin'

A bold and bright opening statement, 'Skin' seems to inhabit a 'private world' that forms the obverse of the final track 'Now Lover'. If the later cut evokes a visionary, almost futuristic dream world of sexual ecstasy, 'Skin' offers a more personal depiction of intimacy, one in which the 'electric shiver in the spine' of 'Now Lover' is transmuted into a 'shiver down the spine of the body map.' There's a solid drum machine beat to anchor the track, but Evans soon emerges to add his own distinctive rhythms around Hammill's resonant voice and darting guitar work. As Hammill writes in the notes to the *Storm (Before The Calm)* compilation, the song also sees 'the last bow of [his] cha-cha-in-the-living-room organ', previously heard to variable effect on songs like 'Handicap and Equality' and 'She Wraps It Up'.

'After The Show'

'There are several onion skin layers of reality here', writes Hammill of this song in the notes to the *Calm (After The Storm)* compilation, 'and some of them are obviously self-referential.' In other words, this is another take on the situation in 'The Mousetrap (Caught In)' from *The Future Now* (1978), in which a troubled actor is faced with the uncomfortable truth that he's 'not really going anywhere.' The actor in 'After The Show', on the other hand, seems comfortable with a life of 'drinking in the café on the corner' as a means of winding down from a performance. I particularly like the reference to Samuel Beckett's *Waiting for Godot*, the last word in theatrical cyclicality. As for the cryptic reference to 'that philosophy in German', my money's on Nietzsche's theory of eternal recurrence. As Nietzsche wrote: 'Your whole life, like a sandglass, will always be reversed and will ever run out again.'

In a 1998 documentary, Hammill told of how 'a singer is like an actor in that he has to go through a process of change, and readiness, in order to become convincing in terms of the songs – to play the roles of the songs.' Those who have seen Hammill live over the years will attest to the way he absolutely assumes a character as he plunges into the performance of each song. In any event, there's a poignant lyricism to the text that's reflected in Hammill's layered vocals, Jackson's smoky sax breaks and the song's sensitive, restrained arrangement.

'Painting By Numbers'

A curious subject for a song, this. Hammill seems very exercised by the risk that the art world establishment might act as cultural gatekeepers, dismissing an artist's work because it lacks a theoretical basis. Not, I confess, an issue that keeps me awake at night, although Hammill's concern is obviously sincere. The lyric is appropriately acid, both in meaning and delivery, and those who have snoozed through various BBC arts documentaries over the years will smile in recognition at the lines 'a programme for the BBC where academic critics can talk of art that's fine, like holy wine – the Blessed Intellectuals!' The DX7 sounds a trifle over-egged here, and the rhythm is on the square side, but it's an exuberant song with a highly catchy tune. This was released as a single, but inevitably it failed to trouble the charts.

'Shell'

If anyone ever tries to tell you that Hammill (a) can't sing properly; and (b) can't write a decent tune, just play them 'Shell'. This lovely song is one of his best ever, haunted by a quality of desperate yearning and with a lyric that unfolds to an unutterably gorgeous rising and falling melody. Hammill's voice has rarely sounded as calm and understated as it does here, cleaving to a text shot through with dazzling, rapturous imagery. The Argentinian writer Jorge Luis Borges, the Dutch artist M. C. Escher (*cf.* 'The Moebius Loop' from *Loops and Reels*) and the English poet William Blake (the 'tiger burning bright') all have walk-on roles, but the key figure in the song, though unnamed, is Charles Darwin. In the sleeve notes to the *Calm (After The Storm)* compilation, Hammill writes that the song 'was originally called 'Galapagos' … [I'm] sure as hell we're writing our own (unknown) histories.' Darwin spent time on the Galapagos islands in 1835; observing the tortoises he found there, he noted that their shells differed in shape, an observation that contributed to the theory of evolution. In the song, the shells of the tortoises (or turtles) merge with the sea shells on the beach, forming 'some kind of history' out of the characters' 'ghost-written lives.'

'All Said And Done'

'One of my better pop songs,' writes Hammill in the sleeve notes to the 2007 reissue, and who am I to disagree. Hammill's voice carries the song's light, airy melody, shadowed by radiant acoustic guitar and frisky piano. The tempo rises as Hammill cuts loose on electric, while multi-layered voices animate the text. Backing himself on vocals is a frequent practice for Hammill, and rightly so, since it allows him to temper his mighty baritone with softer vocal lines in a higher register. This approach pays repeated dividends, nowhere more so than on 'All Said And Done' with the backing vocals sparkling around the verses and chorus. Lyrically, the song's a return to the bitter emotional terrain of 'If I Could' and 'Don't Tell Me'. Painfully aware that his lover is on the brink of leaving him, the narrator is left with the unpleasant fact of there being 'nothing left to say.'

'A Perfect Date'

There's a drum-heavy, almost tribal feel to this one, although the drums were all programmed. Sinuous electric guitar pops up at intervals, but all is not as it seems. As Hammill writes in the notes to the *Storm (Before The Calm)* compilation, what you hear is 'the remnants of an original continuous riff' which he played straight through and then muted from time to time in the finished track. The lyric is opaque, but the line about the Mount of Venus seems to prefigure the erotic tension of 'Now Lover', while the references to Jerusalem and the Jaffa Gate (part of the city wall in old Jerusalem) bring a historical perspective to the song. VdGG organist Hugh Banton plays keyboards, programmed to sound like (to quote the sleeve notes) a 'perfect mad cello'.

'Four Pails' (Chris Judge Smith, Maxwell Hutchinson)

VdGG co-founder Smith wrote this song in partnership with Maxwell Hutchinson, later a renowned architect. Like Smith's earlier 'Been Alone So Long' (from *Nadir's Big Chance*), it's a song so in tune with Hammill's worldview that it's hard to believe he didn't write it himself. Indeed, Hammill had addressed similar themes at least twice before, on 'Red Shift' from *The Silent Corner and the Empty Stage* and 'Still in the Dark' from *The Future Now*. Like those earlier songs, 'Four Pails' sets out to acknowledge the irrefutability of the scientific method, but ends up mired in doubt and confusion. Faced with the death of his lover, the narrator undergoes some kind of spiritual epiphany, moving from a blunt dismissal of the notion of life after death ('when you're dead you're dead, when you're gone you're gone') to a troubled recognition of the possibility of an afterlife. It's a deeply humane song, its journey traced by Hammill's sombre lead vocal and delicate piano. Layered backing vocals glide over the surface, adding to the sense of uncertainty and fragmentation that dwells within the song. Stuart Gordon adds shimmering violin; in the sleeve notes to the 2007 reissue, Hammill writes that 'this was the first time that [he] played for me.' Hammill had apparently forgotten about Gordon's appearance on 'Just Good Friends' from 1983's *Patience* album.

'Now Lover'

'A song about time and the chase of the 'now'', writes Hammill in the sleeve notes to the 2007 reissue. As Hammill's longest song of the 1980s, and certainly one of his most ambitious during this period, 'Now Lover' is a key track in terms of his development as a writer, producer and arranger. Its arresting dynamic shifts, timbral variations and daring lyrical flights are more than enough to invoke the presence of VdGG, while the presence of David Jackson on sax and Guy Evans on drums doesn't do it any harm either. The song's an urgent channelling of sexual desire, visualising the erotic as 'ancient magic', lovers as 'flesh and blood bodies consumed by the catalyst.' It's surely one of Hammill's greatest lyrics, conceptually rich and alive with hallucinatory imagery.

Beginning and ending with the guttural lurch of the didgeridoo (courtesy of British musician David Coulter), the song sets out its case with an introduction fuelled by brisk keyboards, bold strokes of percussion from Evans and, once again, those labyrinthine layered vocals, surging through the neural pathways of Hammill's text. In the calmer middle section, Jackson takes an emotive solo while Hammill's voice retreats into wintry, sorrowful cadences. The last five minutes pass in a glorious maelstrom of ensemble playing, with Hammill, Jackson and Evans tumbling headlong towards the song's passionate conclusion, their co-operation as intuitive and magical as ever.

Bonus track
'You Hit Me Where I Live'

Originally released as the B-side of the 'Painting By Numbers' single, this is a fantastic slice of Hammill at his most pop-wise and refreshing. From its initial cry of 'wah-ooh, yeah!' to its fiery bursts of electric riffing, the song propels Hammill towards the dancefloor like nothing else in this book. And after the anguished balladry of his '70s love songs, it's a joy to hear him express words of love in natural, idiomatic terms. 'When I try to speak, I find my bursting heart full of you' is worthy of McCartney, while lines like 'you're a duellist in your own fashion, eyes that run me through' leave me purring with pleasure. As for the keyboard arpeggiation that whizzes through the track, it was all played through by Hammill rather than sequenced. Take that, 1980s recording technology!

And Close As This (1986)

Personnel:
Peter Hammill: vocals, keyboards
All songs by Peter Hammill, except where noted
Recorded at Sofa Sound, Avon, August-September 1986
Produced by Peter Hammill
UK release date: November 1986
Photography: Anton Corbijn

It's a measure of Hammill's versatility and the sheer scope of his ambition
that within a year of releasing one of his most highly produced and arranged
albums, he came up with this minimalist masterpiece. It's an album of solo
keyboard songs but, characteristically, there's a rigorous theoretical foundation
to it, as described by Hammill in the sleeve notes to the 2007 reissue:

> What would an album be like if derived from one single pass of the hands
> across the keyboard, one single vocal take? Could one create something with
> a diverse sonic palette yet still originated from, tied to, the idea of direct
> performance in its simplest form?

In an attempt to answer these questions, Hammill came up with a cunning
plan. Each of the eight songs on the album was recorded in a single take, both
vocals and keyboards. Two of the eight – 'Too Many of My Yesterdays' and
'Beside The One You Love' – were recorded live at the piano, with the vocals
overdubbed later. Hammill played the remaining six tunes directly into his
Yamaha DX7 synthesizer, thereby creating MIDI data which was saved to disc
by his collaborator Paul Ridout. Hammill and Ridout were then able to use
the computer to create the 'diverse sonic palette' they were after by assigning
different timbres and other sonic treatments to each individual note, always
working with the original fund of notes that had been created in one single
pass of the keyboard.

In practice, most of the timbres chosen for the recorded versions were
not too far removed from piano sounds anyway – an electric piano here, a
harpsichord or organ there. It would, of course, have been possible to assign
pure piano sounds to everything, but that would have defeated the object
of the exercise. Hammill could also have recorded the six MIDI-generated
songs at the piano instead, which might have made for a more conceptually
unified solo piano album. But he has never been one to shirk a challenge,
nor to pass up the opportunity to use whatever technology means are at his
disposal in the service of creative music-making. It's also tempting to speculate
what some of these songs would sound like played by a full band, or at least
an accompanying instrument or two. 'Silver' and 'Confidence', in particular,
almost sound like demos here. Ultimately, though, *And Close As This* is a brave
and thoughtful experiment, and – more importantly – a cracking set of songs.

'Too Many of My Yesterdays'

Another take on the perennial Hammill theme of faltering relationships (*cf.* 'If I Could', 'Don't Tell Me', 'All Said And Done'), this is the first of two songs recorded live at the piano in one unedited take. It's also notable for a stunning vocal performance from Hammill. No singer has ever inhabited a song with such unflinching dignity, such grave attention to the grain and sweep of human existence, as Hammill does here. When he sings 'but seeing you again puts shakes into my soul', to take just one example, it feels shattering to listen to, as though he's living through the experiences he describes even as he's uttering the words of the song.

'Faith'

As Hammill writes in the 2007 sleeve notes, 'there's probably more of dramatic effect to be mined from stories of failed rather than fulfilled romance.' A song like 'Too Many of My Yesterdays' from the former category certainly doesn't lack dramatic effect. But Hammill has also told stories of fulfilled romance, blissfully so in the case of 'Vision' from 1971's *Fool's Mate*, less successfully on 'My Favourite' from 1979's *pH7*. 'Faith' is the first of two such songs on *And Close As This*, its simple message carried by a plaintive melody and unvarnished vocals. Hammill is on dangerous ground here, since the potential for mawkishness undoubtedly exists. But he negotiates the dangers adroitly enough, not least by recognising that 'doubt casts its shadow on every perfect plan that is made' and by the closing plea of 'don't let me down, now that I've fallen completely for you.'

'Empire of Delight' (Hammill, Emerson)

A one-off collaboration with the late Keith Emerson of Emerson, Lake & Palmer, for which Hammill wrote the lyric to a tune by Emerson. Amusingly, when Emerson was asked in 2011 how the collaboration came about, he had no recollection of it ever having taken place. Hammill was a little more forthcoming, recalling in a 1986 interview that '[Emerson] got in touch with me and I went over to see him ... it was a professional and artistic collaboration.' Whatever the precise circumstances of the encounter, 'Empire of Delight' is a highlight of the album, its haunting melody picked out in restrained tones of electric piano and harpsichord. The song imagines the wraithlike presence of a past lover who materialises and then slips away, as though the memory of her is sufficient to bring her back in 'that moment when the fire ignites.' The line 'suddenly I feel you near me, worlds away and close as this' also gives the album its title – an appropriate one for an album cloaked in intimacy and regret.

'Silver'

As I wrote in the introduction to this chapter, some of the songs on *And Close As This* sound less like chamber pieces and more like songs that could happily stand up to fuller arrangements. 'Silver' is one such, an intimidating snarl of a song birthed from raging vocals and maze-like electric piano. The lyric takes venomous aim at some liar, some betrayer; Hammill writes in the 2007 sleeve notes that he 'had no-one particular in mind' when he wrote the song, but that 'life doesn't disappoint in throwing up instances of this kind of behaviour.' With characteristic poetic flair, Hammill seizes on the symbolic associations of silver: Judas betraying Christ for thirty pieces of silver (although Hammill seems to have misremembered it as forty pieces); having one's future told by crossing a fortune-teller's palm with silver; and finally, brutally, the custom of placing silver coins on the eyes of a dead person. On an album mostly characterised by feelings of composure, 'Silver' is a welcome blast of turbulence.

'Beside The One You Love'
The second of the two acoustic piano songs, and another sublime affirmation of romantic love. It's with a song like this that the notion of 'one pass of the hands across a keyboard' really begins to make sense. Hammill's piano playing here sounds cautious, almost tentative, as though he's picking his way gingerly through a minefield of emotions as he performs the song. His voice, too, imparts that fear of evanescence, the same anxiety that haunts 'Been Alone So Long' – the fear that a state of such bliss may not be true after all and is in danger of vanishing like the 'embers now flickering their last.'

'Other Old Clichés'
In the 2007 sleeve notes, Hammill brackets this with 'Too Many of My Yesterdays' as being the two songs on the album in which 'the last nails in the coffins of relationships are hammered home.' The song's also about a perennial Hammill theme, language and the power of words. Faced with the impending end of a relationship, how successful a coping strategy is it to construct defensive barriers made of comforting clichés? The answer appears to be 'not very', since midway through the song, the clichés evaporate and the narrator lashes out with hard, direct questions: 'What do you want? What do you expect? What do you say?' By the final verse, these too have gone, with nothing left but fear and emptiness: 'hold me now, don't let go.'

'Confidence'
Like 'Silver' before it, this is a song infused with high-wire drama that is crying out for a band arrangement. In the absence of such, Hammill and Ridout use the full panoply of DX7 and other sonic treatments to flesh out this arch tale of outer confidence masking inner turmoil. Electric piano and spacey synth timbres shore up Hammill's rich, sonorous voice, insistent falsetto running rings around the primary vocal line. As the song takes hold, hypnotic Philip Glass-like arpeggios battle for supremacy against echoing vox and drums.

'Sleep Now'

In 1973, Hammill wrote 'Wilhelmina' for the infant daughter of VdGG drummer Guy Evans. Not yet a parent himself, he was concerned in that song to warn the little girl that she was entering a 'cruel world' in which 'people can really be strange'. Thirteen years later, he was to write 'Sleep Now', a disarmingly beautiful lullaby to his own young daughters with an emotional weight capable of affecting even its composer. At a 2008 concert in Israel, Hammill prefaced a performance of the song with an announcement that his youngest daughter was about to turn 21, rendering him no longer a 'biological necessity'. Overcome by emotion, he broke down and cried onstage during the performance. The song has an almost unbearable tenderness at its heart, a vulnerability inscribed in the gentle turns of its melody and in exquisite lines like 'these eyes that gently flicker in some lost childhood dream.' As the parent of two children myself, all I can say is that I know how he feels.

In A Foreign Town (1988)

Personnel:
Peter Hammill: vocals, guitar, keyboards
Stuart Gordon: violin
All songs by Peter Hammill, except where noted
Recorded at Sofa Sound, Avon, October 1987-January 1988
Produced by Peter Hammill
UK/US release date: November 1988
Cover design by Paul Ridout
Photography by Hilary Hammill and Armando Gallo

Hammill's 1986 album *Skin* had seen him use computers and sequencing software as tools for music-making for the first time. Two years on, *In A Foreign Town* was very much a development of that sequence-driven sound. As Hammill writes in the notes to the album on his website: 'this is an absolutely crucial set of recordings in terms of my development ... if I had not undertaken them in exactly this way and with this result, much of my subsequent work would not have come about.'

In other words, Hammill was still on something of a learning curve when he made this album, and unfortunately, it shows. The record is unpopular with many Hammill fans, less due to the quality of the songs themselves than to their production and instrumentation, which in many cases veer towards the clunky and overbearing. It's instructive to compare the album to *Skin*, which also made extensive use of sequenced keyboards and drum machines. The earlier album, however, had a lightness of touch and a certain swagger that is mostly absent from *In A Foreign Town*, as though the record is being weighted down by the seriousness of its concerns.

This brings me to the other notable aspect of the album, which is that several of the songs mark a return to the social and political themes of the *Future Now/pH7* era from 1978-79. When *pH7* was released, the Conservative government of Margaret Thatcher had just come to power; nine years later, they were still there, still enacting socially divisive and morally bankrupt policies. In addition, seismic events such as the 1987 stock market crash and the rise of the anti-apartheid movement were raising the global temperature. Against this backdrop, it's not surprising that Hammill felt the need to address social and political issues on the album. Despite a certain stodginess and uniformity of sound, Hammill's social conscience and lyrical inventiveness are in full flight here.

'Hemlock'

The Japanese CD release of *In A Foreign Town* contained a booklet in which Hammill wrote short notes on each of the songs. With regard to 'Hemlock', he describes it as 'a song confronting some of the lies and half-truths we must swallow in order to retain a semblance of unity in the modern world.'

Heavy stuff, borne out by gravely intoned lyrics such as 'The earth is flat, and pigs can fly – swallow hard and believe the lies.' The song itself, on the other hand, never quite takes flight, hamstrung as it is by a ponderous melody and thumping programmed drumbeats. Stuart Gordon tries to liven things up with some scurrying violin runs, but he's fighting a losing battle. A live version on the 1990 *Room Temperature* album, with Gordon on violin and Nic Potter on bass, reveals the underlying power of the song when cut loose from the moorings of those drumbeats.

'Invisible Ink'

This is more like it. A sleek pop song that wouldn't have sounded out of place on *Skin*, 'Invisible Ink' benefits greatly from its easygoing vocal and catchy, memorable hooks. The song's a disarming plea for directness in public discourse and an admission of confusion in the face of endless messages that are so esoteric that 'they might as well be printed in invisible ink.' But it wears its concerns lightly, its effervescent synth melody dancing around an infectious beat, while Hammill's voice diffracts smoothly into lead and backing vocals. Indeed Hammill notes on his website 'the continuing evolution and importance of backing vox' on this album. 'Invisible Ink' is a fine example, the darting interplay between voices in different registers key to the full, inviting soundworld of the song.

'Sci-Finance (Revisited)'

This track is a revised and updated version of 'Sci-Finance', a cut from the riotous 1978 Van der Graaf live album *Vital*. Whereas the original version was all rough edges and fuzzed-out guitars, the remake is an altogether slicker proposition fuelled by blaring synth and half-buried acoustic guitar. The stock market crash of 1987 had just happened when Hammill began work on the album, giving the original song a grim relevance that required updating only to reflect the computerisation of the money markets. The fortune that 'shines on the VDU' vanishes 'when the last of the deals have been cleared away.' The song received a vigorous live treatment during a 1993 European tour, its hookline 'there goes the daylight' giving the resulting live album its title.

'This Book' (Hammill/Colombo/Ameli)

The unusual writing credits to this one tell their own story. Spanish singer Miguel Bosé had recorded a song called 'Abrir y cerrar' on his 1984 album *Bandido*, with music by two Italian composers, Roberto Colombo and Gianpiero Ameli. For 'This Book', Hammill used the same tune but wrote a new lyric to go with it, in the process giving *In A Foreign Town* one of its few optimistic scenarios. It's a highlight of the album, its persuasive melody and stylish mid-tempo rhythms exerting a considerable emotional pull. When Hammill sings, 'we are breaking the mould, we are rapture', there's a real sense of euphoria to his voice, while the delightful chorus and its line 'find I'm befriended in a foreign town' bestow a title on the record.

Musically, the song sees silvery threads of acoustic guitar wrap themselves snugly around discreet synth parts. In the notes to the album on his website, Hammill relates that he 'was learning all the time, particularly in the area of putting together keyboard and guitar parts into a structured whole.' On the evidence of 'This Book', he was learning fast.

'Time To Burn'

Tony Stratton-Smith passed away in 1987, having founded the Charisma label on which most VdGG and early Hammill albums were released, and having been VdGG's manager for many years. 'Time To Burn' is a moving elegy for 'Strat', a sombre ballad dominated by looming synthesised strings. Stratton-Smith died at the tragically young age of 53, and the song is haunted by the troubling thought that there was 'so much left undone' in his life. I'm reminded of Hammill's other great elegy, 'Not For Keith' from 1979's *pH7*, in which he mourns that Ellis 'deserved more time.' So, too, did Stratton-Smith.

The song's string arrangement is appropriately funereal, but there's a rinky-dink keyboard line that doesn't sit particularly well alongside it. One might also have hoped for a little more finesse in the rhythm track, which frequently threatens to overwhelm the vocals and keyboards. The song is often performed live at solo concerts, where its stripped-down piano accompaniment illuminates its disquieting sense of loss and regret far more than the studio version.

'Auto'

In the notes to the album on his website, Hammill describes this song as a 'vignette from my days of touring.' He puts a more metaphysical spin on things in the notes to the Japanese edition, writing that 'the Drive, and its philosophical implications is ... both purposeful and purposeless, juxtaposing a sense of timelessness with intimations of mortality.' In either case, the song can be seen as a kind of sequel to 'Sitting Targets', albeit one that trades that song's punky energy for a lively synthesized brass arrangement. As is so often the case on this album, the drum machine is unwieldy and invasive, but there's a fine sense of helter-skelter motion implied by those synths and by the exhilaration in Hammill's voice. Close your eyes and you could almost be pedal to the metal, 'up ahead on the autobahn.' It's a very different sound of movement from that of Kraftwerk's 'Autobahn', or the endless vistas imagined by Klaus Dinger's *motorik* beat for Neu!, but it's equally appealing – and it moves closer to that context in the German version on the *Offensichtlich Goldfisch* album.

'Vote Brand X'

As noted in the introduction to this chapter, *In A Foreign Town* came in the midst of a long and bleak period of Conservative government in the UK. In

1979, Hammill had written 'The Old School Tie' as a broadside against career politicians; by 1988 his scorn had escalated further into vitriolic condemnation of 'the modern political man' for whom politics is 'just like selling soap powder.' Although the sentiment is unimpeachable, 'Vote Brand X' is a gruelling low point on the album. Devoid of melodic interest and held together by a lumbering rhythm, the song rightly expresses indignation but forgets to include anything that might make it worth listening to.

'Sun City Nightlife'

And speaking of indignation, here's a righteous denunciation of apartheid South Africa, as symbolised by the Sun City entertainment complex that became the focus of the cultural boycott of that country in the 1980s. Ten years earlier, Hammill had been one of the first western musicians to write about apartheid, on the caustic 'A Motor-Bike In Afrika' from *The Future Now*. Making explicit the connection with the earlier song, he recites its opening lines towards the end of 'Sun City Nightlife'. In a 1990 interview, however, Hammill clarified the later song by saying that it's 'not just about South Africa, it's about a certain mentality which can occur away from apartheid.' Be that as it may, the impact of the song is fatally weakened by its strident keyboards, galumphing drumbeats and everything-but-the-kitchen-sink production.

'The Play's The Thing'

As we saw in earlier chapters, Hammill drew shrewd parallels between the life of a musician and that of an actor in his earlier songs 'The Mousetrap (Caught In)' and 'After The Show'. It's natural, therefore, that he would pay tribute to Shakespeare in this sober ballad, a welcome moment of tranquillity on an album where everything else seems to be pushed into the red.

In the notes to the Japanese edition, Hammill writes of Shakespeare's 'deep understanding of the human heart and nature.' However, this acquiescence to Shakespeare's supposed timeless genius is deeply contentious. When I was studying English at Sussex University in the late 1980s, at the time *In A Foreign Town* was released, it was clear to me (via the teachings of Jonathan Dollimore and the late Alan Sinfield) that Shakespeare was inescapably political, and that essentialist depictions of his work as 'human' and 'eternal' were in fact ideologically loaded. This is the trap that Hammill falls into in 'The Play's The Thing'. Instead of wondering 'what is it Shakespeare'd say if he came back today?', he should have been asking how the plays function as critiques of Elizabethan society and ideology. But that might have made for a less interesting song.

'Under Cover Names'

The original LP ended here, with this exuberant anthem that once again demonstrates Hammill's ability to write a great left-field pop song. The synthesised horn parts are almost funky and just about survive the onslaught of the decidedly inert rhythm track. The voice is in fine shape, blasting its way deliriously through tides of percussion and sequenced keyboard patterns. You're almost tempted to pump your fist in the air, as Hammill's impassioned finding that we're 'lost in a jungle of our own creation, lost in a labyrinth of cover names' gives way to another heady flourish of brass. The song speculates on what happens when 'we keep on skirting round the edge of darkness, with fresh identities and best-laid plans.' However hard we try to hold on to a sense of who we are and our place in the world, at the end of the day we're all living in a foreign town.

Bonus tracks

'Smile' (Hammill/Grönemeyer)

I think of this as a bonus track because it doesn't appear on the original vinyl LP release of *In A Foreign Town*, although it does appear on the original CD and the later reissue on Fie! Its presence on the album feels unearned, partly due to its gestation (it's a translation of 'Lächeln' by the German superstar singer and actor Herbert Grönemeyer, from his 1986 album *Sprünge*), and partly because its puny arrangement is so far removed from the vibe of the rest. Pottering along on a flimsy rhythm track, the song takes a swipe at 'fat cats [who] get fatter day by day' but is not able to summon up much at all in the way of conviction.

'Time To Burn' (instrumental)

An instrumental version of Hammill's poignant elegy for Tony Stratton-Smith was, for some reason, tacked onto the end of the CD.

Out of Water (1990)

Personnel:
Peter Hammill: vocals, guitar, keyboards
John Ellis: guitar
David Jackson: saxophone
Nic Potter: bass guitar
Stuart Gordon: violin
All songs by Peter Hammill
Recorded at Sofa Sound, Avon and Terra Incognita, Bath, January-August 1989
Produced by Peter Hammill
UK/US release date: February 1990
Cover: John Ellis

A new decade brought changes to Hammill's working methods, including a new studio. He began recording *Out of Water* at his home studio, but roadworks (!) meant that it could not be completed there. Hammill then took over the lease of David Lord's Crescent studios in Bath and completed the recording and mixing of the album there, renaming the studio Terra Incognita in the process.

Recording and production technology, too, was advancing all the time. Inevitably, this meant that the sound of Hammill's albums began to change in ways that would continue to be apparent throughout the 1990s. Writing about the album on his website, Hammill notes that he 'felt on top of the technology and able to use it as part of the palette ... all sorts of hybrid ways of working, of composition, of subject matter, are on offer here.'

Having taken the sequenced keyboards and drums approach as far as it could go on *Skin* and *In A Foreign Town*, there was a more organic band sound to these recordings. Hammill began to make significant use of electric guitar for the first time since the K Group period, while the keyboards and percussion were less in-your-face than they had been on *In A Foreign Town*. Speaking of the K Group, John Ellis of that outfit plays lead guitar on several tracks, not to mention contributing the cover painting, which depicts the Meoto Iwa rocks off the coast of Japan. Other musicians appearing on the album are VdGG alumni Jackson and Potter on sax and bass, respectively, and violinist Stuart Gordon on one track.

In terms of the music business side of things, Hammill's public profile had been up and down for most of the 1980s, and the release of *Out of Water* did nothing to change that. His 1980s albums had been released on a bewildering variety of labels. Having left Charisma after the release of *pH7* in 1979, he formed his own short-lived record label, S-Type, for the release of *A Black Box*. His next album, *Sitting Targets*, was released on Virgin, but the two K Group studio albums appeared on Gordian Troeller's Naïve label. It was then back to Charisma (which was now part of Virgin) for *The Love Songs*, only for his next two albums (the live K Group set *The Margin* and *Skin*) to come out on the independent British label Foundry. He did one more album for Virgin (*And Close As This*) before signing to the American label Enigma for the release of *In A Foreign Town*, *Out of Water* and the double live CD *Room Temperature*. His tenure at Enigma, however, was not a happy one in terms of his (lack of) public visibility, a state of affairs that was to pave the way for him to start his own label Fie! in 1992.

Finally, I have a soft spot for *Out of Water* because it was the first new album Hammill released after I became a fan. I was living in Brighton at the time and went to Rounder Records in the Lanes (which, of course, is no longer there) on the day of release to pick up a copy. Enigma may not have done Hammill too many favours in terms of his public profile, but they managed to get some copies of *Out of Water* to southern England, so they must have been doing something right. More importantly, listening to this album on repeat was what convinced me that Hammill was the world's greatest singer and songwriter, an opinion I've never had cause to revise. Once he's got you, he's got you for life.

'Evidently Goldfish'

Not for the first time, one is confounded from the start of this album by questions of genre. What is 'Evidently Goldfish'? It's too minimalist to be progressive rock, too combative to be art rock, too finely wrought to be pop. In the notes to the album on his website, Hammill writes that the song 'originated from a tune I'd had since 1967 at the latest, but had never got round to working'; as we've seen in previous chapters, he's often raided the cupboard for tunes he hadn't used before or felt could be improved upon. In any event, this is an uncompromising statement of the need for scepticism 'in the mental sphere', an appeal to question one's environment and cut loose from 'circular experience'. Hammill delivers his text over a biting synthesizer and drum arrangement, while John Ellis contributes a spiralling solo. What is 'Evidently Goldfish'? It's another great Peter Hammill song, that's all.

'Not The Man'

Throughout his career, Hammill has never been content to trade on past glories. For almost thirty years, he refused all offers to reform Van der Graaf Generator, even though taking such a path would almost certainly have been more lucrative than the path he chose to take. When VdGG did finally reform, it had to be on the basis that they would not be another 1970s nostalgia act but had something new and vital to impart. In his solo career, too, Hammill has consistently made musical choices on the basis of artistic integrity rather than commercial appeal. 'Not The Man' could almost be his rejoinder to anyone who might wish him to revert to the classic 1970s PH/VdGG sound, a reminder that 'there can be no returning to the scene of the crime' if 'for perfection you're yearning.' Driven by crystalline keyboard arpeggios and sparkling acoustic guitar, the song makes a compelling case for not looking back.

'No Moon In The Water'

A transcendentally beautiful song, with a graceful vocal by Hammill and exquisite sax by Jackson. The refrain is based on a Zen koan – a short story or fable used as an object of study in Zen Buddhism. The koan of the nun Chiyono tells of how she was carrying a pail of water one moonlit night and noticed the full moon reflected on the surface of the water. The pail broke and the water ran out, so she could no longer see the reflection of the moon. Realising that she had been looking at a mere reflection, not the moon itself, Chiyono achieved enlightenment. The koan ends with a poem: 'No water in the pail! No moon in the water!'

One might add that Leonard Cohen, in my view Hammill's only serious rival as the world's greatest songwriter, was an adherent of Zen Buddhism. Cohen's famous line from his 1992 song 'Anthem', 'there is a crack in everything, that's how the light gets in', effectively makes the same point as Hammill's 'broken water pail, no moon in the water.' Cohen's album *The Future*, on which 'Anthem' appears, was released two years after Hammill cut *Out of Water*. It contains a song called 'Democracy', which begins with the lines 'It's coming through a hole in the air, from those nights in Tiananmen Square.' Which brings us to:

'Our Oyster'

In his 1967 polemic *The Society of the Spectacle*, Guy Debord wrote that 'all of life presents itself as an immense accumulation of spectacles ... everything that was directly lived has moved away into a representation.' Like Debord, Hammill is acutely aware of the power of the mass media to influence our response to external events. In 2001, soon after the 9/11 attacks, he wrote that 'our fixation and dependence on news as entertainment is implicit in all this. The impact of the second plane on the WTC was, of course, scheduled to be in effective prime time.' 'Our Oyster' makes a similar point about the Tiananmen Square massacre: 'six o'clock entertainment, tears of anguish and rage/In the zoos of the media, the spirit of moment is caged.'

In the notes to the album on his website, Hammill states that he 'didn't feel a compulsion to stick rhythm parts on everything,' an evident change from his practice on *In A Foreign Town*. Indeed there is no percussion on 'Our Oyster', which sees Ellis' guitar swirl in eddies around an emphatic keyboard figure. The electric piano is too clunky by half, but the song's sense of moral outrage is powerfully conveyed by the baleful sting of Hammill's vocal.

'Something About Ysabel's Dance'

Violinist and occasional guitarist Stuart Gordon first played with Hammill on 'Just Good Friends' from 1983's *Patience* album and frequently collaborated with Hammill on both live and studio work until his tragic death in 2014. 'Something About Ysabel's Dance' is a showcase for Gordon's inspired violin playing, its vertiginous cadences swooping around Hammill's restrained acoustic guitar. The anti-folk setting vividly imagines the fevered atmosphere of an after-hours cantina 'where there's every chance that she might show', drawn with precision by Hammill's evocative lyric. The title and the line 'there's no Charlie Mingus, his Tijuana's gone', refer to 'Ysabel's Table Dance' from Mingus' 1962 album *Tijuana Moods*, parts of which Hammill and Gordon would incorporate into live performances of the song.

'Green Fingers'
The only out-and-out rock song on the album is 'as much an admonition to myself as anyone else … got to stay engaged, got to stay passionate, got to stay in the real', as Hammill writes in the notes on his website. As philosophies of life go, it's a pretty good one, and it's one that Hammill has adhered to faithfully throughout his long working career. You need green fingers to be an expert gardener, but if you really want to experience life in all its burning intensity, you'll need to 'blood those hands with passion.' David Jackson is a towering presence, his molten tenor sax cascading around Hammill's stormy baritone and shards of electric guitar.

'On The Surface'
A song with a 'systems music basis', according to the notes on the website. What Hammill seems to mean by this is that 'a note sequence or rhythm is distended, altered, repeated, laid over itself… like a riff viewed through a kaleidoscope.' Indeed the song is constructed from a short, constantly repeated sequence of notes which undergoes subtle shifts of timbre and phrasing throughout the piece. It seems to me, however, that Hammill is guilty of a category error here. Systems music, insofar as it exists as a term at all, is really just another term for minimalism (let's leave 'process music' for another time), as exemplified by the early work of Steve Reich and Philip Glass. And the whole point of cornerstone works of minimalism like Glass' *Music in Twelve Parts* and Reich's *Music for 18 Musicians* is precisely that although they may sound repetitive to the casual listener, they are actually not repetitive at all, but are constantly changing over an extended period of time.

In any case, the trancelike repetitions of 'On The Surface' give the song a seductive, durational feel that is entirely appropriate to its lyrical quest for 'dreaming of long-lost childhood' and 'hoping for better days'. Recalling the meditative imagery of 'No Moon In The Water', the song plumbs oceanic depths of self-doubt, illuminated by a closing solo from Ellis that is almost Gilmourish in tone.

'A Way Out'
The album closes with an emotionally charged song of farewell that rightly takes its place as one of Hammill's greatest moments. The song is a hard reckoning of tragedy, haunted by a brokenness that lives and breathes in every syllable of Hammill's vocal. As lyrically audacious as it is melodically

sublime, it unflinchingly itemises absence and loss and excludes any possibility of redemption. The song having been a staple of live solo sets since its release, where its path is marked out in fallen crosses of piano, it's startling to reacquaint oneself with the studio version, wreathed in majestic washes of synthesizer and tendrils of Knopfleresque guitar. As the song nears its ending, the line 'out of reach of all family, all friends' banishes whatever glimmer of light remained: a bleak iconography of despair that cuts as deep as anything Hammill has ever written.

The Fall of the House of Usher (1991/1999)

Personnel:
Peter Hammill: vocals, guitars, keyboards
Andy Bell: vocals
Sarah-Jane Morris: vocals
Lene Lovich: vocals
Herbert Grönemeyer: vocals
Stuart Gordon: violin (1999 only)
Music by Peter Hammill
Libretto by Chris Judge Smith
Recorded at Sofa Sound, Avon and Terra Incognita, Bath, 1989-1990
Produced by Peter Hammill
UK release date: November 1991/November 1999
Cover: Paul Ridout

The Fall of the House of Usher is unlike anything else in Hammill's catalogue. Eighteen years in the making, the work is an adaptation of Edgar Allan Poe's 1839 short story of the same name, with music by Hammill and libretto by VdGG co-founder Chris Judge Smith. To get the question of definition out of the way: this is an opera. It's not a 'rock opera', 'rock musical', 'song cycle' or 'concept album'. It meets all the formal criteria for an opera, in that it's a theatrical work scripted for acting, where music is fundamental and the dramatic roles are taken by singers.

Usher has a long and tortuous history. It has been recorded twice but never performed. As Smith writes in the notes to the 1999 re-recording, Hammill 'began writing *Usher* in 1973 ... work had proceeded intermittently ever since, with most years seeing at least a few weeks' collaborative work on the project.' As the work neared completion, there were plans both to record it and to perform it live. In 1989, discussions were held with the city of Barcelona regarding a full staging of the opera, but they came to nothing.

At around the same time, Hammill began work on the recording, which was substantially complete by the spring of 1990. Finding a record company prepared to release it, however, proved to be a challenge. As we saw in the previous chapter, Hammill's relationships with record labels during the 1980s had been sporadic at best; it's unsurprising, therefore, that few record companies saw a 76-minute opera adapted from Poe as a viable commercial proposition. The opera was, however, eventually released on Some Bizzare in 1991 on CD, cassette and a limited run of 500 double LPs. Some Bizzare were an unusual partner for Hammill, as they were previously best known for releasing work by key figures in the post-industrial underground – groups such as Coil, Psychic TV, Test Dept, Swans and Einstürzende Neubauten. But they deserve credit for releasing the opera at a time when Hammill's commercial appeal was not exactly at its height.

Hammill gathered an eclectic group of singers to perform the various roles in the opera alongside himself. The contralto Sarah-Jane Morris had appeared on a No. 1 single in the UK in 1986, singing on The Communards' 'Don't Leave Me This Way'. She was introduced to Hammill by her husband David Coulter, who had played on the *Skin* album. Lene Lovich had also enjoyed top five chart success in the UK, with her 1979 hit 'Lucky Number', and had worked previously with Smith. Herbert Grönemeyer, on the other hand, had never troubled the UK charts but was the biggest selling artist in German music. Most surprisingly, Hammill (at the suggestion of Lovich) drafted in Andy Bell of British synth pop duo Erasure to sing the key role of Montresor. At the time, Erasure were one of the most popular bands in the UK, having had three consecutive number one albums. One might have expected Bell's presence to raise the commercial profile of the opera somewhat, but it was not to be.

Eight years after the opera's release, Hammill regained the rights to the recording and planned to re-release it on his own Fie! label. But before the opera could take its rightful place alongside the rest of his back catalogue, there were some aspects of the original recording that could be improved upon. As Smith wrote in the 1999 sleeve notes: 'the austerity of the musical arrangements [of the 1991 recording] and its understated production techniques made for an uncompromising and demanding listening experience.' Hammill made the point more succinctly in a 1999 newsletter: 'the original version of *Usher* had been done to the best of my abilities at the time, but today seems, especially in comparison to some of the recent work, a little bit clunky at least.'

Hammill, therefore, carried out significant structural work on the original recording in what amounts to an entirely new version of the opera. The main changes were to remove the sampled percussion, add layers of electric guitars and re-record several of Hammill's vocal parts (the other singers' parts were kept from the original). The result is a distinct improvement on the 1991 version – in Hammill's words, 'at the same time much more lush and ordered and much darker, denser and forbidding.' Although the 1999 version is now out of print (as is the 1991 version), Hammill regards it as the definitive version of the opera. The commentary on the following pages, therefore, refers to the 1999 version.

A word on Smith's role as the librettist. The credits of the opera state: 'An opera by Peter Hammill, libretto by Chris Judge Smith.' This is in accordance with operatic tradition, in which the librettist receives second billing, the libretto being regarded as secondary to the music. It would be incorrect, therefore, to refer to Hammill and Smith as the joint authors of this work. Undoubtedly, however, Smith's work is a major achievement, a libretto of extraordinary power with ritualised terror lurking at every turn.

The Fall of the House of Usher stands some distance apart from the rest of Hammill's work by virtue of its status as an opera and an adaptation, the length of its gestation and the fact that the text was by another hand. There are, nevertheless, traces of the opera's Gothic imagination elsewhere in Hammill's work, particularly the cold-hearted isolation of 'House With No Door' and the agonised visions of 'A Louse Is Not A Home'. It's also worth noting that the evil, threatening house or castle is a standard trope of both Gothic literature and film, the latter exemplified by the work of the Hammer production company. I've long been struck by the echo of 'Hammer horror' in Hammill's name, and nowhere is the connection made clearer than in *The Fall of the House of Usher*.

Act I
'An unenviable role'

The first voice heard in the opera is that of Sarah-Jane Morris as the Chorus – 'the silent accomplice of all', as the libretto puts it. The Chorus explains that Montresor is on his way to visit his childhood friend Roderick Usher, who has written to him urgently to request his presence. Morris' rich, dark voice perfectly captures the sense of mystery and foreboding that greets Montresor as he journeys through 'a singularly dreary tract of country'. Smith's elegantly formal libretto, here and elsewhere in the opera, quotes directly from Poe's original text. The section also introduces the soundworld of the opera – resonant keyboards and massed orchestral guitars, the latter reminiscent of the work of New York composers Glenn Branca and Rhys Chatham.

'That must be the House'

Montresor (Andy Bell) arrives at the House of Usher. He describes its forbidding exterior – a 'great crumbling façade', with 'windows just like vacant eyes.' Understandably, he is reluctant to enter the house, but is reassured by a light at the window. This section is beautifully sung by Bell, who makes the role of Montresor his own with a performance of extraordinary sensitivity. It's hard to believe that anyone else was ever in contention for the part, but in fact, at least three other singers were considered at one time or another. British singer David Luckhurst had sung backing vocals on 'A Perfect Date' from *Skin*, and at one point, auditioned for Montresor. Fish from Marillion also had a go, but ultimately Hammill felt that his and Fish's voices were too similar, which would not have worked well since Hammill would be singing the role of Roderick Usher. Art-pop cabaret singer Marc Almond also unsuccessfully auditioned for the role, having previously recorded mediocre cover versions of 'Vision' and 'Just Good Friends'. In the end, though, Hammill made the right choice. Bell's remarkable range and the tone of wounded passion in his voice made him perfect for the role of Montresor.

Act II
'Architecture'

Hammill is heard for the first time, chanting the Voices of the House in deep, menacing tones. These multi-layered voices introduce themselves as they lie in wait for Montresor, each one an architectural feature of the House. Some of the architectural terms used here are well known, others less so. Smith was not an architect himself but had hung out with a group of architecture students in his post-VdGG band Heebalob. These included Maxwell Hutchinson, who later became president of the RIBA and co-wrote the song 'Four Pails' from *Skin*.

'The Sleeper'

Like the House, Usher is waiting for Montresor to arrive, and he passes the time by singing to himself. This is the opera's first major aria, sung by Hammill in a deep, macabre register to a swelling organ accompaniment. The text is an extract from a poem by Poe, first published in 1831, which anticipates the fate of Usher's sister Madeline later in the opera. 'The Sleeper' was one of the first sections of the opera to be completed, and was performed live by Hammill in 1974. It also formed the first part of a twenty-minute 'Usher Suite' which Hammill played at a number of concerts in 1992 – the closest the opera has ever come to being performed live.

'One thing at a time'

Montresor enters the House of Usher and is fulsomely welcomed by Usher. There's some sly comic business going on here, in what is otherwise a fairly serious opera. Montresor gets straight to the point, pressing Usher on why he has summoned him so urgently to the House, but Usher keeps trying to change the subject. Eventually, he caves in, leading to:

'I shun the light'

Usher finally tells Montresor what the problem is – that he is suffering from a morbid acuteness of the senses, and believes (rightly, as we know from 'Architecture') that the House is a living, breathing entity. This is one of Hammill's great vocal performances in the opera, every word invested with visceral anguish and terror. The section formed the second part of the 1992 'Usher Suite', which tells the story from Usher's point of view.

'Leave this House'

Montresor speculates on the cause of Usher's condition, and prescribes a holiday. An attractive option, you would think; but Usher is adamant that he cannot leave because 'the House is I.' Usher and Montresor are joined by the Chorus and then by the House itself, both of whom confirm Usher's fear that he will never leave. The interweaving of Bell's and Morris' voices with Hammill's in this section is uncannily beautiful, as Montresor finds himself beset by malign forces beyond his control.

Act III
'Dreaming'

Usher's sister Madeline (Lene Lovich) enters for the first time, lost in a dreamlike trance. In fact, she seems to be having two dreams at once, the first of a birthday party with a lover (possibly Montresor), the second of drowning in a lake. As Madeline delivers the lines of each dream in turn, they merge into one oceanic fantasy: 'floating in the icy darkness, hold him tightly, I can feel myself dissolving, oh how lovely, deep beneath the lapping water...' There's an icy purity to Lovich's voice here, underpinned by Stuart Gordon's flowing violin work. Those with long memories will recognize the main melody of this section, since it first appeared on 'My Pulse' from the 1983 *Loops and Reels* album.

'A chronic catalepsy'

Montresor and Usher discuss Madeline's condition. Usher tells his friend that Madeline experiences a series of deathlike comas, followed by episodes of sleepwalking like the one we have just seen. While she is sleepwalking, she violently resists any attempt to restrict her movements. Montresor wonders if she is receiving treatment for her condition, to which Usher replies that her doctor is 'one of the foremost rank.' Like most of the opera, this section is in recitative, the style of opera singing that adopts the rhythms of everyday speech. Smith's libretto, however, is anything but everyday in the way it echoes the elegant 19th-century formality of Poe's style.

'The Herbalist'

Usher and Madeline leave together, and Montresor is joined by Madeline's doctor, the Herbalist (Herbert Grönemeyer). It rapidly becomes clear to Montresor, however, that this 'doctor' is no more than a quack, selling dubious remedies for non-existent conditions. Grönemeyer sings the role with relish, offering some welcome comic relief in the midst of the looming horror. This is one of the few sections of the opera where the 1991 recording is preferable to the 1999 version. In most cases, the removal of rock drums was to the benefit of the piece. The percussion on the earlier version of 'The Herbalist', however, gave the section a demented swagger that is mostly absent from the later version, despite the lusty orchestration of the keyboards.

'The evil that is done'

The seriousness of the situation facing Usher and Madeline begins to dawn on Montresor, who sings, 'somehow I must help these two tormented souls, for if I cannot, who will?' In duet with the Chorus, he admits that he is tempted to leave the House, but realises that he 'cannot, because it is too late': the House now controls him as surely as it controls Usher. Grinding metallic sheets of guitar emerge from the walls as the Voices of the House close in on Montresor. This section forms the halfway point of the opera, as night falls on the House. One can imagine the dramatic climax that would be created if a performance were to pause here for the interval.

Act IV
'Five years ago'
The following morning Madeline greets Montresor, apparently recovered from her episode of sleepwalking but aware that 'I am not enjoying the good health I used to.' She is vivacious and charming and seems more concerned about Usher's health than her own. Lovich sings beautifully here, the ringing clarity of her voice contrasting with the weighty pull of the keyboards. Montresor joins Madeline to set up the following duet, saddened by his recollection of 'the fragile hour, the silent walk with a friend.'

'It's over now'
Montresor and Madeline reminisce over their past love for each other. This is one of the most compelling sections of the opera, a grand duet sung by Bell and Lovich in gorgeous two-part harmony. If Smith's libretto tends mostly towards the formal and literary, here it's transformed into a deeply poignant poem of lost love, missed opportunity and a past that can never be recaptured. In an opera dominated by mental disturbance and deep-rooted anxiety, 'It's over now' offers a rare glimpse of something pure and fleeting, a trace of what Philip Larkin called 'the glare of that much-mentioned brilliance, love'.

'An influence'
Madeline leaves the stage just as Usher re-enters. He tells Montresor that Madeline will die from her condition (although there has been no diagnosis, least of all from the Herbalist), but is unaware of her impending death. Montresor urges Usher to leave the House and take Madeline with him, but Usher is convinced that his destiny is intertwined with that of the House.

'No rot'
Usher reacts angrily to Montresor's last-ditch plea to let him take Madeline away. He is convinced that it is his inevitable fate to die in the House, and finally persuades Montresor to stay with him. Finally, the Voices of the House confirm that 'we shall not let him go.'

Act V
'She is dead'
The whole of Act V is given over to this single movement, sung by Hammill as the third part of the 1992 'Usher Suite'. The Chorus relates how Madeline has succumbed to another deathly coma during the night. Usher, with the Herbalist by his side, then wakes Montresor with the news that Madeline has passed away. Montresor agrees to help Usher to carry Madeline's body to one of the vaults beneath the House, there to be entombed. This, for my money, is the most spellbinding part of the entire opera, fuelled by the uncanny

power of Smith's libretto. Sarah-Jane Morris sings with icy precision, her richly expressive contralto laced with the chill inevitability of death. The section in which Usher and Montresor mourn Madeline (although Usher, of course, knows that she is not dead) and plan her burial, followed by an extended instrumental passage, is indescribably moving. As sampled strings play out a stately melody, guitars uncoiling in anger around them, we hear the sound of Madeline's coffin being nailed shut.

Act VI
'Beating of the heart'
The Chorus describes 'a sudden change in Usher's demeanour', in which he appears to be listening for hidden sounds that fill him with terror. The Voices of the House claim that the sound is the beating of the House's heart. A storm breaks, causing the waves on the lake to crash into the walls of the House and make them tremble. Montresor persuades the increasingly agitated Usher to calm their nerves by playing a song, an idea that doesn't exactly go according to plan.

'The Haunted Palace'
The ballad sung by Usher is a poem by Poe, originally published as a stand-alone text and later incorporated into *The Fall of the House of Usher*. The text anticipates the fall of the House: 'evil things, in robes of sorrow, assailed the monarch's high estate.' Montresor begins to hear the same terrible sounds that Usher had heard, and interrupts the song; but Usher continues playing in a doomed attempt to drown out the sounds.

'I dared not speak'
In the terrifying dénouement of the opera Usher, unable to hide the truth any longer, confesses to a horrified Montresor that they had buried Madeline alive. We realise that the sounds they have been hearing are the sounds of Madeline emerging from the tomb. Hammill's singing voice, which has remained in its lower register for most of the opera, transforms into a blood-curdling shriek as the keyboards pound rhythmically against his words. Finally, the voices of Montresor, the Chorus and the House itself combine in a nightmarish chorale of calamity and betrayal. This section formed the climax to the 1992 'Usher Suite', which can be seen in full on the essential *In The Passionskirche* live concert DVD.

'She comes towards the door'
Madeline emerges from her tomb, her mind lost in a childhood game of hide and seek. Her voice weaves unsteadily among those of Usher, Montresor and the Chorus, who utter fragments of lines from earlier in the opera. Echoing their earlier love song, Montresor finally accepts that 'it's over now.'

'The Fall'

The House disintegrates and sinks beneath the waters of the lake, taking its occupants with it and making good on its promise that 'we shall not let him go.' For Usher, too, the collapse of the House confirms his fear that he 'can never leave', while Montresor – the tragic hero of the opera – dies with the thought that 'the evil that is come could not be prevented.' The opera ends with the Voices of the House asserting their victory, as the keyboards and guitars form a wall of noise that looms over the scene and fades away.

Fireships (1992)

Personnel:
Peter Hammill: vocals, guitar, keyboards, percussion
John Ellis: guitar
David Jackson: saxophone, flute
Nic Potter: bass guitar
Stuart Gordon: violin
David Lord: keyboards, orchestration
All songs by Peter Hammill, except where noted
Recorded at Terra Incognita, Bath, November 1990-August 1991
Produced by Peter Hammill & David Lord
UK release date: March 1992
Cover: Paul Ridout (photography by Martin Bailey Reynolds)

In 1991 Hammill started his own record label, Fie!, for the release of his own music and that of a few trusted friends and collaborators. As we have seen, Hammill's relationships with record companies during the 1980s had been up and down, to say the least, so starting his own label seemed like a logical step. As he wrote in his newsletter: 'if I'm not going to be promoted in any tangible way, I might as well undertake the lack of promotion myself.'

Furthermore, the move was the logical conclusion of the self-sufficiency that Hammill had espoused as far back as 1973's *Chameleon in the Shadow of the Night*, which had been partly recorded at home; not to mention that he had recently taken over the lease of the Crescent studio in Bath, now renamed Terra Incognita. The studio was owned by David Lord, whose contributions to Hammill's live and studio work in the early 1990s were significant. (In a bizarre postscript to the story, Lord was convicted in 2015 of running a brothel out of his house in Bath.)

Fireships was the first of Hammill's albums to be released on Fie! It was also described in the CD booklet as 'Number One in the BeCalm series'. As we have seen in earlier chapters, Hammill had never had a problem in the past with mixing up energetic and reflective songs on the same record; indeed, such eclecticism had always been key to his appeal. It came as something of a surprise, therefore, when he announced that he intended to corral his calmer songs on one series of albums (which would be known as the BeCalm series), while the more dynamic songs would henceforth be released on a parallel run (to be known as the A Loud series), the first of which would be *The Noise*, 1993's follow-up to *Fireships*. Much to everyone's relief, the idea was soon abandoned. The booklet of the 2006 reissue of *Fireships* retains the original line about the album being the first in the BeCalm series, adding wryly that the series 'stopped at One'.

Musically, then, the album represents something of a departure for Hammill in its overall mood and pace. After the arresting mid-tempo opener, 'I Will Find You', the album settles into a more or less unified soundworld defined by

Above: Hammill live at La Maroquinerie in Paris, May 2006. *(Seán Kelly)*

Left: Hammill's début album *Fool's Mate* (1971) includes the classics 'Vision' and 'The Birds', both live favourites to this day. *(Virgin)*

Right: *Chameleon in the Shadow of the Night* (1973) is a mix of solo acoustic numbers, dynamic rockers and prog epics. *(Virgin)*

Left: *The Silent Corner and the Empty Stage* (1974) is one of Hammill's most celebrated and enduring albums. *(Virgin)*

This page: Hammill pictured recording a live session for Swiss TV in 1974, performing 'The Lie', 'Forsaken Gardens' and 'A Louse Is Not A Home'.

Left: Hammill used to wear the cloak on the cover of *In Camera* (1974) on his way home from shows. *(Virgin)*

Right: The truculent proto-punk attitude of 1975's *Nadir's Big Chance* famously earned the approval of John Lydon. *(Virgin)*

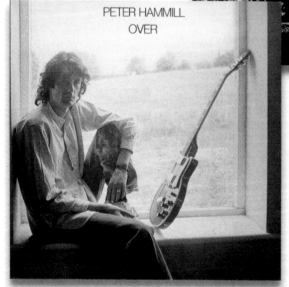

Left: The harrowing *Over* (1977) strikes the perfect balance between progressive ambition, scarred balladry and stinging punk rawness. *(Virgin)*

Right: *The Future Now* (1978) incorporated elements of noise, electronics, unconventional production techniques and a heightened sense of social awareness. *(Virgin)*

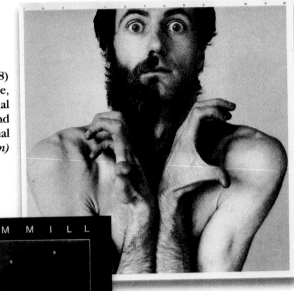

Left: The cover of *pH7* (1979) evokes a scary encounter in New York: 'we ran into some trouble from which we were lucky to escape.' *(Virgin)*

A BLACK BOX

Peter Hammill

Right: *A Black Box* (1980) is an intense, claustrophobic album, full of dark atmospheres and including the side-long epic 'Flight'. *(Virgin)*

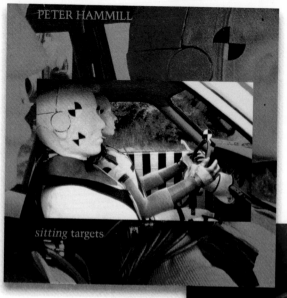

Left: The punchy new wave style of *Sitting Targets* (1981) paved the way for Hammill's future direction with the K Group. *(Virgin)*

Right: The first K Group album *Enter K* (1982), showcased the acute and artful new songs that Hammill was writing. *(Fie!)*

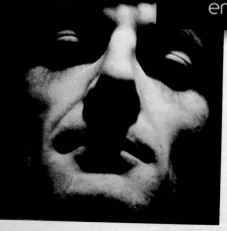

Left: The second and final K Group album *Patience* (1983) contains several tracks that have remained live favourites over the years. *(Fie!)*

Right: *Loops and Reels* (1983) was the first of three albums on which Hammill showcased his more experimental side. *(Fie!)*

Left: *Skin* (1986) is one of Hammill's most appealing and accessible albums, ranging from reflective ballads to uptempo synth-driven numbers. *(Virgin)*

Right: *And Close as This* (1986) is an album of solo keyboard songs, some recorded directly at the piano, others using MIDI technology. *(Virgin)*

Left and below: Hammill appeared on the Italian TV pop music show *Discoring* in 1984, miming to 'Just Good Friends'.

Peter Hammill - In A Foreign Town

Left: *In A Foreign Town* (1988) marked a return to the social and political themes of the *Future Now/pH7* era. *(Fie!)*

Right: Guitarist John Ellis painted the cover of *Out of Water* (1990), depicting the Meoto Iwa rocks off the coast of Japan. *(Fie!)*

Left: Eighteen years in the making, Hammill's opera *The Fall of the House of Usher* has never been performed. *(Some Bizzare)*

Right: The cover of *Fireships* (1992) is based on a painting by Turner. There's a ghostly image of Hammill superimposed on the painting. *(Fie!)*

Left: The raucous *The Noise* (1993) was touted at the time as 'Number One in the A Loud series'. *(Fie!)*

Right: Hammill's best album of the 1990s, *Roaring Forties* (1994), contained another side-long epic, 'A Headlong Stretch'. *(Fie!)*

Left: *X My Heart* (1996) was recorded with the PH Quartet of Hammill, David Jackson, Stuart Gordon and Manny Elias. *(Fie!)*

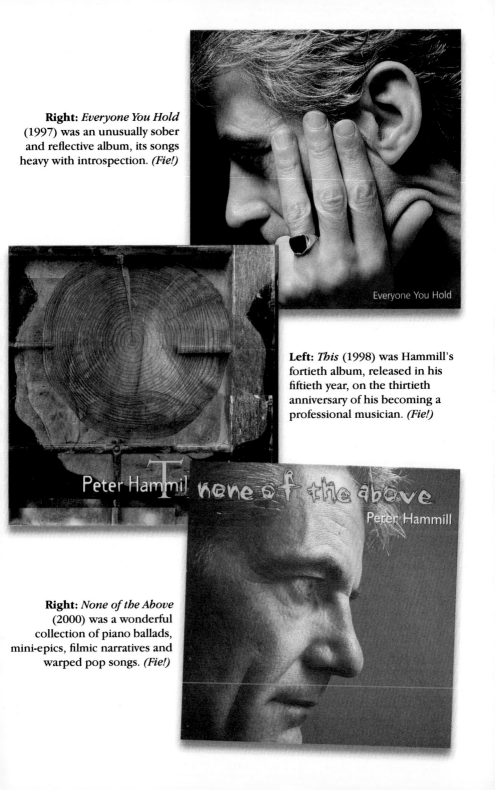

Right: *Everyone You Hold* (1997) was an unusually sober and reflective album, its songs heavy with introspection. *(Fie!)*

Left: *This* (1998) was Hammill's fortieth album, released in his fiftieth year, on the thirtieth anniversary of his becoming a professional musician. *(Fie!)*

Right: *None of the Above* (2000) was a wonderful collection of piano ballads, mini-epics, filmic narratives and warped pop songs. *(Fie!)*

Left: With three condensed epics, *What, Now?* (2001) leans more towards progressive rock than any Hammill album since *Roaring Forties*. *(Fie!)*

Right: *Clutch* (2002) was Hammill's first album containing only acoustic guitar songs – a return to first principles. *(Fie!)*

Left: *Incoherence* (2004) is a single 42-minute piece, Hammill's most sustained and argumentative interrogation of language. *(Fie!)*

Right: With intimations of mortality in almost every line, *Singularity* (2006) was Hammill's first album since his 2003 heart attack. *(Fie!)*

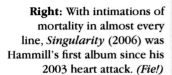

Left: One of Hammill's finest albums of recent years, *Thin Air* (2009), was inspired by the September 11 terrorist attacks. *(Fie!)*

Right: In a change to his usual way of working, Hammill wrote all the songs on *Consequences* (2012) before recording began. *(Fie!)*

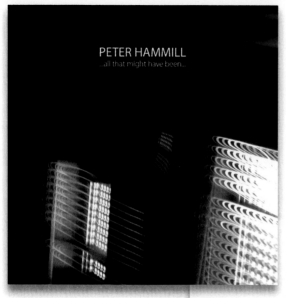

Left: The ambitious *…all that might have been…* (2014) was a concept album about a man adrift in a world of shadowy, neon-lit zones. *(Fie!)*

PETER HAMMILL

Right: Hammill described *From the Trees* (2017) as 'probably as close to conventional song structure as I get.' *(Fie!)*

Left: *In Translation* (2021) is an album of songs from the Great American Songbook, German *Lieder* and Italian popular song. *(Fie!)*

Right: *The Margin* (1985) is an essential live album from 1982-83, documenting the short existence of the K Group. *(Fie!)*

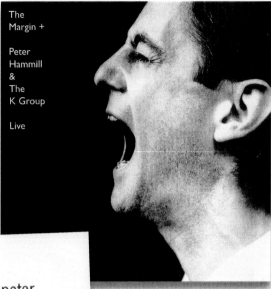

The
Margin +

Peter
Hammill
&
The
K Group

Live

peter
hammill

skeletons
of
songs

Left: *Skeletons of Songs* (1978) is an important Hammill bootleg, documenting an edge-of-the-seat solo show in Kansas City, USA. *(Author's collection)*

The Love Songs

Peter Hammill

Right: *The Love Songs* (1984) contained re-recorded versions of love songs from Hammill's previous solo albums. *(Virgin)*

Left: Hammill live and close-up at Café Oto in London, March 2017. *(Author's photo)*

Right: Taking in the well-deserved applause: Hammill live at the Queen Elizabeth Hall in London, April 2018. *(Seán Kelly)*

tranquillity and introspection, with the lyrical content focused for the most part on romantic (dis)entanglements and sexual attitudes. Stuart Gordon is a major presence, his weeping violin present on five of the album's nine cuts. There are guest appearances from Hammill regulars Jackson, Potter and Ellis, but the other main contributor is David Lord, who earns a co-production credit on the album and even a co-writing credit on one (albeit inessential) track. More than anything else, it's Lord's sampled strings and keyboard orchestrations that define the sound of the album – along, of course, with Hammill's restrained yet commanding vocal presence. As he wrote in his newsletter at the time: 'it kicks, but in slow motion.'

The cover, by Paul Ridout, is based on the British Romantic artist JMW Turner's painting *The Slave Ship* (1840). Many people don't notice that there's a photograph of Hammill faintly superimposed onto the painting.

Oh, and why Fie!? The logo of the label is the Greek letter φ (phi), hence PH – I!

'I Will Find You'

The album kicks off in fine style with this highly catchy tune, one of Hammill's freshest and most appealing pop songs. The track is a perfectly balanced amalgam of acoustic guitar riffing, springy bass (courtesy of Nic Potter) and a discreet string arrangement, all held together by the emotive warmth of Hammill's voice. The 'you' to whom the song is addressed remains obscure, which has led to a certain diversity of interpretation. Some claim that the song has sinister undertones, with lines like 'you can run and hide, but surely by and by' casting the narrator as some kind of stalker. This reading, however, misses the serenity and elegance of the arrangement, not to mention that lines like 'don't be afraid, when you're lost and most alone' point to a relationship of closeness and fellow feeling. The song could conceivably be a sequel to 'Sleep Now' from *And Close As This* (q.v.); in any case, the relationship it depicts is clearly one based on mutual love and empathy.

'Curtains'

We've seen in previous chapters how some of Hammill's songs are like little audio screenplays – 'Breakthrough' and 'Film Noir', for example. Here, though, is a song that would be perfect as a one-act play for the stage since it takes place in a single room and even has an appropriately theatrical title. The protagonists, Sylvia and Tommy, have 'packed their bags, ready for the road', looking for 'some kind of thrill.' But some lack of inner strength stops them from leaving their room, and 'the curtains and the bedroom door stay closed.' There are hints of Pinter and even Beckett in the enveloping stasis of the characters, traced by Lord's delicate chamber music arrangement. Some have tried to argue that Sylvia is Sylvia Plath and Tommy Ted Hughes, despite there being no evidence either within or outside the text to support this claim.

'His Best Girl'

I know very little about cars. From my research, it appears that a GTi Cabriolet is not a specific model of car, but could be one of any number of makes from a Volkswagen to a Peugeot. For the purposes of this song, however, I'd like to think that the vehicle in question is a 1962 Maserati, which certainly has the sense of European glamour evoked by the couple's holiday destination of a villa in the south of France. But as the song progresses, the glamour fades, with the young woman's 'golden curls' supplanted by a fake tan and extravagant jewellery. Eventually, the man trades in his girlfriend for a younger model, just as he would his car. The song drifts past at a glacial pace, led by that rinky-dink keyboard sound of which Hammill was so fond. There's not much to ruffle the surface here, but the song just about retains a sense of intrigue thanks to Hammill's alluring voice and those ethereal backing vocals.

'Oasis'

Along with 'I Will Find You', this, for me, is the standout track on *Fireships*. As with the earlier song, the 'you' to whom it is sung is unclear, lending the track a bewitching and mysterious ambience lit by soft percussion and Jackson's vaguely middle Eastern-sounding sax. And the lyric is just exquisite. I don't want to get into the old Dylan-inspired debate about the extent to which song lyrics can be appreciated as poems in their own right, shorn of their musical context and delivery. Clearly, however, Hammill sees his lyrics as having some kind of extra-musical life, as his occasional appearances at 'poetry readings' of his work testify. I will say that 'Oasis' is one of the most strikingly beautiful texts he has ever written, its blissful imagery of stars, water and moonlight interwoven with a deeply personal summoning of secrecy and intimacy.

'Incomplete Surrender'

Fireships is a rather front-loaded album, if the truth be told. After four almost uniformly excellent songs, the album takes something of a nosedive in quality, starting with this listless study of human relationships. The song wonders 'where's the bridge to take us across the sexual divide'; but whereas a song like 'Now Lover' thrillingly captured every tremor of 'the magic and the wonderful', 'Incomplete Surrender' draws up a lacklustre balance sheet of male and female attributes. There's some nice Floydian guitar from Ellis, and touches of shivery violin by Gordon, but the song can barely muster up a melody to carry it through its almost seven-minute running time.

'Fireships'

Here's another song that outstays its welcome, a messy track that limps from one section to the next without ever managing to cohere. Tying in with the cover image of a ship in stormy seas, the song conjures an 'armada of souls' in peril, then casts its net wider to suggest that, dogged by complacency, 'we never think that we'll get burned.' Hammill invokes the sinking of the Titanic in the line 'keep a stiff upper lip, the band play on through the raising of the toast', referring to the accounts given by some survivors that the house band continued to play as the doomed ship went down. (The British composer Gavin Bryars used these accounts as the basis for his minimalist composition *The Sinking of the Titanic*.) Jackson and Gordon play with their customary verve, but the song is crippled by its awkward structure and Hammill's overwrought vocal.

'Given Time'

Writing on his website about the song 'On The Surface' from *Out of Water*, Hammill described it as 'hovering between dream/hope/consciousness/ fate', noting that it 'fits squarely in my long-running lyrical concerns.' Indeed these are subjects that have long preoccupied Hammill, not least here on 'Given Time'. Fully justifying its inclusion on an album originally described as 'Number One in the BeCalm series', the song unfolds at a calm and measured pace, with the introduction alone lasting over two minutes. Those first two minutes are marked by a lovely guitar solo from Hammill that drifts by on clouds of delay and sustain. Carefully, he sets out the song's argument before lifting skyward on the key line 'caught in the clay of material need.' The end of the song sees a characteristic Hammill lyrical twist, where a line is almost repeated but with a word or two changed in the repeating: 'we make the lives we lead' becomes 'we make the lives we leave.' Examples of this kind of subtle change recur throughout Hammill's work, the certainty of repetition undermined by the grit of the unfamiliar.

'Reprise' (Hammill/Lord)

A frankly unnecessary restatement of themes from 'I Will Find You', 'Oasis', 'Fireships' and 'His Best Girl'. The album would have been better off without it.

'Gaia'

The album ends in grand style with this dramatic ballad honouring the 'whole, connected world.' There's a lot to unpack here, beginning with James Lovelock's Gaia hypothesis, the notion that the Earth is a system that constantly regulates itself so as to ensure the continuing survival of the planet. Hammill associates Gaia with the butterfly effect, an idea from the chaos theory of Edward Lorenz, which states that small changes in one state can have significant consequences on a later state, even though the two theories are not actually related to one another. And the opening line of the song, 'butterflies on the wheel', refers to the quotation 'Who breaks a butterfly upon a wheel?' from Alexander Pope's long poem *An Epistle to Dr Arbuthnot* (1735). Pope was saying that one should not make intensive efforts in order to achieve something trifling, a point echoed by the editor of *The Times*, William Rees-Mogg, when he used the quotation as the heading of a 1967 editorial about the prosecutions of Mick Jagger and Keith Richards of the Rolling Stones for drug possession.

A lyric of such vaulting ambition deserves an impressive setting, and Hammill and Lord more than do justice to the text with their lush, detailed instrumentation. Hammill's sensitive piano melody gathers in clusters around Lord's swirling orchestral arrangement, while his solemnly intoned vocals sound like fragile ripples in the vastness of space.

The Noise (1993)

Personnel:
Peter Hammill: vocals, guitar, keyboards
John Ellis: guitar
David Jackson: saxophone, flute
Nic Potter: bass guitar
Manny Elias: drums
All songs by Peter Hammill
Recorded at Terra Incognita, Bath, January-September 1992
Produced by Peter Hammill
UK release date: March 1993
Cover: Paul Ridout

Having situated the largely reflective *Fireships* as 'Number One in the BeCalm series', it was inevitable that Hammill would follow it up with a more raucous set of songs in *The Noise*. This set was described in the CD booklet as 'Number One in the A Loud series', and consisted of rockier material than we had seen from Hammill in some years, much of which had been written at the same time as the *Fireships* material. The problem was a simple one: the prolific Hammill had more songs than he knew what to do with. As we now know, the idea of parallel 'calm' and 'loud' releases did not survive beyond *The Noise*. One useful side-effect of this temporary alignment, though, was that Hammill's former record label Virgin came out in 1993 with two similarly themed compilations of his work for the Charisma/Virgin stable, *The Calm (After The Storm)* and *The Storm (Before The Calm)*. These are still among the best introductions to Hammill's work.

If *Fireships* had largely been about sexual politics and personal relationships, *The Noise* turned its attention outward, in a series of what Hammill described in his newsletter as "external', observational pieces.' On several songs, this attention manifested itself in the arena of money and fame, while other cuts evoked the life of the performer. Finally, just as *Fireships* had ended with a widescreen epic on the subject of the survival of the planet, so *The Noise* closed with a similarly ambitious speculation on the life and death of the author and Holocaust survivor Primo Levi.

An album of rock songs needs a band, of course, and Hammill put together an excellent one for *The Noise*, albeit one that had a familiar look about it. Joining Hammill in the studio were John Ellis and Nic Potter on lead guitar and bass, respectively, meaning that three-quarters of the K Group were represented. It had been ten years since the second and final K Group album, *Patience*, and elements of that quartet could be found in the punchy riffing and forceful dynamics of *The Noise*. The key addition was drummer Manny Elias, who had seen Top 10 action in the 1980s as a member of Tears for Fears. More of a straightforward rock drummer than Guy Evans, Elias' unfussy approach was arguably more suited to the material than Evans' probing style would have been. The ubiquitous David Jackson guested on a few tracks.

If *The Noise* has a flaw, it's that it's not quite noisy enough. The title of the album promises some arch heaviosity after the relative calm of *Out of Water* and *Fireships*, while Hammill titled his 1993 newsletter about the album 'Guitars, guitars, guitars!' as though we were in for some kind of Glenn Branca symphony. In reality, for those of us who came to love noise and industrial music in the 1980s – artists like Test Department, Whitehouse and Einstürzende Neubauten, to name just three – the idea that there's any kind of real noise on *The Noise* is risible. The playing is energetic enough, but the material is mostly sub-standard, with two outstanding exceptions. 'Like A Shot, The Entertainer' and 'Primo on the Parapet' are at opposite ends of the spectrum, the poppiest and heaviest songs on the album, but both are worthy of much more than passing attention.

The cover, by Paul Ridout, has the dubious distinction of being probably the worst cover of any Hammill album – a horrible lime green and pink composition. The key elements of it, though, are worthy of note. The microphone on the front cover is a vintage studio mic at Terra Incognita, while the speaker cabinet on the back page of the booklet is an old Hiwatt used by VdGG. Finally, the guitar seen on various pages of the booklet is Meurglys III, the subject of the song by that name on the VdGG album *World Record* – an instrument that also graces the cover of 1977's *Over*.

'A Kick to Kill the Kiss'

A lively opener to the album, this cut is dominated by some delightful blues-rock guitar from Ellis. Eschewing the tight post-punk playing of his work with the K Group, here the guitarist stretches out with a slew of Claptonesque licks that keep the song nicely on the boil. For his part, Hammill further enlivens the track with caustic observations on 'the original self-made man', who seems to be some kind of unreconstructed ladies' man. Recalling 'the smirk of the macho man' from the previous album's 'Incomplete Surrender', Hammill's sardonic vocal drips with scorn and derision.

'Like A Shot, The Entertainer'

Since the 1980s, Hammill, the archetypal cult artist, has made occasional gestures towards gaining wider appeal and even stimulating sales of his music. A few singles were released in the 1980s, such as 'My Experience', 'Paradox Drive' and 'Painting By Numbers'; cannily, these were among his most commercial songs. There were other album tracks, such as 'All Said And Done' (from *Skin*) and 'Invisible Ink' (from *In A Foreign Town*), which amply demonstrated Hammill's ability to conjure up catchy hooklines and simple yet persuasive melodies. There was also 1984's *The Love Songs* compilation, which might have been designed to appeal to Radio 2 listeners. Inevitably all of these initiatives flopped, leaving Hammill firmly in the grip of his dedicated cult following.

Nevertheless, Hammill has never abandoned his quest for the perfect pop song, as numerous examples from the 1990s and 2000s will attest. But in my view, the relatively unheralded 'Like A Shot, The Entertainer' is the greatest pop song he has ever written, and in an alternate universe, would have been a million-selling hit single. (In fact, it *was* released on a single, an EP to be precise, but only in Germany, where of course, it failed to trouble the charts.) From Elias' first splash of percussion to Hammill's burrowing acoustic guitar riff, from the irresistible foot-tapping rhythm to Hammill's lissom vocal and the multiple hooks that draw you in, the song represents Hammill at his most genial and engaging.

'The Noise'

'It's clear,' writes Hammill about this song in his newsletter, 'that a great deal of my public growing up was on/with Noise.' There's a strong flavour of the VdGG years here, from the Bantonesque organ flourish that kicks off the song to the memory of the 'bug-eyed overnight drive' that characterised the group's relentless touring schedule in the 1970s. If that wasn't enough to make the connection, David Jackson seals the deal by popping up on flute and tenor sax. I do wonder, though, what the point of bringing in Jackson was when he's so low in the mix that he can barely be heard over the general din.

'Celebrity Kissing'

A classic example of a song where the music is let down by the lyric. In musical terms, this is one of the highlights of the album, with Ellis soloing in formidable Clapton/Beck style over Elias' powerhouse drumming and acid vocals from Hammill. But 'celebrity kissing, this has got to stop'? Really? I find it hard to get worked up about the idea of celebrities doing whatever it is they do, and the fact that 'you know and I know this is only pretence' doesn't make the song's concerns any more pressing or less trivial.

'Where The Mouth Is'

'Another frame from the continuing Sci-Finance story', as Hammill writes in the 1993 newsletter. Indeed this song could be seen as the third instalment of a story that began with 'Sci-Finance' (from the 1978 VdGG live album *Vital*) and continued with 'Sci-Finance (Revisited)' from 1988's *In A Foreign Town*. Picking up where the earlier songs left off, this is a splenetic rant against sharp-tongued, smooth-talking money men – 'pigs in the trough', as Hammill scathingly puts it. The line 'everything you got fell off the back end of the yacht' refers, of course, to the late Robert Maxwell, media mogul and fraudster, who drowned after apparently falling from his yacht into the Atlantic Ocean. The song's a gruelling blues exercise that sees Hammill emote unnecessarily over Elias' lumpy rhythms. Ellis livens up the last couple of minutes or so considerably with a scorching solo.

'The Great European Department Store'

In 1992, as *The Noise* was being recorded, the leaders of the European Union signed the Maastricht Treaty, described as 'a new stage in the process of creating an ever closer union among the peoples of Europe.' Hammill, however, sees danger in 'mass consumption and conformity', the increasing homogenisation of a Europe in which it doesn't matter what you consume because 'they're all exactly the same.' (Little did anyone know, back then, that almost 30 years later, the UK would turn its back on Europe, a decision which itself seemed to be motivated primarily by a petty distrust of cultural difference.) While Hammill has a point, this is another case where the natural response is to shrug one's shoulders with indifference. What's more, the song's presence on *The Noise* feels unearned since there's nothing very noisy or unruly about it. It's an easy-paced, amiable canter with a rather flat keyboard sound and half-buried sax interventions by Jackson.

'Planet Coventry'

To 'send someone to Coventry' means to shun them by deliberately ignoring and not speaking to them, as some kind of social punishment or revenge. In 'Planet Coventry', the shunned person seems to be an actor or entertainer, and the shunning takes place in some kind of dream world. In some ways, then, the song is a partial return to the fractured dream logic of K Group cuts such as 'Paradox Drive' and 'The Unconscious Life', filtered through the theme of performance which we saw in songs like 'The Mousetrap (Caught In)' and 'After The Show', to say nothing of 'The Noise' from this album. Musically, too, there's a hint of the K Group in the biting hooks, fierce ensemble playing and vague sense of foreboding that lurks here, notwithstanding that lead guitar chores were undertaken by Hammill this time rather than Ellis.

'Primo on the Parapet'

Talking of the K Group, here's a song that bears more than a passing resemblance to one of that outfit's greatest moments, 'Patient', in its jarring transitions from acoustic to electric states and its meticulous mapping of psychological terror. As noted in the introduction to this chapter, the song is a meditation on the life and death of the author and Holocaust survivor Primo Levi, who died in 1987 when he fell from his third-floor apartment window. His death was ruled a suicide (hence 'climbing up upon the parapet'), although some believe it was accidental. Having recounted his experiences at Auschwitz in his memoir *If This Is A Man* (1947), Levi dedicated the rest of his life to ensuring that the horror of the concentration camps would never be forgotten.

After the slick inconsequentiality of much of *The Noise*, 'Primo on the Parapet' hits you like a body blow. Inflamed by its insistence that 'we must learn not to forget', the song's a grim warning that 'raw barbarity sleeps, spore in soil.' Hammill's ominous vocals and fluttering sax by Jackson give way to a mighty guitar riff that twists and turns on the gravitational force of Elias' drumming. Live versions of the song, such as the one on the live album *There*

Goes The Daylight, would often last for ten or more minutes, as the group would lock into the main riff and repeatedly grind it out. The studio version is no less compelling, its mantric repetitions casting harsh light on a dark chapter in human history.

Roaring Forties (1994)

Personnel:
Peter Hammill: vocals, guitar, keyboards
David Jackson: saxophone, flute
Stuart Gordon: violin
Simon Clarke: Hammond organ
Nic Potter: bass guitar
Manny Elias: drums
All songs by Peter Hammill
Recorded at Terra Incognita, Bath, August 1993-May 1994
Produced by Peter Hammill
UK release date: 12 September 1994
Cover: Paul Ridout

By this stage, it should be clear that one can never write off Hammill. In 1992 and 1993, he released two albums in contrasting calm/loud styles, *Fireships* and *The Noise*, and announced that he intended to release future albums in parallel according to those styles. As noted in the previous chapter, Hammill had a glut of songs and apparently decided to release them all over two albums, rather than doing what might have been preferable, i.e. taking the best eight or nine and making a single album out of them. (It would be an interesting exercise to compile one's own 'best of *Fireships* and *The Noise*' album; mine, for what it's worth, would be 'I Will Find You'/'Like a Shot, the Entertainer'/'Curtains'/'Celebrity Kissing'/'Oasis'/'Planet Coventry'/'Given Time'/'Primo on the Parapet'.)

By the following year, however, Hammill had abandoned the idea of the BeCalm/A Loud series. His 1994 album *Roaring Forties* saw him blend uptempo songs with ballads again, with the same Potter/Elias rhythm section that had graced *The Noise* and instrumental colour provided by the ubiquitous Jackson and Gordon. Hammill himself took on guitar and keyboard duties, with the former more prominent than the latter throughout the album. As he wrote in his 1994 newsletter on the album, 'since this is for the most part, not a sequenced/ordered work, six strings seem best.' In fact, Hammill's guitar playing here, on both acoustic and electric, is excellent, adding to the feeling of air and space that marks out the album in contrast to the rather overcooked sound of *The Noise*.

The Roaring Forties are strong prevailing winds in the southern hemisphere, blowing between the latitudes of 40° and 50° south. On the one hand, the title forms part of the nautical imagery that runs through 'A Headlong Stretch' and 'Your Tall Ship' (and which allowed Paul Ridout to produce one of his best Hammill album covers). On the other hand, Hammill, well into his own forties when he made this record, is talking about himself, and asking whether the inevitable process of ageing should be allowed to compromise the act of living in and for the present. For Hammill, who has never cared much for compromise, the answer is clearly that it shouldn't.

Those who like their Hammill complex, knotty and prog-flavoured will find much to their liking here, not least in the multi-part epic 'A Headlong Stretch' that forms the centrepiece of the album. But the whole album is shot through with a melodic sensibility and an organic sound that renders it highly fresh and listenable. Hammill is at the absolute top of his game on this album as a singer, lyricist, guitarist and producer/arranger, and the other musicians (especially Jackson and Gordon) make fine contributions. With the long piece bookended by three songs in the 'classic rock' vein and an exquisite ballad, Hammill knocked it out of the park and made his best album of the 1990s.

'Sharply Unclear'
Recognize that riff? Of course, you do, it's 'I Want You (She's So Heavy)' from the Beatles' *Abbey Road*. After that neat little quotation, the song pitches headfirst into a zone of gale-force guitar and swooping violin runs, underpinned by Potter's unobtrusive bass and Elias' vigorous drumming. A tightly controlled verse/chorus structure frames this portrayal of a not especially sympathetic character. I love the flash and gusto of this song, the way it takes the Beatles riff and hammers it repeatedly and decisively home. Halfway through, Hammill's exuberant cry of 'yes!' tells you all you need to know about the sheer energy and commitment at work here.

'The Gift of Fire'
The song begins with a short instrumental passage for flute, keyboards and acoustic guitar that reminds me, for some reason, of Dire Straits at their most tranquil. Nothing wrong with that, but after a couple of minutes, the calmness gives way to a galloping romp of a song, driven by jaunty sax by Jackson and glowing Hammond organ from guest musician Simon Clarke. The subject of the song is a woman whose 'derangement runs deep.' Her identity is (sharply) unclear, but given the vitriol with which Hammill addresses her, I suspect that it's the late Margaret Thatcher in his sights. Mrs. Thatcher was no longer Prime Minister by 1994 but was still making public speeches in which her own 'prescience' was a regular topic. 'What a windfall of wickedness when truth gets warped to perversion', rages Hammill in sulphurous tones that recall the political engagement of records like *In A Foreign Town*.

'You Can't Want What You Always Get'
Having borrowed from the Fab Four on 'Sharply Unclear', it would have been churlish for Hammill not also to acknowledge that other legendary British rock band, the Rolling Stones. As well as mangling the title of 'You Can't Always Get What You Want', there's a touch of Stones swagger to this lengthy, hard-rocking cut. The whole group is on fire here, from Gordon's tempestuous violin to Hammill's strutting lead guitar and Potter's magisterial bass. Elias varies his rhythmic attack with dashing tom-tom fills, while Jackson dominates the three-minute instrumental outro with furious blurts of sax. Hammill's lead

and backing voices, meanwhile, engage in some wonderful call-and-response singing. According to the 1994 newsletter, the central tenet of the song is that 'one must live the present life, between Known and Unknown.' Or, as Hammill puts it in the last verse: 'better live the life you're living' (*cf.* the last line of 'Flight': 'better think on today'). It's hard to argue with such a message, especially one delivered with as much vigour and zest for life as we find here.

'A Headlong Stretch'

'A Headlong Stretch' is Hammill's third long-form piece, following 'A Plague of Lighthouse-Keepers' (VdGG, 1971) and 'Flight' (1980). Inevitably it's not as fêted as those two, but there's much to admire here, from the tight ensemble playing and disconcerting shifts of tempo to the rhapsodic imagery that runs through the piece. Indeed there's a line that connects Hammill's perception of the sea and maritime navigation as portals to hidden depths and mysteries, from 'Plague' via *Out of Water* and *Fireships* to 'A Headlong Stretch' and 'Your Tall Ship'. Here, the limitless stretch of the ocean finds its correlative in the 'uncharted waters' of life itself. In the 1994 newsletter, Hammill wrote that the piece 'is to do with 'living in the now'' ... an element of that involves getting older and acknowledging (if not necessarily celebrating!) the fact.' As noted in the introduction to this chapter, the title of the album is a neat pun on the fact that Hammill was now in his forties. Having sung about 'pushing thirty' on 1978's *The Future Now*, an update was clearly overdue.

(i) 'Up Ahead'

In 1971, Jackson darkened VdGG's 'A Plague of Lighthouse-Keepers' with cold blasts of sax that chillingly evoked the warning sound of a stricken oceangoing vessel. Twenty-three years later, Jackson begins 'A Headlong Stretch' with similar sax tones that, this time, give way to unhurried electric and acoustic guitar figures. Hammill sings the opening verses with great sensitivity and restraint, his immaculate baritone ripened by a new maturity of tone.

(ii) 'Continental Drift'

Tension begins to rise in this section as electric guitar and keyboards trace a path through Hammill's mordant reflection on the price and the limits of free will. For his part, Elias opens up space with vectors of flowing percussive activity. Towards the end, a haunting melodic figure emerges, leading to an outburst of arch scepticism ('surely we look ripe for a fall') fuelled by aggressive guitar arpeggios.

(iii) 'The Twelve'

A short, bracing part propelled by spiky Jackson sax and thunderous drumming from Elias. The section pivots on a central verse, sung in agitated falsetto, that reels off various contexts for the number twelve – twelve signs of the Zodiac, twelve apostles, twelve notes of the chromatic scale and so on. To which one might add the twelve members of the jury which we are told is 'out upon the matter', deliberating on 'every vital pro and con' of planning one's life versus 'living in the now.'

(iv) 'Long Light'

If 'A Headlong Stretch' has a precedent in Hammill's work, it's with the vast and troubling canvas of 'Flight', another multi-part suite that takes inspiration from the elements. But whereas 'Flight' looks upwards to the air and down towards the earth, the later piece here finds itself lost in 'dark water, dark fire down below', all the while conscious of 'signs serial, adrift in the air.' Musically, too, there's a desperate urgency to 'Long Light' that recalls the 'Nothing is Nothing' section of 'Flight', all splintering guitar and hammered-out percussion.

(v) 'Backwards Man'

The older we get, the more we look back upon the lives we've led. This is the position in which the Backwards Man finds himself, beset by self-doubt, asking, 'did I really do that? Was I ever so young?' A wintry sadness descends upon the piece in this section, an unbridled fatalism etched in every grave syllable of Hammill's voice and the elegiac turns of Gordon's violin.

(vi) 'As You Were'

As the piece nears its conclusion, the figure from 'Continental Drift' re-emerges, first on piano, then on acoustic slide guitar. There's something very moving about the way this short leitmotif settles in fragments around Hammill's yearning vocal, as though drained of life and seeking a place to rest: 'that'll end the sentence, the time I've served.' The phrase 'serious fun' in the next verse, by the way, is one that Hammill has often used in newsletters and interviews to describe his attitude to making music, an attitude characterised by total commitment but never at the expense of sheer enjoyment.

(vii) 'Or So I Said'

It seems to me that 'A Headlong Stretch' is structured like a storm and its aftermath, with the unearthly calm of 'Up Ahead' and 'Continental Drift' followed by the danger and turbulence of 'The Twelve' and 'Long Light', and then the clear air of 'Backwards Man' and 'As You Were'. 'Or So I Said' is a kind of epilogue, a short, affecting chorale for piano, guitar and layered voices. 'How strange they seem, the lives I've never led,' broods Hammill, and in his words, we hear the echoes of all we know, or all we think we know.

'Your Tall Ship'

This, in my opinion, is one of Hammill's greatest ever songs. It's another nautically minded piece to link with the title of the album (quoted in the lyric) and the maritime imagery of 'A Headlong Stretch'. But if the long piece saw the ocean as a region of imminent finality, 'Your Tall Ship' sees the sea as a place where 'the succession never ends', an infinite horizon of possibilities. Hammill picks out a radiant melody on the piano, cradled by vibrant organ tones. At around three minutes in, the song cuts loose with ecstatic currents of organ and wired drumming from Elias, ascending in giddy harmony with Hammill's impassioned vocal. Animated by its defiant insistence that 'all rites of passage make us strong', the song is a magnificent end to the album.

X My Heart (1996)

Personnel:
Peter Hammill: vocals, guitar, bass, keyboards
David Jackson: saxophone, flute
Stuart Gordon: violin, viola
Manny Elias: drums
All songs by Peter Hammill
Recorded at Terra Incognita, Bath, February-November 1995
Produced by Peter Hammill
UK release date: 18 March 1996
Cover: Paul Ridout

In 1994 and 1995, Hammill toured the UK, Europe and Russia with the nucleus of the *Roaring Forties* band, Jackson, Gordon and Elias, a group that became known as the PH Quartet. As it turns out, those concerts – plus a few in 1996 – represent the last time Hammill trod the boards with a full band under his own name. Since VdGG reformed in 2005, all live band activity has been under the VdGG banner, while 'solo' PH shows were for several years presented as duos with Gordon and have, in recent years, been completely solo.

With the PH Quartet fully bedded in as a touring outfit, it was a no-brainer to head for Terra Incognita and make a record. And as with 1983's *Patience*, which followed a heavy bout of K Group touring, *X My Heart* has a 'live', played-in feel to it. As Hammill wrote in his 1996 newsletter about the album: 'there are moments of soloing, but for the most part, these are ensemble pieces … some of them almost sound like live recordings.' Indeed there's a delightful interplay between the instruments on these songs, with Jackson's woodwind and Gordon's strings coiling like woodsmoke around Hammill's fleet-footed guitar and piano. Hammill's singing voice, too, reaches some kind of peak with these 1990s records. It's still as fearsome an instrument as it was in the 1970s, but its tone has a new depth and maturity that is ever more appropriate to the weighty nature of Hammill's songwriting. Increasingly, too, we see Hammill use layered backing vocals in a higher register, lending a reverberant choral timbre to many of these songs.

X My Heart would turn out to be the last Hammill album with this kind of ensemble band sound. Although Jackson, Gordon and Elias would all go on to grace later albums such as *This* and *What, Now?*, their contributions on those records were essentially as individuals rather than as members of a group. Starting with the following year's *Everyone You Hold*, Hammill's albums became much more about Hammill with a range of sidemen rather than Hammill with a band. As such, *X My Heart* represents the end of an era that began with the formation of the K Group.

Lyrically, the songs on *X My Heart* cover familiar Hammill territory. He wrote in the 1996 newsletter that 'the subject matter [of the songs] falls fundamentally into two camps: sense of memory, and sense of time and place.'

Ever the tease, Hammill doesn't actually go on to say which of the songs fall into which camp, leaving the listener to work that out for himself. In some cases, such as 'Amnesiac' and 'A Better Time', the category is fairly obvious, while in others, it's harder to discern. What is clear, however, is that these songs are borne of a serious, mindful engagement with human identity – what T. S. Eliot called 'the impossible union of spheres of existence'.

After his excellent cover design for *Roaring Forties*, Paul Ridout rather let the side down this time with a design that's almost, but not quite, as bad as his cover for *The Noise*. Featuring a bulbous green heart, thick red bars and cartoonish lettering, it's inelegant, inharmonious and nothing at all to do with the music.

'A Better Time (Acapella)'
The first of two versions of the standout track on the album, here presented in a multivoiced *a cappella* arrangement.

'Amnesiac'
In terms of the distinction between 'sense of memory' and 'sense of time and place' songs, this brilliant track falls firmly into the former group. These songs, Hammill writes in the 1996 newsletter, 'focus more on what is lost than on what remains or is gained; and therefore on what identity one can patch together from the gaps which increasingly occur.' If the narrator of 'Amnesiac' is indeed suffering from some kind of dementia, it's accompanied in the song by flashes of certainty and loyalty amongst the painful self-awareness of memory loss. The line 'I'm terrified to admit, to let go, to accept I don't know' is especially moving, turning as it does on a bare internal rhyme. Musically speaking, the song is quintessential late-middle period Hammill, with flickering violin and flute cushioned by luminous acoustic guitar. At around the two-minute mark, the song bursts into life with heated acoustic chords and descending flute runs, only for Jackson to rein things in with a tender sax solo. The last couple of minutes pass by in a rush of dizzying violin and slashing electric guitar, a compelling way to end this essential cut.

'Ram Origami'
Another 'sense of memory' song, albeit a less striking one than 'Amnesiac'. This track never really gets going, hampered as it is by a flimsy melody and sluggish mid-tempo rhythm. Hammill tinkers away on piano and guitar without making much of an impact, while Jackson's sax is frustratingly tentative. The central image, though, is lovely – a sheet of paper, folded in origami, holding memories that are lost when the paper is unfolded.

'A Forest of Pronouns'
In his 1996 newsletter, Hammill writes that one of the musical elements present on *X My Heart* is 'systems music.' As we saw in the case of 'On The

Surface' from 1990's *Out of Water*, Hammill sees systems music as 'a note sequence or rhythm … distended, altered, repeated, laid over itself.' He doesn't specify the track from *X My Heart* on which systems music is present, but my money's on 'A Forest of Pronouns', in which a fidgety percussive line steps its way through chattering vocals and jagged electric guitar. On an album otherwise dominated by space and acoustic textures, this song is a bustling hive of sequenced activity. It also marks a return to the lyrical territory of 'Losing Faith In Words', reaching out for something to hold onto on the slippery slope of language.

'Earthbound'

It had been a while since Hammill had released a love song in the manner of those collected on *The Love Songs*, so 'Earthbound' was welcome evidence that he hadn't abandoned the genre. A swooning piece in the vein of the *Fireships* material, the song makes some deliberately clichéd statements of romantic *frisson* – 'my heart flew in my mouth', 'my heart stopped in its tracks' – only to deconstruct them in more expressive terms. If 'gravity's cruel tax' leaves us earthbound, maybe it's only love that can 'spring [us] free to flight.' Jackson's distant sax and Gordon's understated violin wrap tenderly around Hammill's piano and vocals. This is a fine example of what Hammill meant by the songs being 'ensemble pieces'. There's no soloing here, no individual grandstanding, just exceptional levels of empathy and sensitivity to the needs of the song.

'Narcissus (Bar & Grill)'

Every so often, it's my duty to report, Hammill comes out with a really duff song. Most of these, it has to be said, can be found on two albums, *In A Foreign Town* and *The Noise*, released within five years of each other. 'Narcissus (Bar & Grill)' is another one, a track so greasy that you wouldn't want to eat at the bar and grill that prepared it. The song takes almost seven minutes to set out its depiction of a self-absorbed narcissist, its scorn prodded by leaden guitar and braying sax. As a review in *The Wire* noted at the time, The Beat's 'Mirror in the Bathroom' made the same point more incisively in half the time.

'Material Possession'

After the unfortunate excesses of the previous track, the album ends on a high note with three immensely enjoyable songs. 'Material Possession' is the first of these, a surging gallop of a song that simultaneously manages to sound both like classic Hammill and like nothing he's ever done before. The song's a seductive whirl of ensemble playing, with Gordon's violin dancing around cascades of acoustic guitar and saxophone. At about two and a half minutes in, a delightful Celtic-flavoured interlude adds weight to the argumentative passion of Hammill's vocal.

Hammill's text is an eloquent and comprehensive evisceration of consumerism, arguing that true pleasure and reward comes from the memories of things, not from the things themselves. I know a few record collectors who might dispute that, and who might even recognise themselves in the line 'if the owning becomes an obsession.' Personally, I gave up the vinyl chase years ago, and am perfectly happy to listen only to digital files these days. Having said that, if anyone reading this has a copy of the original *Skeletons of Songs* bootleg on vinyl, feel free to contact me via the publishers.

'Come Clean'

'In my dream world,' writes Hammill in the 1996 newsletter, 'these are what might almost pass for pop songs.' We've seen in previous chapters how Hammill cleaves to the notion of the perfect pop song, seeing it half-buried in much of his work. That said, I don't hear much poppy stuff on *X My Heart*, with the exception of this enchanting ballad. Once again, ensemble playing is to the fore, the song's quirky melody shaped by deft touches of piano, sax, acoustic guitar and violin. The lyric, too, is a gem; warm and conversational without ever lapsing into cliché, it convincingly argues that 'we can only do our best with an open heart.' Since the past is gone and the future unknown, we should 'try to make a brand new start' with each new turn of the pages that make up our lives.

'A Better Time'

In terms of songs from *X My Heart* which are regularly played live, only 'Amnesiac' and 'A Better Time' have troubled the scorers. No great surprises here, since these are the album's two undisputed masterpieces, opening and closing the record on guitar and piano, respectively (discounting the *a cappella* arrangement of 'A Better Time'). If 'Amnesiac' is key to the album's sense of memory and forgetfulness, 'A Better Time' does the same for its sense of time and place, finding itself locked into an infinite and infinitely troubling present. There's a devastating ambiguity at the heart of this song, ruthlessly exposed by Hammill's grave vocal: if 'I'll never find a better time to be alive than now', then while things certainly couldn't be any better, they also couldn't get any worse. The song cloaks this ambiguity in a sublime string arrangement by Stuart Gordon, forging something hard and unforgiving out of raw tenderness and beauty.

Everyone You Hold (1997)

Personnel:
Peter Hammill: vocals, guitar, keyboards
Stuart Gordon: violin
Hugh Banton: organ
Manny Elias: drums
David Lord: keyboards
Holly & Beatrice Hammill: backing vocals
All songs by Peter Hammill, except where noted
Recorded at Terra Incognita, Bath, April 1995-June 1997
Produced by Peter Hammill
UK release date: 13 October 1997
Cover: Paul Ridout
Photography: Leo Vaca

As noted in the preceding two chapters, both 1994's *Roaring Forties* and 1996's *X My Heart* were essentially full band albums and were accompanied by significant amounts of touring with the PH Quartet. *Everyone You Hold*, by contrast, is very much a solo record in atmosphere and temperament, notwithstanding the presence of Stuart Gordon, Manny Elias and even Hugh Banton. Hammill's guitar and keyboards are often used tonally rather than structurally, and his voice is pushed to the forefront with layered backing vocals prominent in the mix. It's a reflective, autumnal sound that feels entirely appropriate for an artist entering the fourth decade of his recording career.

The recording dates of April 1995 to June 1997 are unusual in that it's unheard of for Hammill to spend more than two years recording an album. In his 1997 newsletter about the album, he writes that 'the work done in 1995 was sketchy in the extreme.' Nonetheless, there's a meticulousness about the way the record sounds that bespeaks great care and attention to detail: this does not sound like an album that was knocked out in a fortnight.

In keeping with the hazy, indeterminate sound of the album, the subject matter of these songs is heavy with abstraction. The songs speak of inner worlds, of psychological states of mind, of coming together and being alone. Perhaps this is why Hammill plumped for a series of close-up photographic portraits in the cover art, of a kind not seen since *Enter K* and *Patience*. Taken against an inky black background, the photographs seem to show the artist hopeful of human contact, stranded somewhere between solitude and togetherness. As the title track says: 'If everyone is with you, then you can never be alone at all.'

'Everyone You Hold'

Fans of Hammill's 1992 album *Fireships* will find much to admire on *Everyone You Hold*; indeed, the album could easily have been number two in the BeCalm series, had Hammill decided to persevere with that schema.

David Lord's spectral keyboards, so prominent on *Fireships*, reappear as part of the moody atmospherics of this opening track. Like most of the songs here, the ambience is slow, meditative and dreamlike, with undercurrents of strangeness disrupting the glacial flow of Hammill's piano and guitar. Much of the guitar, here and elsewhere on the album, is ebow, to an extent not heard on a Hammill album since 1978's *The Future Now*. Its buzzing presence brings a sense of liminal space to Hammill's darkly intoned reflection on the value and price of human contact. In spite of a certain anxiety, the song has a message of hope: 'when every sweet embrace has faded ... still you stay in everyone you hold.'

'Personality' (Hammill/Hammill)

In the 1997 newsletter, Hammill writes that the songs on *Everyone You Hold* are 'in the tradition of looking hard at reality in order to deal with it rather than turning away.' It's a sentiment that certainly applies to 'Personality', which recalls 'Amnesiac' in its depiction of a soul in the throes of disintegration: 'I feel I'm losing sight of all I've known,' admits the narrator. This is one of the more uptempo and fully realised songs on the album, with Hammill hitting the wah-wah pedal amid shimmering organ from Banton and Elias' fluid stickwork. The track features a rare co-writing credit with Hammill's daughter Holly, who pops up later in the album on backing vocals.

'Nothing Comes'

Often performed live at solo concerts in recent years, this song sees the much-missed Stuart Gordon deliver his usual scintillating violin over Hammill's wistful piano and vocals. It's the shortest song on the album by some distance, yet still manages to incorporate at least three of Hammill's characteristic lyrical tropes: ships ('It's all plain sailing in the dry dock'), lost love ('you remind me of the girlfriend I never had') and film ('the wrap's about to happen, the scene is already blocked'). But the real heavy lifting is done by the line 'nothing comes as a shock', which hinges on a disquieting ambiguity: the standard sense of 'nothing comes as a shock anymore', but also the idea that nothing comes, and that's a shock. Broken by negation and loss, the track ends with an echo of Chris Judge Smith's 'Four Pails' from 1986's *Skin*: compare the closing lines 'once I would have answered clearly, now I only think I'm nearly sure' and 'once I thought I knew it all, now I just don't know.'

'From the Safe House'

The problem with the resolutely downbeat approach adopted by *Everyone You Hold* is that without the sustained melodic and harmonic invention that we have come to expect from Hammill, it becomes challenging to retain the interest of the listener. Certainly, the album has a painterly, impressionistic quality that, in the right set of listening circumstances, may have a soothing effect. Nevertheless, for an artist whose work has always relied for impact on drama and intensity, the effect of a whole album's worth of such melancholia is muted – like David Sylvian or Talk Talk without their avant-garde and jazz-inflected leanings. The problem comes to the fore on 'From the Safe House', a six-minute dirge whose wintry subject matter ('last secrets to be whispered and the dying of the light are all that we have left now') is reflected in its gaunt arrangement for guitar and piano.

'Phosphorescence' (Hammill/Cosentino)

This is more like it – a delightful, slow-burning love song with words by Hammill and music by Italian singer-songwriter Saro Cosentino. Channelling the mystical spirit of 'Oasis' from *Fireships*, the track imagines an 'ocean of the night' where two lovers meet for the last time, their encounter leaving traces of phosphorescent light. Gordon's orchestral violin passes elegantly through the song, shadowed by Hammill's serene guitar. The cut also sees the first instance of female backing vocals on a Hammill song, and not just any female backing vocals either – the pure soprano voices we hear are those of Hammill's daughters Holly and Beatrice, carrying the song aloft into the stratosphere.

'Falling Open'

Like 'From the Safe House', here's another song that fails to make much of an impact over its allotted six minutes. The lyric is striking, and has a density of language that the rest of the album never quite musters: 'out of my grasp the future floods my fingers: the blood that binds the bone for us a given, unforgiving known.' But the arrangement for ebow guitar and voice is heavy going, weighted down by ponderous voices and with barely a rhythmic pulse to animate the song until it's almost over.

'Bubble'

Along with 'Nothing Comes', this is the other song from *Everyone You Hold* that Hammill has regularly dusted down for live performance, and with good reason. It's not only the appearance of Hugh Banton, raising the roof on organ as only he can, that evokes the presence of Hammill's classic 1970s work on this searingly powerful track. One is struck by the similarity between the line 'I surfaced from a lifetime's worth of sleep' and the line 'I rise from lifelong sleep' on VdGG's 'Pilgrims', not to mention that the line 'all solid faith seems nothing but conjecture' echoes the phrase 'our only conjecture what lies behind the dark' from 'Childlike Faith in Childhood's End'. What's more, the whole of the 'I fell off the raft of self-assurance' section, from which the quoted lines are taken, scans in a way that is strangely reminiscent of 'No More (the Sub-Mariner)' from the *In Camera* album. Whether any of the above is deliberate or merely accidental, the song makes a compelling case for living a life of conviction in the knowledge that 'the bubble's going to burst.'

'Can Do'

And speaking of conviction, here's a song that urges 'don't you say you can't do it; till you try you don't know what you can do.' The sentiment may be unarguable, but the almost seven minutes of this track are a leaden trudge indeed, only partly enlivened by Hammill's combative electric guitar. Hobbled by an annoying stop-start rhythm, with truisms baked hard into the lyric and little to show for itself in the melody line, 'Can Do' is a wearisome low point of the album.

'Tenderness'

Patchy though Hammill's 1990s output may have been, he never lost the knack of ending an album on a high note. Following 'A Way Out', 'Primo on the Parapet', 'Your Tall Ship' and 'A Better Time', 'Tenderness' is another emotional *tour de force*, a wrenching and heartfelt offer of comfort to a bereaved friend. Grief-stricken to the point of paralysis, the song acknowledges the uselessness of words as a form of consolation, the only possible comfort being a sympathetic presence and the holding out of kindness. Hammill's voice is tenderness itself, rising and falling with the soft contours of the text, its sighing cadences accompanied by subdued piano and strands of ethereal guitar. The song ends with a little flurry of alien sound, a final note of affirmation in the face of unbearable loss.

This (1998)

Personnel:
Peter Hammill: vocals, guitar, keyboards
Stuart Gordon: violin
David Jackson: saxophone, flute
Manny Elias: drums
All songs by Peter Hammill
Recorded at Terra Incognita, Bath, January-July 1998
Produced by Peter Hammill
UK release date: 26 October 1998
Cover: Paul Ridout

An album marked by the serendipitous alignment of several key milestones in Hammill's life. *This* was released in Hammill's fiftieth year, was his fortieth album (by his reckoning at least, including the VdGG records) and came on the thirtieth anniversary of his becoming a professional musician. As a result, there's a certain amount of retrospective thinking going on here, although not noticeably more so than on any other Hammill album since the 1970s. As Hammill wrote in his 1998 newsletter devoted to the album, 'the subject matter is fundamentally the passage of time, nowness and the singularity of our individual lives.' No change there, then; but, as always, Hammill managed to find new and arresting ways to approach these perennial topics.

There's a certain sonic diversity to the album, after the candlelit atmosphere of *Everyone You Hold*. The album is notable for the inclusion of a 14-minute piece, 'The Light Continent'. For those keeping score, this is Hammill's longest ever solo song, apart from the multi-part epics 'Flight' and 'A Headlong Stretch'. There are also three short instrumental fragments that incorporate elements from some of the other songs. In a 1998 interview, Hammill described these as 'little pieces [that] serve as glue', helping to smooth the sequencing of these varied songs.

This marked a return to the quartet line-up that made *X My Heart*, with Hammill joined once again by Jackson, Gordon and Elias. As Hammill writes in the notes to the album on his website, though, 'this is not in any sense a 'band' disc' as *X My Heart* had been.

The album was, of course, self-produced and recorded at Terra Incognita in Bath. There is, it has to be said, a touch of familiarity about all of this. No two Hammill albums are alike, yet his regular use of the same few trusted collaborators, and his insistence on retaining total creative control over each project, have resulted in a certain uniformity of sound over the years. Clearly, this is how Hammill likes to work, and there is something to be said for the certainty it brings and the sense of confidence it engenders. But I've often wondered how sparks might fly if Hammill were to bring in a new instrumentalist – someone like guitarist Bernard Butler or drummer Chris Cutler – or even an outside producer like Nigel Godrich to shake up the recording process. I'm not, however, holding my breath.

For those who enjoy visual puzzles, there's a certain amount of enjoyment to be gained from close scrutiny of Paul Ridout's cover art – uniquely presented as a fold-out poster this time. The thirty rings of the tree trunk may represent Hammill's thirty years as a professional musician. Elsewhere on the cover, we find: pennies minted in 1948 (the year of Hammill's birth) and 1998 (the year of the album's release), a cricket ball (as noted in previous chapters, Hammill is something of a cricket fan), corks from Spanish, Italian and French wines (Hammill has always seen himself as a good European), a car (*cf.* 'Sitting Targets'?), a group of blurred figures who may or may not be audience members, a vehicle tachograph disc from a European tour, and a watch that belonged to Hammill's father. There are other elements whose symbolic significance escapes me; as always in Hammill's work, a sense of mystery endures.

'Frozen in Place (fragment)'

A short introduction for layered choral vocals.

'Unrehearsed'

Not many of the songs on *This* have regularly been performed live. 'Unrehearsed' is the exception, a beautifully structured mini-epic that opens starkly with lone voice and piano over dark clouds of violin and sax. As so often on Hammill's 1990s records, here Jackson and Gordon bring vast reserves of empathy and experience to bear, their warm sonorities never overwhelming in tone but always carefully deployed in the service of the song. Three minutes in, the song explodes into life, as Hammill's vocal hits its stride and Elias' muscular drumming ratchets up the tension. In a fiery middle section, Hammill calls up the spirit of Rikki Nadir with truculent lead guitar, stoked by Jackson's bristling sax work. The track ends as it began, with a lonesome piano melody unfolding around Hammill's becalmed vocal.

'Stupid'

The album takes a sudden dip in quality with this laborious jazz-rock exercise. Jackson's squalling sax falls into lockstep with Elias' jerky rhythm track, while Hammill smears his arch and orotund vocal all over a wobbly piano figure. The song seems to suggest that although we all do stupid things from time to time, these mistakes form part of our 'pilgrim's accidental progress' through life. No quarrel with the sentiment, but still this kind of bluster tries the patience, coming after the similarly feeble 'Narcissus (Bar & Grill)' from *X My Heart* and 'Can Do' from *Everyone You Hold* (whose tune Hammill seems to have reheated for 'Stupid').

'Since The Kids'

Most of the keyboards on *This* are electric, with the notable exception of the piano on 'Since The Kids', which is Hammill's grand piano and was recorded at home – a rare throwback to the days of the Sofa Sound home studio. The instrument brings untold passion and gravitas to this delicate portrait of a married couple and how they are affected by their children growing up and leaving the family home. Three crashing chords announce the song, which then forms itself into a classic Hammill piano ballad with no other instruments in evidence, only his impeccable baritone and the fractured backing vocals that reinforce and amplify his presence – 'these fragments I have shored against my ruins', as T. S. Eliot wrote. A kind of sequel to 'Autumn' from 1977's *Over*, the song ends as it began with dramatic pounding of the keys announcing the mending of the broken chord.

'Nightman'

This song and the one after it form a pair, a gathering of crepuscular moods and shadows. In the 1998 newsletter, Hammill describes the two songs as 'snapshots of passing moments of clarity.' Certainly, there's a vividness to 'Nightman' despite its night-time setting, a sense of uneasy revelation in the midst of escaping and unspoken dreams. Hammill excels himself as a lyricist here; there's not a word wasted, the text pulsating with sharply evocative imagery. The key line 'by day I'll have clay in my hands', repeated with slight variations later in the song, recalls 'Given Time''s 'caught in the clay of material need.' There's a sense here of gloom giving way to moments of intense lucidity, a sense mirrored by Gordon's miraculous violin solo and the artful thrumming of Hammill's acoustic guitar.

'Fallen (The City of Night)'

The second in this diptych of night-time songs trades 'Nightman''s fevered visions for a heightening of recollected detail, described by Hammill in the 1998 newsletter as 'the ghosts of cities and lives past.' Indeed there are half-buried autobiographical elements here, starting with the echo of *A Black Box*'s 'Fogwalking' in the song's urban setting, and continuing with fleeting lyrical references to '70s Hammill classics 'Forsaken Gardens' and '(In the) Black Room'. But the real pleasures here are musical, as Gordon's skirling violin dances around Elias' ominous drums and Hammill's shadowy multi-layered vocals. Towards the song's end, Gordon and Elias cut loose amid waves of heavy riffing, bringing matters to a wild conclusion.

'Unready (fragment)'

A second short instrumental piece lifts from Stuart Gordon's sensitive violin work on 'Unrehearsed'.

'Always Is Next'

On what is sonically a very varied collection, 'Always Is Next' is perhaps the strangest and most jarring four minutes. Coming across like a proggy New

Order with its pounding electro rhythm and sharp snare drum crack, the song has a crazed intensity that feeds off its ferociously sexual lyric. The track bears some resemblance to early '80s PH cuts like 'What I Did' and 'Accidents', but trades their exuberance for a barbarity that fails either to impress or to convince. As for the puzzling reference to 'the Demiurge Avenger', Hammill described it in a 1998 interview as 'a kind of primal force ... not a godhead, but a kind of primal disinterested force.'

'Unsteady (fragment)'
The third and final of these short interludes takes vocal and instrumental elements from 'Nightman'.

'The Light Continent'
Forty years into Hammill's career as a professional musician, it's remarkable that he was still taking risks, still showing a willingness to experiment, and still making music that sounded like nothing he had ever done before. 'The Light Continent' is a prime example, a 14-minute driftwork that recalls German ambient producer Thomas Köner's early '90s masterpieces *Teimo* and *Permafrost* in its monolithic evocation of desolate Antarctic landscapes. Layering slow, deliberate vocals over bleak mists of keyboard noise, Hammill conjures an endless expanse of frozen fields, lit by 'a horizon of light' that 'blurs the boundaries of whiteness.' Jackson and Gordon make unobtrusive appearances, the frosty timbre of their instruments settling like ice into the sunken crevices of the piece. In the 1998 newsletter, Hammill relates how their contributions were improvised over the piece as it then stood: 'the final contributions of David and Stuart were made without their having had the benefit of hearing a note of the track played to them in advance.' He goes on to describe 'The Light Continent' as 'a tone poem ... stretching and extending the sentiments of a moment.' A challenging listen for sure, but one that amply repays the close attention it requires.

None of the Above (2000)

Personnel:
Peter Hammill: vocals, guitar, bass, keyboards
Stuart Gordon: violin, viola
Manny Elias: drums, percussion
Holly & Beatrice Hammill: backing vocals
All songs by Peter Hammill
Recorded at Terra Incognita, Bath, January 1999-February 2000
Produced by Peter Hammill
UK release date: 15 May 2000
Cover: Paul Ridout
Photography: Dinu, Paul Ridout

Hammill's first album of the new millennium is a wonderfully fresh and invigorating collection of songs. *This* had been an ambitious but rather demanding set, rich in texture and atmosphere but short on hummable tunes. That's not an accusation you could level at *None of the Above*, which contains enough searing piano ballads, condensed epics, filmic narratives and warped pop songs to satisfy the most discerning of Hammill fans. Along with 2009's *Thin Air*, I rate *None of the Above* as Hammill's best album since the turn of the millennium.

Taking care as ever not to repeat himself, Hammill followed up the pensive self-awareness of *This* with an album of first and third-person stories, described in the 2000 newsletter devoted to the album as 'a number of tales of people in earthy and/or earthly circumstances.' This direction is reflected in the title *None of the Above*, which may be read as 'there is nothing of a spiritual or otherworldly nature here', as well as playing on the difficulty of categorising Hammill's music.

The promised attention to earthly detail is manifested in the subject matter, some of which is unusually explicit for Hammill: a violent husband ('Like Veronica'), a demented stalker ('Somebody Bad Enough'), a rose grower mourning the death of his wife ('Naming the Rose'). (Hammill's next two albums, *What, Now?* and *Clutch*, would continue in this vein with songs about Catholic sexual abuse, anorexia and paedophilia.) These are vivid domestic dramas in which Hammill's gift for idiomatic phrasing is matched by settings that range from the sombre to the pulsating, always foregrounding the elegance and mutability of the voice.

Hammill plays most of the instruments here, with a good deal of orchestral guitars in evidence and even a few touches of bass. Stuart Gordon contributes strings on three tracks, with Manny Elias weighing in on drums on one. The soundworld is endlessly vital and fascinating: shape-shifting changes of mood and timbre; instrumental colouring by turns delicate and brutal; the tightly arranged and the purely improvisational fruitfully juxtaposed.

The photographs in the booklet are of ladders and staircases, hinting at the possibility of ascension to some celestial sphere which never quite materialises in these songs. And there's a playful reference buried in the credits: the cover photo, evidently a self-portrait, is credited to 'Dinu'. This is short for Dinu M'Brela, a pseudonym for Hammill as cover artist which he hadn't used since 1975's *Nadir's Big Chance*. The elusive Dinu would go on to make another appearance in the credits for 2006's *Singularity*.

'Touch and Go'

A large part of Hammill's genius as a songwriter is his ability to render new and unexpected angles on subjects that have obsessed him over the years. Identity, memory and personality form one such group; language, its slipperiness and its inherent unreliability, a second. But Hammill's central obsession is love – its beauty, its pain, its perfection and its terror. 'Touch and Go' is the fifth in a series of songs (the others being 'If I Could', 'Don't Tell Me', 'Too Many of My Yesterdays' and 'All Said And Done') that isolate the traumatic moment in a relationship where love turns to avoidance and mistrust. 'If I Could' had begun with the startling line 'you must be crazy to stay here'; now, the narrator of 'Touch and Go' admits that 'you've got no reason to stay', before contemplating whether it's even worth putting up a fight to save the relationship, and ultimately concluding that it's not. This harrowing interior drama is played out in long fields of synthesizer, abstracted guitar tones and skeletal threads of piano. Hammill's voice is, still, an instrument of astonishing strength and flexibility; the way he hits the high note on the word 'headed' in the extraordinary line 'across the leaden hammer-headed sky' chills me every time.

'Naming the Rose'

'A bittersweet love story of devotion,' writes Hammill in the 2000 newsletter. Indeed this tale of how a rose grower memorialises his dearly beloved and departed wife by developing a new rose cultivar, returning her ashes to the soil where it grows, and finally naming it after her, is one of Hammill's most touching narratives. Appropriately, the song is a model of elegiac reserve and composure. Reciting the exotic names of other roses called after women, including the splendidly named Zephirine Drouhin, Hammill sings in a layered choral style, his daughters once again brought in on soprano backing vocals. Stuart Gordon's string arrangement hovers around the narrative, as shapely and delicate as the roses of the song.

'How Far I Fell'

In Samuel Beckett's 1958 play *Krapp's Last Tape*, an old man listens to tape recordings of himself at a younger age. Among the last words spoken by the younger Krapp are: 'Perhaps my best years are gone. When there was a chance of happiness. But I wouldn't want them back. Not with the fire in me now.' The narrator of 'How Far I Fell' might sympathise with Krapp, being an old man looking back over his life, recognising his past hubris and regretting the mistakes he has made. The song opens with Hammill as a kind of Greek chorus, introducing the characters and commenting that 'we're born to be fools in life.' The rest of it feels like the kind of un-folk song that we'll see more of on *Clutch*: predominantly acoustic guitar-based and structured around some kind of refrain, but wired with a tension that places it well outside the folk tradition. Incidentally, Hammill notes in the 2000 newsletter that the guitars used in this song date from VdGG days: Meurglys III for the electric parts, and a Yamaha acoustic that was used on *The Least We Can Do Is Wave To Each Other*.

'Somebody Bad Enough'

What a taut and chilling song this is, John Fowles' *The Collector* set to music. The narrator is a stalker who follows the object of his obsession and plans to initiate contact with her. The title plays on the contrasting meanings of 'bad enough' and 'badly enough', and the song turns on the stalker's deranged conviction that the girl will accept him for what he is. The idea of an obsessed individual keeping a 'website stocked with pictures' seems somewhat dated today, but in 2000 would have seemed like the epitome of internet-era creepiness. Sonically, this is one of those songs that demonstrates Hammill's unswerving commitment to originality and creative invention, propelled as it is by ticking percussion and feathery electric guitar. Hammill takes a concise solo at around the three-minute mark, and the whole thing is constructed around an addictive, unexpectedly lyrical chorus.

'Tango for One'

Someone evidently got on Hammill's nerves here. 'Tango for One' is a long and eloquent diatribe against a nameless individual who seems oblivious to the fact that the world does not 'revolve around whatever problem [they] want solved.' What's impressive about this song is the sheer scope and commitment of Hammill's invective: by the time he barks 'every time you call me, your self-obsession grows' you think he must be just about done with his condemnation, but in fact, he's barely halfway through it. Hammill's menacing piano stalks the song in vituperative clusters, while Gordon's sweeping violin forms a bulwark against the increasingly don't-fuck-with-me tone of Hammill's voice. The title of the song may contain a coded reference to the individual who inspired it.

'Like Veronica'

The only song on the album to be regularly performed live, 'Like Veronica', is also the album's only full-on rock number, with energetic drums from Elias cutting across Hammill's sharp-tongued guitar. Veronica Lake (1922-1973) was an American actress whose trademark was a hairstyle that cascaded over her right eye. The song makes brilliant use of this image, conceiving a battered wife who adopts the same hairstyle to conceal the bruises on her face. While the brutal violence it describes is something we've not previously seen in Hammill's writing, it nevertheless represents one possible outcome of the kind of obsessional thinking that's often portrayed in his work. Simmering electric guitar accompanies the song's introduction, falling into choppy riffage as the text descends into cruelty and psychosis.

'In A Bottle'

The longest track on the album at just over eight minutes, 'In A Bottle' drifts past on multi-layered choral voices, spare keyboards and restrained flurries of percussion. As Hammill puts it in the 2000 newsletter, the subject of the song is 'a hedonist [who] finds himself staring in the mirror by guttering candlelight' and who can't bring to mind the essence of his past adventures. The lyric is, as ever, impeccable in its precise depiction of a mind in a state of dislocation, while the disparate registers of voice form a highly effective channelling of the text's fractured sense of time and place. Nevertheless, the song is an unmemorable low point on the album, encumbered as it is by a dawdling melody and a general sense of lethargy.

'Astart'

Another inexpressibly lovely closer in the vein of 'Your Tall Ship' and 'Tenderness', this gets my vote as Hammill's most beautiful song of the 2000s. In its calm, rational insistence that 'life is neither cruel nor fair, at random or well-planned', it seems to gather up the strands of all the songs that have preceded it and weave them into a vast, overarching expanse of connections and possibilities: 'every action, every passion, forms a little chain reaction...' The song settles into an unforced rhythm and a tender, forgiving melody, exquisitely rendered in warm vocals and gentle keyboard swells. Hammill's daughters once again add soprano backing vocals to the mix, their angelic voices rising in perfect harmony with Hammill's mellifluous baritone. After all the darkness and damage we've seen on the album, this last song holds out a promise of hope wrapped in a classic piece of Hammill wordplay: every breath is 'astart', sudden, as well as 'a start', a new beginning.

What, Now? (2001)

Personnel:
Peter Hammill: vocals, guitar, bass, keyboards
David Jackson: saxophone, flute, whistle
Stuart Gordon: violin, viola
Manny Elias: drums, percussion
All songs by Peter Hammill
Recorded at Terra Incognita, Bath, autumn 2000-March 2001
Produced by Peter Hammill
UK release date: 25 June 2001
Cover: Paul Ridout

Who else releases an album every year? A quick glance at the PH/VdGG discography shows that there have been very few years since 1970 in which there was no new studio album. Those rare gaps, moreover, are almost always accounted for either by the appearance of a live album or by extensive touring. There is surely no other artist in rock who has released so much material over such an extended period of time.

Hammill's work rate continued to be prodigious throughout the 2000s, at a time when most of his progressive rock-era contemporaries had already slipped into comfortable retirement. Barely a year after the release of *None of the Above*, he came out with another highly diverse and listenable album in *What, Now?* One might have thought that quality control would suffer as a result of the sheer quantity of material being released, but not a bit of it – *What, Now?* contains some of Hammill's best work of the decade.

Recording of the album took place, as ever, at Terra Incognita in Bath. In his 2001 newsletter devoted to the album, Hammill notes that he 'took some time away from the analytical world of the studio to remind myself of the immediacy of the stage. It's my feeling that a lot of the playing has an extra looseness as a result of this.' That looseness is also, no doubt, in part due to the presence of the other members of the long-established PH Quartet – Jackson, Gordon and Elias – alongside Hammill on several tracks. In fact, this would turn out to be the last album on which the four of them played together.

The album is notable for containing three longish (8-10 minutes) tracks that could be described (using a favourite Hammill prefix) as 'neo-epics'. In the shifting time signatures, elaborate lyrical conceits and extended instrumental passages of 'Here Come The Talkies', 'Lunatic In Knots' and 'Edge of the Road', *What, Now?* cleaves more to the progressive end of things than any Hammill album since *Roaring Forties*.

As for the title, Hammill acknowledges in the 2001 newsletter that it has 'a degree of joke' to it and is 'open to several interpretations.' At least some of these interpretations turn on the strategic placement of the comma between the first and second words of the title. Without the comma, the question means 'what's happening next?' But with the comma, it can be read as something like 'so he's doing this *now*?' or even 'so you want me to do this *now*?' In any case, the point is surely the emphasis on 'now', an insistence on living in and for the moment that is a recurring theme in Hammill's work.

The cover artwork is a series of long-exposure motion photographs of Hammill all in white, as he often appears in concert. Flick the pages of the CD booklet quickly and you might be able to see him dancing. It's worth a try, anyway.

'Here Come The Talkies'

Back in 1983, Hammill had set a murderous love story against a backdrop of 1950s 'Film Noir'. This time, the setting is the silent film era – specifically the tail end of it, as the genre was heading towards obsolescence in the face of the 'talkies'. In this case, however, the cinematic context is more metaphorical than literal. Speculating that the legendary silent film star Rudolph Valentino might have felt 'something alien in the air', the song suggests that 'something new is always bound to come along and upset our cosy conceptions of how life is and will ever be', to quote Hammill in the 2001 newsletter. This perfectly formed mini-epic is bookended by lovely sparkling piano, dreamy violin from Gordon and sympathetic drumming from Elias. In a convulsive middle section, Hammill splits the song open with blistering vocals and manic Nadir-esque riffing.

'Far-Flung (Across The Sky)'

Originally released in a different version on a charity compilation, *The Sky Goes All The Way Home*, this is a short and rather slight interlude for guitars and voice. Layers of fingerpicked acoustic emerge from a cloud of treated and ebow electric. The setting is atmospheric enough, but the text's appeal that 'if we just raise our eyes we'll share the sky' is not, shall we say, Hammill at his most lyrically acute.

'The American Girl'

The second in a triptych of shorter, reflective pieces slotted in between the three neo-epics on the album. Here we find an unnamed American woman who experiences feelings of displacement and hostility when she goes to live in the 'old world' of Britain. Jackson makes the first of two appearances on the album, his lambent soprano sax gliding over the polished surfaces of Hammill's keyboards and Gordon's violin. Hammill's half-spoken, half-sung enunciation of the verse lines is a joy, filled with the classical English precision that makes his singing voice so unique. As for the identity of the woman in the song, Hammill has remained tight-lipped but issued a barely necessary denial in the 2001 newsletter that it was about an 'ambitious blonde', i.e. Madonna. Wallis Simpson would seem to be the most likely candidate, or possibly Nancy Astor.

'Wendy and the Lost Boy'

A bittersweet evocation of childhood, lost love and broken promises – but then again, what is adulthood but an endless series of betrayals of the certainties we felt as children? Drawing on J. M. Barrie's *Peter Pan*, the song centres on the character of Wendy, who in the novel takes on the role of mother to the Lost Boys and, it is implied, is in love with Peter Pan. Peter, though, being a boy who never grows up, is unable to return Wendy's love. Swirling pizzicato strings – presumably sampled, since Gordon is not credited – deepen the elegiac moods of Hammill's piano and voice, adding to the tone of nostalgic regret that suffuses the song.

'Lunatic In Knots'

The album really gets down to business here, with the first of two linked neo-epics that descend to some fairly wild and dangerous places. The lunatic of the title forms part of the narrator's splintering identity, and seems to take pleasure in making him question his grip on reality. This intense psychological warfare is played out against a hulking acoustic guitar figure that's gradually engulfed by urgent group activity, reminiscent of 'Primo on the Parapet' in its unstoppable drift towards illogic and insanity. Gordon and Elias work wonders here, interlocking with Hammill's sheets of electric guitar over the song's blazing final minutes.

An aside: in the 2001 newsletter, Hammill describes the 'keep him away from me' section towards the end of the song as 'a *Krebs-technik* transition', a term he also used to describe the ending of 'Fallen (The City of Night)' from *This*. In a 1998 interview, Hammill defined *Krebs-technik* as 'an old modern classical composing technique' in which you 'start with motif one or riff one and actually then have [two] running simultaneously and then merge.' Now, I'm no musician, but it seems to me that Hammill has made another category error here. All the reference works I've consulted point to *Krebs* being the German term for what is known in music theory as 'retrograde motion', i.e. taking a single melodic line and playing it in reverse. Clearly, what happens towards the end of 'Lunatic In Knots' and 'Fallen (The City of Night)' is as Hammill describes; that is to say, two riffs merging into one. But I wouldn't call it *Krebs-technik*.

'Edge of the Road'

In the 2001 newsletter, Hammill draws a clear line from 'Lunatic In Knots' to this song: 'the lunatic is out there with the wildest of eyes set on the horizon, and it's doubtful that he'll ever make it back.' Still suffering from 'the murmur of an alien disease', he's now shadowed by a woman who hopes that he'll come to his senses 'if she just paid out plaits of flaxen rope' (*cf.* the Rapunzel fairy tale). But there's not much chance of a romantic ending to this story, not when the man is still 'chasing after a thrill that'll take him out beyond all sense of time and place.' This song is, for me, the highpoint of *What, Now?*, a widescreen epic that slowly unfolds over ten dramatic minutes with Jackson in magnificent form on saxophone and flute. Hammill's voice shapes the song in passionate drawn-out cadences, while his electric slide guitar brings a sense of inexorable forward motion to the piece.

'Fed to the Wolves'

One of Hammill's most truly disturbing songs, this angry condemnation of child sexual abuse by Catholic priests, shocks you like nothing else in his work. With rage and disgust boiling from every pore, Hammill denounces this 'hell on earth' amid waves of guitar-driven feedback and controlled, sinister drumbeats. The obscenity of the language in the first verse is amply justified by the obscenity of the acts described and the magnitude of the betrayal they involve. Yet, as ever, there's a forceful intelligence at work here, structuring the sonics for maximum impact. Halfway through the song, Hammill's voice softens to a pitch of muted outrage, certain that 'the damage that is done is worse than unholy.'

'Enough'

The album ends with a searching, oddly troubled piece for layered choral voices and treated electric guitar. Hammill sings two verses in his higher register, only to find his provisional conclusions ('this alone will have to be enough … this alone will never be enough') undermined by a Beckettian paring down of language to its barest essentials. Attempting to make sense of the permutations available to him (that/this, why/how, if/when, soon/now), Hammill concludes by asking the same question posed by the title of the album – 'what now?' But the song fades away in plumes of guitar noise, leaving the question unanswered.

Clutch (2002)

Personnel:
Peter Hammill: vocals, acoustic guitar, lute
Stuart Gordon: violin, viola, FX
David Jackson: saxophone, flute
All songs by Peter Hammill
Recorded at Terra Incognita, Bath, August 2001-July 2002
Produced by Peter Hammill
UK release date: October 2002 Cover: Paul Ridout

Those fortunate enough to have seen Hammill live in a solo context will know that his concerts invariably consist of two piano (or keyboard) sets with a guitar set sandwiched in between. His work can be divided into piano and guitar songs, depending on the instrument on which they were composed, with most of his studio albums containing a more or less equal mix of the two. The 1986 album *And Close As This* was the first he had released consisting solely of keyboard songs, but it wasn't until 2002 that he made *Clutch*, his first album consisting exclusively of guitar songs.

In a sleeve note, Hammill points out that the acoustic guitar was the instrument on which his earliest songs were written and performed. In making *Clutch*, then, he returned to 'a discipline of first principles, informed by the passage of time.' Indeed it's possible to trace a direct line from *Clutch* back to early acoustic guitar offerings on albums like *Fool's Mate* and *Chameleon in the Shadow of the Night*.

Hammill is also at pains to point out in the sleeve notes that 'this was not intended to be and has not turned out as any kind of folk or roots collection.' Needless to say, a song written and performed on acoustic guitar is not necessarily a folk song, and Hammill has always worked well outside the folk tradition. Without getting too deeply into issues of genre, it's clear that the defining characteristics of contemporary folk music – its sense of an oral tradition, of something culturally specific and rooted in collective experience – are largely absent from Hammill's work.

Along with the usual crop of Hammill themes – memory, identity, language and the lessons of experience – there are also three songs here that deal with specific real-world issues – religious terrorism, paedophilia and anorexia. Having sung about domestic violence and Catholic sexual abuse on his two previous albums, Hammill was clearly not in the mood to shy away from difficult and sensitive topics. As ever, his engagement with these subjects is serious, committed and startling in its tone.

Paul Ridout's cover booklet provides an ingenious visual key to the album, the red dots on the fretboards showing the opening chords of the songs (some of them, at least). And I very much like the way the lyrics are printed as prose, making them seem like short stories or polemical tracts. (The lyrics of 2012's *Consequences* are printed in the same way.)

'We Are Written'

Remember the Beatles riff at the start of 'Sharply Unclear' from *Roaring Forties*? Well, here's another possible homage to the Fab Four: the opening chord of this song sounds remarkably similar (to my untrained ear, at least) to the opening chord of 'A Hard Day's Night'. And if Hammill isn't quoting The Beatles here, he certainly quotes himself lyrically elsewhere in the song. The phrase 'we are written' sounds like a partial echo of 'we are written in the star-crossed sky' from 1992's 'I Will Find You', while the closing phrase 'unconsciously pre-planned' recalls the line about 'unconscious pre-planning' from the 'Continental Drift' section of 1994's 'A Headlong Stretch'. If this sounds like I'm accusing Hammill of resting on his laurels creatively, nothing could be further from the truth. In fact, this is one of the most powerfully attractive songs on the album, with Hammill's agile vocals tracked by a skittish chord progression and a scampering top line.

'Crossed Wires'

Talking of recurrent imagery, the grinning Cheshire cat from *Alice's Adventures in Wonderland* makes the second of its three appearances in Hammill songs here, the first being in 'Sharply Unclear' and the third in 'Our Eyes Give It Shape' from 2006's *Singularity*. This is one of the album's more uptempo moments, with Hammill alternating between frantic fingerpicking and slashing chordal runs over Gordon's exuberant violin. Meanwhile, Hammill's lead and backing voices trade overflowing vocal lines to mesmerising effect. The song's a return to the theme of language, and its ability to drive a wedge between what we say and what we mean – a theme previously explored in 1980's 'Losing Faith In Words', and which would go on to be explored in greater depth on Hammill's next album *Incoherence*.

'Driven'

In his 2002 newsletter devoted to the album, Hammill wrote that 'one of my subsidiary aims in this project was to increase the available stock of guitar songs for live performance.' With most recent additions to the live repertoire having been piano songs, Hammill clearly felt it was time to redress the balance somewhat. As it turns out, however, 'Driven' is the only song from *Clutch* to have received regular live airings since the album's release. It's certainly worthy of this accolade, being an engrossing four minutes shaped by a lovely melody and a glowing chord sequence to which Jackson adds misty layers of saxophone. If 1981's 'Sitting Targets' had pictured the car as the perfect place to hold a serious conversation, by the time of 'Driven' the journey has turned into a lifelong one, thwarted by plans undone and dreams unfulfilled.

'Once You Called Me'

In 1986 Hammill had released 'Sleep Now', a tender and emotive lullaby dedicated to his young daughters. Sixteen years later, 'Once You Called Me' is a kind of sequel to that song, a beautiful and heartfelt reflection on one daughter's growing up. There's nothing mawkish or sentimental here, just a painful awareness of how precious and fleeting childhood is, expressed in terms that any parent (this writer included) will easily recognise. Stuart Gordon's radiant string arrangement perfectly complements the introspection of Hammill's guitar and his deeply affecting vocal performance.

'The Ice Hotel'

The fundamental aural building block of *Clutch* is the use of two acoustic guitars in double-tracked form, a fact crucial to the album's rich and resonant sound. 'The Ice Hotel' is a good example; its mazelike picking style pushed to the front of the soundworld with Jackson's saxophone drifting hazily into the spaces in between. That said, this is by some way the least successful track on the album, lacking melodic interest and without much of a rhythm to help it along. Recalling the environmental mysticism of 'Gaia' from 1992's *Fireships*, the track declares that 'impermanence marks the man-made ... each year another team will build it up anew.' A fine lyric but a laborious song.

'This Is The Fall'

In the 2002 newsletter, Hammill wrote that his aim with *Clutch* was 'to collect a group of songs with as wide a range of styles as possible within the self-imposed instrumental restrictions.' The benefits of this approach are made clear on 'This Is The Fall', a sulphurous diatribe against religious terrorism and its betrayal of faith. Roused to indignation by terrorist atrocities committed in the name of God, Hammill demands to know 'in what book of what religion is the blood-lust sanctified?' The strafing blasts of Hammill's guitar intensify the force of the track, reinforced by Jackson's coiled saxophone and Gordon's stormy violin. One can hardly imagine a full band treatment of this song having a greater impact than this acoustic arrangement does. Indeed the song I'm most reminded of when I listen to 'This Is The Fall' is 'Modern' from 1973's *The Silent Corner and the Empty Stage*, which in its savage declaration that 'the city's lost its way, madness takes hold today...' seems to prefigure the violence and bloodshed of the later cut.

'Just A Child'

No comment needed here, except to note that the song is a brutally effective denunciation of this most abhorrent of crimes. Gordon adds slabs of treated, discordant violin to the impassioned hammering of Hammill's guitar.

'Skinny'

As the father of three daughters himself, Hammill would have been acutely aware of the constant presence of idealised images of young people, especially girls, in the media. The harmful effect of such images is well documented as one of the causes of anorexia. In 'Skinny' Hammill rages against the pernicious influence of 'every glossy fashion shot' on the mind of a vulnerable young woman suffering from anorexia. I could have done without the rather heavy-handed pun on the word 'magazines', but otherwise, this is a scathingly powerful track on a difficult subject. Unaccompanied by violin or sax this time, Hammill issues lightning bolts of acoustic guitar at restless angles to the discomforting barks and howls of his voice.

'Bareknuckle Trade'

As a collection of solo acoustic guitar songs, *Clutch* naturally foregrounds the voice and the text as the primary means of expression. Appropriately enough, Hammill's lyrical gifts are at their height here, not least on the closing track 'Bareknuckle Trade'. Lines such as 'not for the first time I'm here in some disarray, and returning in spades are the hands that I've played with the tools of the trade' are dizzying in their brilliance, evoking card games and manual labour as stealthy correlatives of music-making. Indeed there are numerous references to hands, fingers and thumbs scattered throughout the album, reflecting the physical act of playing the guitar even as they spin layer upon layer of metaphorical meaning.

As the final track on *Clutch*, 'Bareknuckle Trade' is a major piece of work – not only for its lyrical complexity but for the way it unfurls over eight long minutes in tense and unforgiving strands of melody. Opening with slow, glistening fingerpicked guitar over eerie violin, Hammill kicks the song into life halfway through with salvos of torrential riffing, while Gordon's feedback-drenched violin sounds as heavy as any electric guitar. Finally, we're back in the ring with the bareknuckle fighter who never gives in: 'timidity be damned – hang on to that towel, never throw it.' Timidity is not something you could accuse Hammill of, nor is he likely to throw in the towel.

Incoherence (2004)

Personnel:
Peter Hammill: vocals, guitar, keyboards
Stuart Gordon: violin
David Jackson: saxophone, flute
All songs by Peter Hammill
Recorded at Terra Incognita, Somerset, March-December 2003
Produced by Peter Hammill
UK release date: March 2004
Cover: Paul Ridout

The year 2003 was an eventful one for Hammill. In the early part of the year he moved out of the studio in Bath, where he had recorded every album since 1991's *Fireships*. In newsletters from 2003, Hammill noted that the departure from Bath 'was not exactly a stress-free experience,' without elaborating further; he did, however, mention that the move was partly the result of 'looking for more mobility, [having] shrunk the recording hardware down in both size and complexity.' So he moved to a new, smaller studio near Frome in Somerset and set to work on the recordings that would become *Incoherence*. In all probability, he intended to retain this as his working environment for the foreseeable future. Life, as usual, had other ideas.

At midday on 7 December 2003, Hammill had a heart attack while walking down by the Thames at Henley. Happily, he suffered no lasting ill-effects (although the roll-ups he could occasionally be seen smoking after concerts were now a thing of the past). The experience did mean, however, that it was not advisable for him to be working away from home for extended periods of time, so he took the decision to move the studio back under his own roof – bringing the story full circle, as he had first begun recording *Chameleon* at home (not the same home, of course) way back in 1973.

Having completed work on *Incoherence* only two days before his heart attack, it would turn out to be the only album Hammill recorded at Frome. It's notable for other reasons as well, primarily that it's a single 42-minute piece, his fourth long-form work after 'A Plague of Lighthouse-Keepers', 'Flight' and 'A Headlong Stretch'. Although it's divided up into sections, the album makes most sense when listened to at a single sitting; in this respect, it resembles *The Fall of the House of Usher*. And the parallels don't end there, since several passages from *Incoherence* recall the sung-through vocal style of *Usher*, not to mention that the album was recorded, like the 1999 version of *Usher*, without any drums or percussion.

The paradox of *Incoherence* – and it's an album riddled with paradoxes – is that although it cleaves closer to that hoary old progressive rock trope, the concept album, than any other Hammill album, its fourteen sections contain more than enough winning melodies, driving rock passages and wintry ballads to satisfy any Hammill fan. It's also Hammill's most sustained and argumentative interrogation of language, its unreliability and its treachery. Earlier songs like 'Losing Faith In Words' and 'Other Old Clichés' had signalled Hammill's interest in this topic; never before, though, had he subjected the problem of language to such intense scrutiny.

But when we talk about the problem of language, what exactly do we mean? Hammill came closest to an answer in the 2004 newsletter about the album: 'I grow more and more aware of how often and how strikingly I fail to get my point across precisely, of how often I fail to express myself with clarity. In other words, I wonder about my own fluency in English.' With peerless contributions from the ubiquitous Jackson and Gordon, *Incoherence* is the sound of Hammill coming to terms with that inevitable failure to communicate.

Paul Ridout's beautifully designed lyric sheet is a graphical representation of the Tower of Babel, which according to the Book of Genesis, stood at the origin of the world's different languages. It's also a 'calligram' (text arranged as an image), in the style of the early 20th-century French poet Apollinaire.

'When Language Corrodes'

A strange little orchestral introduction, and fluttering saxophone by Jackson, give way to what sounds like the start of a classic PH piano ballad. 'What truths are there left to be told, when we're all lost for words?' asks Hammill, raising a question to which we already know he's unlikely to proffer an answer.

'Babel'

The lovely piano melody from the first section flows seamlessly into this part, with Hammill's grave baritone rising to an emphatic falsetto. Jackson lends further tonal colour here; indeed, his contributions to the album as a whole are significant, his sax and flute adding vivid clarity to Hammill's weighty ruminations on the failings of language. We're 'uncertain when it all goes south if we mean what we say,' Hammill suggests, setting himself up nicely for the next section on ... crosswords?

'Logodaedalus'

By his own admission, a solver of cryptic crosswords, Hammill would no doubt be aware of the guiding principles of clue-setting as set out by Ximenes, a British crossword compiler. Among these is 'I need not mean what I say, but I must say what I mean', a principle perhaps more achievable in the world of crosswords than it is in everyday discourse. Anyway, this section depicts a wily crossword setter who enjoys outwitting his solvers, 'certain that we'll all agree with his definition ... an obsolescent word from 1663.' It's probably not a coincidence that 'Logodaedalus' (literally, one who manipulates words with cunning), itself an obsolescent word with no later

Oxford English Dictionary entry than 1663, was the pseudonym of a setter of cryptic crosswords in the *Guardian* newspaper at the time this album was written. Recalling the 'systems music' basis of 1990's 'On The Surface' and 1996's 'A Forest of Pronouns', the section sees sparks of electric guitar emerge from a headily repetitive keyboard figure.

'Like Perfume'
A short, *Usher*-like passage for layered electric guitars and voices.

'Your Word'
Another brief linking passage with sax and violin surrounding bright flickers of piano and acoustic guitar. In a typically Hammillesque piece of wordplay, the sense of 'giving your word' as making a promise gets tangled up with the notion of not being able to take back your words once you've said them, thereby giving *up* your word. As he writes in the 2004 newsletter: 'the word, once spoken, [is] forever in the air.'

'Always and a Day'
When we give our word, we say 'I will' as though we mean it to last forever. But what if there's an implied 'until…' buried in there that we feel compelled to deny? This is the premise of 'Always and a Day', a stark interlude for piano (some of it backmasked), acoustic guitar and choral voices.

'Cretans Always Lie'
The album really gets down to business with this pulverising section, again reminiscent of the 1999 *Usher* in its swirling guitars and heated repetitions. The paradox that 'Cretans always lie' was advanced by the Greek philosopher Epimenides, who was himself a Cretan; hence, it's not possible to tell whether Epimenides was telling the truth or not. As if this weren't enough, the section tells us that 'just as Zeno's arrow flies, the snake is eating its tail.' The paradox of Zeno's arrow states that at any moment in time, a moving arrow is at the place where it is, but *is not moving*, since it has no time in which to move. Since the same holds true for any other moment during its 'flight', the arrow never moves. As for the snake eating its tail, this is the *ouroboros*, a Gnostic symbol of cyclical renewal.

'All Greek'
Another pulsating uptempo section, in which the synthesised instrumentation comes over like Tangerine Dream in their 1980s sequence-driven heyday. Nothing wrong with that in my book, and Hammill sings darkly of a 'cacophony of linguistic dismay' over the top, even throwing in a few words of Greek for good measure. Jackson enters towards the end, his dynamic sax adding to the exuberant energy of the section.

'Call That A Conversation?'

After the lyrical and philosophical wordplay of the previous two sections, it's no surprise to hear Hammill slip into a more idiomatic form of language for this acerbic passage. We've seen in earlier songs like 'Silver' and 'Tango For One' how caustic Hammill can be when describing a clash with some real or imagined adversary. Here the conflict stems from a failure of communication, couched in the matter-of-fact terms of everyday conversation: 'I can't believe what you just said … let's forget it now.' Musically, this section evokes the late '70s *pH7* era of songs like 'Faculty X', with a strong melodic lift bolstered by punchy keyboards.

'The Meanings Changed'

The aftermath of the argument in the previous section; bile and cynicism give way to brokenness and regret. This short passage sounds like part of a classic PH song of failed romance, with Jackson's smoky sax curling around Hammill's atmospheric keyboards.

'Converse'

This, the album's only instrumental section, consists of a lively violin passage followed by a reprise of the main melody from 'Call That A Conversation?'

'Gone Ahead'

'Gone Ahead' is the only part of the album that Hammill has performed live. This comes as no surprise since it's both the longest section of the album and the one that most closely resembles a self-contained song. And what a song it is. Constructed from a gorgeous piano melody and wreathed in a dense pall of violin, it turns on the conviction that the only appropriate response to the problem of language is not to say anything at all: 'when the time comes to be silent … one by one the jaws all drop.' The final words of the song are particularly affecting in the knowledge that Hammill survived a heart attack not long after recording them: 'so much I'm losing now, so many things left unsaid.'

'Power of Speech'

There's not a whole lot of acoustic guitar on *Incoherence*, but after a brief piano introduction, this section settles into a rugged acoustic groove with weaving sax accompaniment from Jackson. The album's working its way towards a conclusion by this point, and there's an air of finality about Hammill's defiant declaration that '[we] blow up the flowering of sense with the power of speech.'

'If Language Explodes'

Continuing the imagery from the previous section, this strangely serene passage brings the album to a close. The opening section, 'When Language

Corrodes', had wondered 'what truths are there left to be told, when we're all lost for words?' As expected, no easy answers have been found forty minutes later, only a realisation that we're 'still in the search for the words.' In an extended instrumental outro, silvery Spanish guitar and flute dance fleetingly around each other before trailing off into silence.

Singularity (2006)

Personnel:
Peter Hammill: vocals, guitar, keyboards, bass, drums, percussion
All songs by Peter Hammill
Recorded at Terra Incognita, Wiltshire, January-August 2006
Produced by Peter Hammill
UK release date: December 2006
Cover: Paul Ridout
Photography: Dinu

A gap of over 2½ years between Hammill albums is unheard of; in this case, however, it's perfectly understandable. Hammill was in recovery from his heart attack for much of 2004, while most of 2005 was taken up with the Van der Graaf Generator reunion. It wasn't until early 2006, therefore, that Hammill turned his attention to the next set of solo recordings, which would become *Singularity*. As noted in the previous chapter, Hammill moved his studio back home for this and all subsequent solo releases.

Both the VdGG reunion and Hammill's brush with death were to have a significant impact on the shape of *Singularity*. In terms of the sonics, Hammill decided from an early stage that he wanted to make an entirely solo record with no other musicians on board. Partly this was due to the VdGG reunion; as Hammill notes in the 2006 newsletter devoted to the album, 'it became clear that whatever I was going to do in solo work had to steer well away from the band's territory.' He had also been engaged in remastering his 1970s albums for reissue, and this work encouraged him to approach the latest set of recordings in a similar spirit to the (almost) solo nature of albums such as *In Camera* (1974) and *The Future Now* (1978). Not to mention that after his last album, the elaborate and conceptually rich *Incoherence*, he felt the need to return to basics somewhat. Yet the pleasures of *Singularity* are due in no small part to the sheer diversity of its approaches, from zestful band-style workouts to sombre ballads via elements of *musique concrète* and full-on electronic experimentation.

Lyrically, the songs inevitably deal with weighty matters; as Hammill writes in the 2006 newsletter, 'intimations of mortality are present in almost every line.' Those intimations go beyond Hammill's own near-death experience to songs about the decline of his mother due to dementia, and the death of his piano tuner in a car crash.

As for the title *Singularity*, on one level, it refers to the fact that this is an entirely solo album. There's also an element of scientific inquiry at work here: in quantum physics, a singularity is a location where the density of an object is predicted to become infinite and form a black hole. Hammill notes in the 2006 newsletter that 'a couple of lyrics here refer, albeit fleetingly, to quantum theory and to black holes.'

The cover photograph of a gaunt-looking Hammill is a self-portrait – credited, as was the cover of *None of the Above*, to the mysterious Dinu. The starkness of the image is entirely apposite, given the subject matter of the album and its status as an entirely solo recording. This is also the first time we've seen Hammill's distinctive handwriting grace the front cover of a PH album since 1993's *The Noise*.

'Our Eyes Give It Shape'

It comes as a surprise to hear Hammill sing lines like 'I'm so happy I can barely believe it ... a simple pleasure in the simple things makes life great.' We're a long way from the clichéd image of Hammill as an angst-ridden merchant of doom, but a certain breezy optimism is to be expected – he'd just survived a heart attack, after all. This fantastic opening number brims with zip and confidence, mediated through a lifetime's experience of songwriting and arrangement. A canny acoustic guitar riff skips through the song, buoyed by (sampled) drums and rapturous vocals. And there's a dazzling moment halfway through where Hammill sings the line 'I am happy just to breathe in the quality of the light', delivering the word 'light' with a Lydonesque sneer, and follows it up with a short, scorching electric solo. Not since 'Crying Wolf' from 1977's *Over* has Hammill opened an album with such bold, in-your-face tenacity.

'Event Horizon'

Having celebrated his return from near-death, Hammill takes us back to the immediate aftermath of his heart attack: 'flat on my back, I can feel myself falling... ' The song refers to his 'singular state of mind' as he falls, and to the 'event horizon' – the line which, once crossed, will render him unreachable. In the newsletter, Hammill writes movingly of drifting through this semi-conscious state: 'I certainly had the feeling that waiting for me in those moments ... was some kind of black hole.' A slow, dreamlike meditation etched in cold shivers of acoustic guitar; the song descends in a claustrophobic middle section into the frightening environment of a hospital, all clanking equipment and metallic frequencies.

'Famous Last Words'

The album takes the first of several sidesteps at this point into the self-serving world of a liar and fantasist. Their own self-congratulatory words are first quoted back at them over an elegant keyboard melody. Hammill then pitches the song into a cauldron of anger and scorn, his withering text wrapped in seething guitar and drums; clearly, his heart attack has not mellowed him in the slightest.

'Naked To The Flame'

Here's a finely drawn character study in the mode of songs like 'After The Show' and 'The American Girl'. The song follows the fortunes of an ambitious actress who, 'though ever eager for the spotlight ... was never quite ready to be burned.' There are some great sonic textures here, particularly in the way Hammill sets jagged acoustic and slide guitar against lurking bass and muted percussion. Better still is the fractured vocal arrangement, in which Hammill's main and higher registers are interwoven with spoken word sections to gripping effect. Nevertheless, the track feels overlong and the fragment of whistling halfway through is faintly absurd.

'Meanwhile My Mother'

This is Hammill's deeply touching tribute to his mother, portraying her decline due to dementia with the greatest empathy and sensitivity. Sung in a voice stripped of artifice and filled with inexpressible tenderness, Hammill's text catches a note of everyday simplicity ('I pack her things up and get them ready to store') even as it depicts his mother's condition in heartbreaking detail ('she won't even realise how everything's passing her by'). There's a warm, Fender Rhodes quality to the keyboards here that perfectly suits the emotions of the song, trailed by glowing embers of acoustic guitar.

'Vainglorious Boy'

There's a certain kind of Hammill song that really gets on my nerves. Lumpy and ungainly in the extreme, these are not the *Nadir*-era proto-punk thrashes, nor are they the slash-and-burn attacks of the K Group era. Rather, they deal in a kind of clumsy swagger that's far removed from Hammill's usual incisiveness and wit. 'Where The Mouth Is' from *The Noise* (1993), 'Narcissus (Bar & Grill)' from *X My Heart* (1996) and 'Stupid' from *This* (1998) are all examples of this unfortunate, and thankfully rare, tendency in Hammill's songwriting. 'Vainglorious Boy' is another; a laboured hard rock workout about a hapless, conceited performer who could well be Hammill himself. I will say that I laughed out loud at the repeated use of the word 'dipshit' in the backing vocals.

'Of Wire, Of Wood'

A short, labyrinthine piano improvisation accompanied by ticking percussion: the wire meets the wood. The piece is a prelude to:

'Friday Afternoon'

A tragic and senseless true story: Hammill's piano tuner was killed when he was hit by a car driven by a drunk driver. His voice haunted by the pointless and avoidable loss of life, Hammill relates the piano tuner's commonplace plans for the weekend, plans that never came to pass. The song takes on a darker tone in the last verse, as Hammill steps into the character of the drunk driver and brutally ends the story. A tentative piano melody and the ticking percussion sound from 'Of Wire, Of Wood' melt into gossamer threads of electric keyboard and slide guitar.

'White Dot'

Concluding the album in uncompromising fashion, this six-minute psycho-ambient mindfuck is as strange and unsettling a piece as Hammill has ever put his name to. If 'Event Horizon' portrayed his near-death experience as some kind of trancelike drift towards the infinite, 'White Dot' depicts the process in reverse, as a gradual and painful contraction of consciousness. On old televisions, a white dot would briefly appear after the set had been switched off, a ghostly afterimage that slowly faded to black. In the song, 'time to think is now at a premium' as the time of the white dot approaches. Damaged by glitchy interference, Hammill's voice lurches through devastated fields of backwards piano and guitar. Some of the vocals are also backmasked, the first thirty seconds or so being the fourth verse played in reverse. As forwards and backwards tracks collide viciously with one another, the song leaves behind cracked and distorted images of unfathomable disorder.

Thin Air (2009)

Personnel:
Peter Hammill: vocals, guitar, keyboards, bass, drums, percussion
All songs by Peter Hammill
Recorded at Terra Incognita, Wiltshire, August 2008-March 2009
Produced by Peter Hammill
UK release date: 8 June 2009
Cover and photography: Paul Ridout

Following the release of *Singularity*, Hammill set about an extended period of touring and recording with VdGG, culminating in the release of *Trisector*, the group's first album as a trio. By this time, it was clear that, having committed himself fully to group work with VdGG, he needed to approach solo work in a different frame of mind – as purely solo work, with no contributions from other musicians. As of 2021, the last solo album involving other musicians was 2004's *Incoherence*; Hammill has released six albums since then, all entirely solo affairs.

Needless to say, this doesn't mean that Hammill has become any kind of folk troubadour. As we have seen throughout this book, he's always been a keen user of new technology, and in recent years has been able to reproduce string arrangements and drumbeats very effectively using sampling technology. Not to mention that he's never shied away from subjecting his main instruments, guitar and keyboards, to studio treatments and manipulations. All things considered, there's plenty going on sonically in the run of late-period albums from *Singularity* to the present, despite the lack of other musicians in the credits. As ever, Hammill's music has remained unique and unclassifiable, existing in a space far from any recognised genre or style. The closest parallel, in philosophy and approach, if not so much in the music itself, would be with Neil Young, another prolific songwriter and musician who combines solo and group work and who has rarely allowed his career path to be governed by commercial imperatives.

His songwriting ability undimmed by the passing of the years, Hammill followed up the excellent *Singularity* with, if anything, an even stronger set of songs in 2009's *Thin Air*. In the 2009 newsletter devoted to the album, he writes: 'it became apparent fairly quickly that strong thematic links were running through the songs' lyrics: disappearance, change, loss, dislocation in various forms.' Two of the songs were inspired by real-world disappearances, those of the doomed sailor Donald Crowhurst and the murdered woman Melanie Hall. Elsewhere, Hammill explores unravelling psychological states in typically acute, questioning manner.

Another inspiration for the album was the September 11 terrorist attacks, which are obliquely alluded to in two linked tracks on the album. In a newsletter from October 2001, Hammill had set down some thoughts on 9/11, including 'I expect that all that has happened and will now come will eventually filter into my work' – as indeed it did, eight years later. The text had also concluded with the powerful words 'I feel my legs scrabbling to find balance beneath me. In thin air.' The record had its title.

'The Mercy'

In July 1969, the yacht *Teignmouth Electron* was found adrift in the Atlantic Ocean, with no sign of its skipper, the British sailor Donald Crowhurst. Crowhurst had embarked on a doomed attempt to win a single-handed round-the-world yacht race, despite being an amateur yachtsman with very little seafaring experience and an ill-equipped vessel. Crowhurst soon realised that he could not win the race, and began an elaborate deception, reporting false positions and planning to shorten his route so that he would appear the winner. But it gradually dawned on him that the deception was sure to be discovered if he claimed the prize. The alternative, of returning home and being seen as a failure, was equally unacceptable to him. Beset by loneliness and faced with an impossible choice, Crowhurst began a decline into mental disorder, which presumably ended with his suicide (his body was never found). His last journal entry included the words 'It is finished – it is finished – it is the Mercy', quoted by Hammill in the opening song of *Thin Air*.

Hammill renders Crowhurst's impossible dilemma in bursts of piano and sustain-heavy electric guitar, his voice alighting with trepidation on the troubling questions posed by the text. At around the 2½ minute mark, the song descends into a zone of nerve-jangling friction, sampled strings and stabs of guitar, as the narrator approaches some kind of realisation: 'this is the moment I must show my hand in mercy.' As if he and Crowhurst are connected by their predicaments, the song ends by quoting the famous last line of Captain Oates as he left his tent in the knowledge of certain death. Gripped by drama and pathos, it's a song that has regularly been performed live.

'Your Face on the Street'

This song was inspired by the case of Melanie Hall, a young woman who disappeared in 1996 following an evening in a Bath nightclub not far from Hammill's studio. The song fictionalises a passer-by who occasionally sees a woman on the street, later spots her image on a 'missing' poster, and finally sees her as 'a ghost apparition.' Starting off as a simple piano chamber ballad, the song changes to something much more sinister as a chorus of backing vocals urges 'don't swim out too far ... don't go in the bar ... don't get in the car', its urgency charged by flashes of electric guitar. Strangely, Melanie Hall's fate having remained unknown for thirteen years, her body was discovered only four months after *Thin Air* was released. The killer was never found.

'Stumbled'

The first of the album's guitar songs is a scintillating blend of acoustic and electric instruments, driven by a hugely authoritative vocal performance. In the

2009 newsletter, Hammill writes that the subject of the song is 'the extent to which we plan or control our unfolding lives.' A familiar PH theme, certainly, but one that is given fresh and appealing context here. Cycling acoustic chords intertwine with Fripp-like soloing while wisps of bass and percussion simmer in the background. Through it all runs the voice, sculpting the long lines of text into a coherent argument: 'still your own footprints are the tracks you stumble on.'

'Wrong Way Round'
Fans of Hammill's occasional forays into molten axe heroics will warm to this trippy instrumental, even though it's under three minutes long. A grinding circular riff animates the piece, hardwired into layers of heated soloing.

'Ghosts of Planes'
The day after VdGG had played in New York City in October 1976, Hammill and Guy Evans ventured as tourists to the observation deck of the World Trade Center, calling themselves The Top of the World Club for the occasion. This is the first of two songs inspired by that day and by the events of 9/11. As Hammill points out in the newsletter, though, neither 'Ghosts of Planes' nor 'The Top of the World Club' is about 9/11 in any direct sense. Rather, this first song draws on what Hammill describes as 'a particular sense of familiar unease' felt since 9/11 when watching a plane flying overhead. Such unease is powerfully evoked by shimmering lines of electric guitar and an insidious bass groove, riding on a sharp snare drum crack.

'If We Must Part Like This'
If you thought Hammill must have said all he had to say by now on the subject of failed romance, you underestimated his ability to bring original and striking perspectives to bear on this frequently visited topic. This is no tear-stained piano ballad, but a blasted folk-blues number with a distinctly contemporary feel. Nimble acoustic slide guitar pushes against economical electric riffing, lit by an insistent percussive sound. Hammill's voice is tense with conviction as he navigates the perilous emotions of the text: 'I feel so strange and restless, dislocated; I'm homesick even though I'm here at home.' The repeated refrain of 'I miss you so' is particularly affecting; there's a sense of profound disquiet here, love put at risk, faith undermined by fear and pain.

'Undone'
If I had to pick one song from Hammill's post-2000 albums to demonstrate the continued brilliance of his songwriting, 'Undone' would be the one without a doubt. This relentlessly savage piece opens with diamond-hard vocals over a tolling piano figure, before rising to a shorter, chorus-like section galvanised by organ, guitar and softly struck percussion. After the second verse, the chorus

section is stated and restated, giving way on the raging line 'all I called my own' to a brief, meteoric guitar solo. In the newsletter, Hammill writes that the song 'acknowledge[s] that all our careful constructs will ultimately be broken', and points out the double meaning of 'undone' – fallen apart, and never achieved. All of that aside, for me this short song contains the essence of everything that's great and true about Hammill's music – its drama, its intensity and its explosive beauty.

'Diminished'

Here's a strange, elusive number formed from interlocking guitar lines that seem to move restlessly in circles around each other – 'drilled, diminished circles,' as the song puts it. The song having set out its conviction, in the first three minutes, that old debts will never be scratched and old scores never settled (*cf.* 'Astart' from *None of the Above*: 'try as you may, your debts all stay unredeemed'), the last three minutes are a shivery *avant-garde* collision of treated and backmasked guitar, fitful percussion and looming industrial drones. It's not the conclusion you'd expect, necessarily, but it's one that demonstrates Hammill's continued love of sonic experimentation.

'The Top of the World Club'

The final track of an album haunted by loss and disappearance, 'The Top of the World Club' returns to the World Trade Center, now riven by unimaginable horror: 'my crawling skin, my crawling skin, what circle of hell are we fallen in?' Yet, as with 'Ghosts of Planes', the song's not so much about 9/11 as it is about all of our possible future losses and misfortunes: 'when the fall comes it will hit you pretty hard.' Carving out the song's melody in forlorn shapes of piano and electric guitar, Hammill sings in a voice fraught with discomfort and closes with an indescribably moving sigh of farewell: 'worlds we thought were ours to own, disappeared and gone.'

Consequences (2012)

Personnel:
Peter Hammill: vocals, guitar, keyboards, bass, drums, percussion
All songs by Peter Hammill
Recorded at Terra Incognita, Wiltshire, 2011/12
Produced by Peter Hammill
UK release date: 16 April 2012
Cover and photography: Paul Ridout

Having delivered one of his finest solo albums of recent years in *Thin Air*, Hammill once again returned to VdGG activity. Extensive tours of Europe and North America took place around the release of *A Grounding in Numbers* in 2011. Once again, since VdGG was still an ongoing concern, Hammill determined that the next solo album should be an entirely solo endeavour.

Hammill has often described in interviews how he consciously makes an effort to approach each project in a different way from the last. Such differences may involve giving an album some kind of overarching concept (*Incoherence*), restricting the available instrumental palette (*Clutch*), or process-based changes such as recording and mixing each song in turn before moving onto the next one (*Out of Water*, *Thin Air*). As well as making the recording process interesting and challenging for Hammill himself, this way of working means that no two Hammill albums sound exactly alike. I can't think of any other artist whose work has shown such sonic variety over the years.

In the case of 2012's *Consequences*, Hammill decided to finalise all the songs, including lyrics, before recording a note. It was the first time he had done this since the 1970s, and stood in marked contrast to his usual method of going into the studio with maybe half-a-dozen songs partially written, and trusting the muse to bring more songs to fruition over the course of the recording. With all the songs in place, it made sense for Hammill to record the lead vocals first and then build the instrumentation around them – principally backing vocals, keyboards and guitar. As a result, there's a certain immediacy to the soundworld of the album.

Lyrically there's much to enjoy here, with songs on favourite Hammill topics – language, memory and the passing of time – alongside songs about real-world situations such as stalking and panhandling. That said, this is not one of Hammill's most successful recent albums, as the low turnout of these songs in live performance bears witness. (Of the post-2000 albums, only 2001's *What, Now?* has been less represented in solo concert setlists.) With a few notable exceptions, the elegance and musicality that made *Thin Air* so essential are mostly found wanting here. Hammill's lyrical acuity is as strong as ever, but the record suffers from a lack of tunes and a certain ponderousness that makes it one for the committed fan.

'Eat My Words, Bite My Tongue'

The first three songs on the album form a kind of sequence about a failing romance and the role of language in its collapse. Back in 1986, 'All Said And Done' from *Skin* had acknowledged the powerlessness of words to repair a faltering relationship: 'All the words in the world wouldn't put us back together … I hold my tongue as you're walking away.' The man in 'Eat My Words, Bite My Tongue' seems not to have learned the same lesson, and is furious with himself as a result: 'I should have listened, for once, to my own advice … by now you'd think I might have learned to bite my tongue.' The song gets rather bogged down in the middle section, but the last two minutes pass by in a rush of acoustic and electric guitars, layered vocals and a final, euphoric drop on the line 'to bite my tongue.'

'That Wasn't What I Said'

In the second song of the sequence, the argument moves beyond what the narrator shouldn't have said, but did, into the realm of 'some things I never did, some words I never said.' Having been on the defensive in 'Eat My Words, Bite My Tongue', he lashes out with anger at his partner's perceived lack of empathy: 'you talk as if you know me: in reality, you haven't got the faintest clue.' The unnerving backing vocals forcefully echo the lead vox in this song, as though forestalling any chance of respite or forgiveness. But there's a plodding quality to the piano arrangement and the song never really moves out of second gear.

'Constantly Overheard'

Some kind of resolution is reached in the third and final part of the sequence, as the narrator finds himself in a position of satisfaction at the way things have turned out: 'benign indiscretions and confidences spilled… sooner or later they'll hold you to account.' Having castigated himself in 'Eat My Words, Bite My Tongue' for saying things he shouldn't have, the narrator takes pleasure in reminding his now ex-lover of the dangers of doing exactly that: 'whatever you say can't be unsaid, not once it's tripped off the tongue.' This track is a highlight of the album, with Hammill's resonant vocals and plangent acoustic guitar set off by emotive flourishes of organ.

'New Pen-Pal'

If the first three songs on *Consequences* form a kind of trilogy, the next two form a pair around the uncomfortable subject of stalking and obsessive behaviour. 'New Pen-Pal' sees clipped electric guitar make its way ominously through fields of percussion and faint traces of piano, while Hammill's lead and backing voices trade unsettling vocal lines. From pen-pal to neighbour and finally girlfriend, there's a looming sense of encroachment here which is unlikely to end well.

149

'Close To Me'

Hammill's first book of lyrics, *Killers, Angels, Refugees* (1974), includes a story about an obsessed fan called Dorothy who comes up to him with a series of increasingly unwelcome and unhinged requests. It's unclear whether Dorothy was real or imagined, although Hammill recalled in a 2013 interview that there were some 'wacky people around' in the 1970s: 'I wasn't exactly stalked, but there were some fairly crazy people in those days.' The girl in 'Close To Me' is someone like Dorothy, a girl who had been 'training her sights on me' and who ends up getting 'dangerously close to me.' With trails of ebow guitar hovering over a repeated piano figure, the song's a concise and vivid portrayal of vulnerability in the face of obsession.

'All The Tiredness'

There's a thread running through the second half of *Consequences* to do with ageing, the prospect of death and facing up to one's fears and anxieties. In the 2013 interview quoted above, Hammill said: 'I'm aware of the finite nature of life ... having a heart attack is brilliant for understanding that you are not, in fact, immortal.' Having celebrated the joy of still being alive on 2006's *Singularity*, it comes as no surprise that subsequent work should stare down mortality. It makes for sobering listening, not least in lines such as 'low, down to the ground I go, beaten down by the years of body blows.' This is Hammill at his most difficult and uncompromising, purged of style, songwriting ruthlessly pared down to a skeletal form. Beginning in flinty sparks of acoustic guitar, the song shifts halfway through to a minimal groove etched from layered vocal lines. Drained of spirit and laced with fatigue, it's heavy-going stuff.

'Perfect Pose'

Here's a strange, fleeting narrative about a man standing on Charles Bridge in Prague, in search of the perfect photo opportunity. Except that he seems mainly interested in taking selfies since 'he's made his only purpose the pursuit of posing for the perfect photograph.' Those who have visited this bridge may raise an eyebrow at the idea that anyone standing there might feel ghosts 'crowding in around him', rather than the tourists who swarm across it at all hours of the day and night. The song's briefly enlivened by a delicate guitar solo that somehow puts me in mind of *Selling England by the Pound*-era Genesis. Other than that, it's a gloomy, overlong affair, low on melodic interest.

'Scissors'

A scary real-life encounter inspired this song, according to Hammill in the 2013 interview. In a car driving through New York City in 1976, he saw a 'massive six-inch pair of scissors threateningly held by a lady as she was begging for food at the traffic lights.' It wasn't until 36 years later that the incident was to surface in a song, drawn with unflinching precision in the text. However, 'Scissors' doesn't really take off until its lengthy instrumental outro, with tough electric riffs hurtling into crazed piano fills. Up to that point, the song's something of a trudge, its rhetorical quality amplified by strident backing vocals.

'Bravest Face'

Consequences is an uneven collection of songs, as we've seen, but it ends on a high note with two stunning ballads. Picking up where 'All The Tiredness' left off, these songs reflect soberly on the approach of mortality – a subject that Hammill, for all his articulate lyrics on the passing of time over the years, had never really addressed in song before now. 'Bravest Face' sees gently strummed electric guitar weave in and out of a halting piano melody, over which Hammill sings with soft, broken eloquence: 'this is the moment when all the fear floods in apace.' Troubled by anxiety and frozen in fear, Hammill's voice takes on a stricken confessional tone even as lucid backing vocals attempt to banish the demons that haunt the song.

'A Run of Luck'

The album ends with this desolate ballad, starkly arranged for piano and voice – no other instruments, and no backing vocals. Not since 1986's *And Close As This* had Hammill recorded a piano song in such stripped-down fashion, but the arrangement seems appropriate to this clear-headed meditation on the consequences of ageing and the shifting sands of (mis)fortune. Countering the bleak pessimism of 'All The Tiredness' and 'Bravest Face', the song turns on the conviction that even though you may be 'in too deep when your luck runs out,' there's nothing for it but to 'wait till your luck turns up'; after all, 'life's still great though the wick's burned up.'

...all that might have been... (2014)

Personnel:
Peter Hammill: vocals, guitar, keyboards, bass, percussion
All songs by Peter Hammill
Recorded at Terra Incognita, Wiltshire, September 2012-July 2014
Produced by Peter Hammill
UK release date: November 2014
Cover and photography: Paul Ridout

The recording dates in the credits tell their own story with regard to the development of this remarkable album. Almost two years in the making, Hammill confirms in the sleeve notes that 'the gestation period for this set of recordings has almost certainly been the longest in my solo career.' This comes as no surprise when you consider the way it was put together, since it's a highly ambitious project quite unlike anything Hammill – or anyone else, for that matter – had ever attempted before.

The complexity of the album is reflected in its multifaceted presentation – it exists as a standard CD, a vinyl LP and a triple CD box set, all of which offer different perspectives on the same material. The music was originally worked up as ten individual songs, self-contained but with a submerged narrative thread running through them, a series of cinematic takes on a relationship. On the occasion of a 2013 tour of Japan, Hammill produced a 40-minute 'work in progress' CD that presented a continuous mix of the songs as they then stood. Having absorbed the material in this form, Hammill hit upon the idea of cutting the completed songs up into pieces, reordering them and presenting the rearranged fragments as a continuous whole. It's this so-called *ciné* version that Hammill regards as the main release of ...*all that might have been*..., and which is presented on the standard CD edition of the album and disc 1 of the box set. The individual songs are presented on the vinyl LP and on disc two of the box set, while disc three consists of a revised version of the 'work in progress' CD.

As well as being the definitive release of the album, the *ciné* version is also the most rewarding way into this material, recalling 2004's *Incoherence* in its sprawling ambition. Like *Incoherence* and *The Fall of the House of Usher* before it, it's best experienced in a single sitting. (For a more relaxed listen, try the individual songs CD, which tells the story, murky as it is, in some kind of chronological order.) Drifting fuzzily in time and space, the *ciné* version takes lyrical and musical elements from all ten songs and stitches them into a single fifty-minute piece. The impact of this technique is striking, cutting the listener adrift from narrative coherence and lending the album a distinctly cinematic, European arthouse quality.

There seems little point in producing a track-by-track rundown of the *ciné* version, since with one or two exceptions, the soundworld varies little between its 21 parts. The overall impression is sombre and nocturnal, with looming analogue synths pierced by shards of electric guitar and augmented by spare, restrained percussion. Occasional nervy grooves and bursts of angry riffing disrupt the mostly glacial and dreamlike tempo. Sounds, images and half-buried melodies coalesce, mutate and burn out. Multilayered vocals comment on the action in different registers, adding to the sense of a tale being told from multiple, fractured perspectives.

As for the story, there's certainly some kind of narrative here, although you'd be hard-pressed to work it out for the most part. As Hammill writes in the sleeve notes, 'there's a male and female protagonist, though their relationship is never exactly clear.' By turns lyrical, reflective and conversational, the text casts the characters into a netherworld of shadowy, neon-lit zones. The story is set partly in Tokyo, a city in which Hammill has spent a certain amount of time in recent years; indeed, the sleeve notes mention that he was there on two separate occasions during the writing of the album.

The path of the relationship is recounted in a series of glancing, allusive scenes, told out of chronology and mostly from the male point of view. It doesn't seem to be going particularly well; at one point ('Rumpled Sheets') 'she moves her thumb to the front of his throat.' Understandably, he gets out and heads ('Alien Clock') for the entertainment district of Kabuki-cho. Unfortunately for him, this area is also a hotspot for crime and clip joints, and it's not long before 'he's in trouble here ... no-one knows if he's ever going to make it out alive.' Things go from bad to worse in 'Washed Up': 'he was bundled in the taxi and he stumbled out the other side.' It's a relief, then, to find him 'taking the back road to the airport ... his luck held out and he's in the clear' ('Back Road'). As for the relationship, 'he knew this was goodbye for good,' but 'he couldn't tell her, just couldn't find the words to say' ('The Last Time').

Since Hammill regards ...*all that might have been*... as a single, album-length piece, it's unsurprising that no part of it has ever been played live. Nor, for that matter, have any of the individual songs from disc two been performed live, emphasising the point that the songs are source material for the definitive *ciné* version rather than an alternate version of the album itself. But however you want to approach it, ...*all that might have been*... is a major achievement. It's a bold, visionary piece of work, requiring the listener's undivided attention but offering multiple rewards in return.

Paul Ridout's artwork for the box set is some of his best work for Hammill. There are two booklets, one for the *ciné* version (let's call it disc one) and one for the songs CD (disc two). Each booklet contains numerous colour photographs that hover between naturalism and abstraction, evoking the dreamlike soundscapes of the music. The booklet for disc two gives each of the ten songs its own unique colour code. These colour codes are also used in the booklet for disc one, in which the lyrics to each of the 21 parts are printed in the colour corresponding to the song from which it is taken. Using the colour codes, it's possible to connect each part to its originating song, as shown in the tables overleaf.

A Concordance to ...*all that might have been...*

This table shows, for each of the *ciné* version's 21 parts, the song from which the part comes and the verse(s) which it quotes. The last part, 'Hooks', is unique to the *ciné* version.

Ciné version part	Song	Verses
'In Overview'	'Upon A Sixpence'	1-2
'The Last Time'	'Until'	1-4
'Never Wanted'	'An Outlier'	1-2
'As For Him'	'Upon A Sixpence'	3-4
'Nowhere Special'	'Vai Lentissimo'	1
'Piper Smile'	'Someday (The Piper Smile)'	1-3
'Wanted To Belong'	'An Outlier'	3-4
'This Might...'	'Passing Clouds'	6-8
'Inklings, Darling'	'Someday (The Piper Smile)'	4-11
'Be Careful'	'Best Wishes'	1-2
'Alien Clock'	'Disrespect (In Kabuki-cho)'	1-9
'Drifting Through'	'Not Going Anywhere'	4-6
'Washed Up'	'The Whole Thing Through'	4
'Rumpled Sheets'	'Vai Lentissimo'	2-3
'Fool-proof'	'The Whole Thing Through'	4
'Can't Get Home'	'An Outlier'	5
'Washed Away'	'Best Wishes'	3
'Back Road'	'Passing Clouds'	1-6
'The Line Goes Dead'	'Not Going Anywhere'	1-3
'He Turns Away'	'Until'	5-7
'Hooks'	-	-

This table shows, for each song on disc two, the parts of the *ciné* version which are taken from that song.

Song	Ciné version parts
'Upon A Sixpence'	'In Overview', 'As For Him'
'Someday (The Piper Smile)'	'Piper Smile', 'Inklings, Darling'
'Vai Lentissimo'	'Nowhere Special', 'Rumpled Sheets'
'Disrespect (In Kabuki-cho)'	'Alien Clock'
'An Outlier'	'Never Wanted', 'Wanted To Belong', 'Can't Get Home'
'The Whole Thing Through'	'Washed Up', 'Fool-proof'
'Best Wishes'	'Be Careful', 'Washed Away'
'Passing Clouds'	'Back Road', 'This Might...'
'Not Going Anywhere'	'The Line Goes Dead', 'Drifting Through'
'Until'	'The Last Time', 'He Turns Away'

From The Trees (2017)

Personnel:
Peter Hammill: vocals, guitar, keyboards, bass
All songs by Peter Hammill
Recorded at Terra Incognita, Wiltshire, late 2016-July 2017
Produced by Peter Hammill
UK release date: 3 November 2017
Cover and photography: Paul Ridout

At the time of writing, 2017's *From The Trees* is Hammill's most recent album
of original material. Once again, he played all the instruments on the record
himself. Following the highly conceptual *...all that might have been...* the
album was something of a return to basics, a collection of songs which
Hammill described in a 2017 newsletter as 'all at the short end of things, and
probably as close to conventional song structure as I get.'

The reader may be permitted an ironic smile at that last comment. Those
who hanker after conventional song structure probably wouldn't start by
going to Peter Hammill for it, and even a relatively straightforward set of
songs like *From The Trees* has little to offer by way of stuff like choruses and
instrumental breaks. What it does have is a lightness and sureness of touch,
a laser-sharp lyrical focus and, of course, Hammill's still mightily impressive
singing voice.

If the album has a precedent in Hammill's work, it's with 2012's
Consequences, another stripped-down set of songs arranged largely for piano
and guitar. In my view, however, *From The Trees* is a considerable improvement
on *Consequences*, in part because the *From The Trees* songs were written
with live performance in mind. As Hammill writes in the sleeve notes to the
subsequent live album *X/Ten*, 'one of the guiding principles behind the making
of [*From the Trees*] was that I'd have performable versions of these songs
in place before I began the process of fully arranging and overdubbing the
pieces.' As a result, there's a certain looseness and vigour to the album, in
contrast to the rather overworked feel of *Consequences*.

Lyrically, the usual Hammill subjects are present and correct – lost love,
the treachery of language, acting and performance, obsessiveness, and the
tightening grip of mortality. Bass and sampled strings are used sparingly
around front-centre piano and guitars, always sympathetic and always in
the service of the songs. Backing vocals are widely and sensitively deployed.
Emphatic, introspective yet highly listenable, *From The Trees* is a worthy
addition to the Hammill catalogue.

'My Unintended'

As close to folk rock as Hammill ever got, this opening cut fairly grabs the
attention with a heady mix of acoustic strumming and Fairport-like electric
soloing. But there's no time to dwell on the instrumentation, because this song

is all about the text, of which there's a lot packed into less than four minutes. The song seems to portray some kind of stalker, or at least a delusional man with his eye on an unsuspecting woman; he has 'no regrets as to how it went', even though he's managed to convince himself that 'such a bright future awaited us.' A perfect little psychodrama and a gripping song.

'Reputation'
Here's a song that drips with mockery and contempt for its nameless subject, someone who has been arrogantly trading on their fame and fortune. But as the text points out, these are just 'falsehoods that'll leave you for dead.' It's unclear if the subject of the song is personally known to Hammill, if these are observations made from a distance, or indeed if the subject is entirely fictional. The critic Richard Williams, in his review of *From The Trees*, writes that 'the degree of autobiographical essence doesn't matter,' but I don't agree; of course it would be interesting to know who Hammill is singing about here, just as it would in the case of earlier broadsides like 'Silver' and 'Famous Last Words'. In any case, the zinger of a last line 'that reputation you traded on no longer means very much to me,' leaves one in no doubt as to the keenly felt nature of Hammill's disdain. Hammill plays a slow dance on piano, the arrangement augmented by gentle touches of strings.

'Charm Alone'
And speaking of autobiography, here's an intriguing take on the personal and confidential: 'this public face I'm prepared to wear; my private thoughts, I keep them all well hidden.' We're back in the territory of 'Eat My Words, Bite My Tongue' from *Consequences*, and its conviction that it's 'best to refrain, don't excuse or explain.' Something has clearly gone awry here: 'I never thought I'd be overheard ... I revealed all my secrets, so my cover was blown.' Nevertheless, there's an upbeat quality to the song that makes it a high point of the album. Hammill's artfully strummed acoustic guitar is immediately seductive, adding luminous weight to an agile vocal performance.

'What Lies Ahead'
A lovely piano intro, reminiscent of Keith Jarrett at his most limpid, ushers in this quiet exercise in self-reflection. Kicking off with the statement that 'underplaying expectations has become my stock in trade', Hammill acknowledges the importance of 'maintaining the vital spark' even while doubting his own continued ability to do so. On 'In The End' (1973), he had sung of what might happen 'when my mouth falls slack and I can't summon up another tune.' Forty-four years later, 'the excuses [are] growing weaker' for his apparent failure to deliver on his audience's expectations. One might well counter that the only expectations held by Hammill's audience are those of quality and commitment; in those respects, as in many others, he has never let us down.

'Anagnorisis'

The dictionary tells me that 'anagnorisis' means 'recognition leading to dénouement' or, more simply, the moment in a drama where a character makes a crucial discovery. In other words, we're back on the stage, location of earlier Hammill songs like 'The Mousetrap (Caught In)' and 'After The Show'. On an album freighted with questions about his future and his ongoing role as a musician, it's no surprise that Hammill would return to the notion of artifice and the peeling away of layers of reality. The play in question is probably *King Lear*, as hinted at by the onstage presence of a king with a papier-mâché crown and a broken heart.

But there's more to this theatre than meets the eye: a 'papered house' is a performance where tickets for an undersold show have been given away free to make the house seem full. In this case, the anagnorisis comes at the moment where the actor catches 'a glimpse of the seating plan' and realizes that he's no longer as popular as he once was. Sketched in wintry shades of piano and energised by rippling electric guitar, the song's a touching portrayal of a performer riven by anxiety.

'Torpor'

The sense of mortality that haunted *Consequences* tracks like 'All the Tiredness' and 'Bravest Face' returns in this disquieting piece for acoustic guitar and voice. A calm middle section with wordless backing vocals sounds like a quote from Pink Floyd's 'Goodbye Blue Sky'; elsewhere, Hammill's deft fingerpicking style leads the song into a downward spiral of introspection and self-doubt. Like much of *From The Trees*, it's far from an easy listen – a song preoccupied with what Hammill described, in a 2010 newsletter, as 'the certain knowledge that at some point I'm not going to be able to carry on enjoying it.' He was writing specifically about live performance, but a line like 'I can't maintain the pace, feels like I'm slowing irreversibly' has wider resonance, speaking to what he described in the same newsletter as 'the last stretch of a working life in recorded music.'

'Milked'

The longest track on *From The Trees* is a gripping neo-epic. Beginning, like 'Anagnorisis', on the stage, the hero of the song finds himself alone 'in the stormcloud night', overrun by 'the driftwood of memory.' I'm reminded of another recent Hammill epic, 'Edge of the Road' from *What, Now?* (2001), in which the (anti)hero crashes 'head on into the unknown ... the man chasing mystery finally missing his own.' This time, though, there's 'not much left of the man to see', only milk that's been spilt and tears that have been shed. The song weaves its dark magic slowly and carefully, setting out its position in swirling forms of guitar and piano clusters made weak by tragedy. Layered backing vocals make their presence felt throughout, casting spectral shadows behind the lead voice. With the lyric 'he's fed out all the lines that once charmed the birds from the trees', the song also gives the album its title, summoning a sense of exhaustion that seeps into the record like an affliction.

'Girl To The North Country'

In 1963 Bob Dylan recorded 'Girl From The North Country', a tender ballad to a former lover. Hammill has never really spoken of Dylan as someone by whom he was influenced or with whom he felt a particular affinity, but 'Girl To The North Country' is a song where the presence of Dylan – specifically, the young Dylan – can certainly be sensed. Hammill also acknowledged, when introducing it at a 2018 concert, that the song 'has a certain personal connection for me with [my] seventeen-year-old self.' He didn't elaborate, but in any event, this is a knotty and complex song that struggles to come up with a rational answer to its key question: 'was she ever your true love of the long ago?' Unlike the Dylan song from which it (almost) takes its title, there's nothing gentle or folky here, just tightly wound coils of acoustic guitar that stalk the piece in tandem with Hammill's blistering vocal attack.

'On Deaf Ears'

If language and its pitfalls have been a recurrent theme in Hammill's work, and age and mortality increasingly so, then what happens when age makes language itself begin to fail? This is the question that 'On Deaf Ears' faces up to; as the song acknowledges, 'no language of precision lasts in these declining years.' Sculpted from falling piano notes and distant washes of synthesizer, the song resists any kind of resolution, with the building blocks of communication 'suspended in mid-sentence.' Hammill's lead and backing voices converse in a call-and-response dialectic, falling into line with the shifting arguments of the text. As so often in Hammill's work, the song is ultimately a call to action: 'you never know the worth of what you have ... you never know when time is running out.'

'The Descent'

For its closing track, the album takes a step back from the questions that have preoccupied it up to this point, and returns to themes that loomed large in *Thin Air* (2009): loss, dislocation and disappearance. In particular, I think of 'The Mercy', of its 'circular descent' and of the way its doomed heroes, Crowhurst and Oates, slipped beyond the point of no return into vast tracts of water and ice. The hero of 'The Descent', too, feels 'the thinning of the air' as he fights for breath and, like Oates, abandons the safety of his tent in favour of an unknown destination. In this deeply moving finale to the album, lowering strings and flickers of electric guitar drill down into lost fragments of piano. Hammill, as ever, inhabits the song to an almost frightening degree, his voice sounding increasingly possessed as the lyric approaches crisis in the fourth verse before the voice loses its hold in the final lines and falls sadly away.

In Translation (2021)

Personnel:
Peter Hammill: vocals, guitar, keyboards, bass
Recorded at Terra Incognita, Wiltshire, March-December 2020
Produced by Peter Hammill
UK release date: 7 May 2021
Design: Paul Ridout
Photography: James Sharrock

With the exception of three songs by VdGG co-founder Chris Judge Smith, Hammill had never previously recorded songs by others. That was to change in 2021 with the release of *In Translation*, an album of cover versions of songs from various sources – the Great American Songbook, German *Lieder*, French classical music, Argentine tango and Italian popular song.

The album was recorded under very specific conditions, as explained by Hammill in an extensive set of sleeve notes. The main influence was, of course, the COVID-19 pandemic, which began in March 2020 and, at the time of writing, is still ongoing. Hammill writes: 'When lockdown began, I found myself in such an unbalanced and uncertain state that I didn't really feel capable of writing and recording new material.' He began working on cover versions to keep himself occupied but initially had no particular project in mind. That said, he had floated the idea of a covers album in a couple of interviews in recent years, so the appearance of *In Translation* was not a total surprise.

The project was given further impetus by what Hammill describes in the sleeve notes as 'the dread of impending Brexit.' With seven of the ten songs on the album coming from continental Europe, *In Translation* is a pro-European, and by extension anti-Brexit, statement. Again, Hammill put it best in the sleeve notes: 'the making of this record is the act of a Briton who was, is and will remain a European.'

In addition, there's a strong Italian influence at work here, from the cover shot of Hammill wearing an Italian rugby fan's fleecy jacket inwards. Three of the songs here are from Italy; Hammill is fluent in Italian, and has received songwriting prizes there; and VdGG were at their most popular in Italy, where Hammill's operatic delivery struck a particular chord.

In terms of the soundworld of the album, the arrangements are not so far removed from those that occupy what passes for a 'normal' Hammill album. The piano takes centre stage, supported by acoustic and electric guitars and sampled orchestral sounds. The pace mostly varies from slow to mid-tempo, although there are a few parts where a more disruptive mood is called for. Hammill's voice, too, modulates from a roar to a croon in the service of the song, with several sections recalling the operatic singing style of *The Fall of the House of Usher*.

It's often said that a good cover version should emphasise the personality of the interpreter, rather than being a mere copy of the original. Although

Hammill has imprinted his distinctive sense of self on these recordings, he also retained a sympathy and respect for the originals. Many of the songs, being standards of one kind or another, don't have an original version in any case, although they do have *previous* versions of varying degrees of prominence. The title of the album not only refers to the fact that Hammill has translated the texts of the seven songs that weren't originally written in English. It also speaks to the root of the word *translation*, from the Latin *trānslātiō* – the act of moving something between two places, and the transfer of ideas between two contexts. We see ten fine examples of that here.

'The Folks Who Live On The Hill' (Kern/Hammerstein)

This 1937 standard, with words by Oscar Hammerstein II set to music by Jerome Kern, opens the album in yearning and wistful style. The intro has a filmic quality to it, sounding almost like a piece of incidental music to a classic Hollywood movie. As the song unfolds, it locates its emotional centre in an idealised vision of an America with 'a view of meadows green', outlined by pastoral strings and moody piano. Yet Hammill writes in the sleeve notes that he finds 'a sense of unease, of something being missing', in the song. Perhaps this unease can be traced in part to the line 'when the kids grow up and leave us', a life event Hammill wrote about with great sensitivity in 'Autumn' (1977) and 'Since The Kids' (1998).

'Hotel Supramonte' (de André/Bubola)

The composer of this song, the Italian songwriter Fabrizio de André, was inspired to write it after he and his partner were kidnapped and held captive for four months in rural Sardinia. For the most part, Hammill's version doesn't depart too radically from de André's original, drifting by on tender acoustic guitar and melancholy strains of violin. Hammill's vocal, however, trades de André's quiet composure for something more disturbed and elemental. And the song takes a dark turn towards the end, with windswept electric guitar warning that 'tomorrow already hangs heavy with unspoken words.'

'Oblivion' (Piazzolla/Tarenzi)

Here's the first of two songs with music by Astor Piazzolla, the celebrated Argentinian tango composer. According to the sleeve notes, Hammill based his translation on a combination of French and Spanish texts written to accompany Piazzolla's music. Hammill's vocal performance here is invested with the rapturous quality of torch song, some distance removed from his usual style. With the text graced by elegant piano and strings, there's a sensuous flush to lines like 'heavy, they weight me down, all the drapes and sheets on your bed.' But there's not much to hold onto in terms of melody, and the rhythm has a fitful quality which makes it one of the less engaging songs on the album.

'Ciao Amore' (Tenco)

The background to this song makes for compelling, if grim, reading. Briefly, the song's composer Luigi Tenco was one of Italy's leading young singer-songwriters (and was a contemporary of Fabrizio de André, the writer of 'Hotel Supramonte'). In 1967 Tenco was found dead in his hotel room after the song had failed to win a major music prize. The verdict was suicide, although doubts remain as to the true cause of Tenco's death. This is one of the highlights of the album, as Hammill's electric guitar seethes in the midst of lurching piano and brass, while his vocal revisits the narrative clout of *The Fall of the House of Usher*: 'one fine day I'll just say 'stuff it', and be gone for good.' The hero of the song makes a life-changing journey from rural to urban Italy, and finds himself burdened by the realisation that 'my pockets are empty, now I know I'll never get home.'

'This Nearly Was Mine' (Rodgers/Hammerstein)

It's back to the Great American Songbook for this emotional cut from the musical *South Pacific* (1949). In the sleeve notes, Hammill recalls that 'this song and its sense of a yearning which is always destined to be unfulfilled' was familiar to him via his parents' record collection. Sincere, unaffected and never straying into the realm of the sentimental, Hammill's reading of the song pays loving respect to those childhood memories.

'After A Dream' (Fauré/Bussine)

For this, the first of two classical pieces on *In Translation*, Hammill translated from the French a poem by Romain Bussine which had been set to music by the composer Gabriel Fauré. There's a wonky cabaret feel to the arrangement, which sees a playful piano melody embellished by romantic violins. The lyric, however, has an overwrought quality which Hammill plays up to in his somewhat ripe vocal performance: 'you call my name and I lift up the planet, flying through heaven with you under the light of the mystery moon.' Hammill acknowledges the problem in the sleeve notes: Bussine's text 'felt a little too highly perfumed for modern sensibility.' His translation struck a contemporary note, as far as possible. But he only had so much to work with.

'Ballad For My Death' (Piazzolla/Ferrer)

You get the feeling that Hammill is more at ease with Piazzolla than he is with Fauré. As an admirer of Piazzolla for many years, Hammill could certainly relate to what he describes in the sleeve notes as 'the sense of straight-backed fatalism' in this paean to the city of Buenos Aires. Indeed, the sense of self-doubt that lies exposed in recent Hammill songs like 'Bravest Face' (*Consequences*, 2012) and 'Torpor' (*From the Trees*, 2017) finds a parallel in the melodramatic anguish of 'Ballad For My Death': 'hold me close, I fear, I feel the death, the ancient death, come to take everything that I once loved away.' Once again, there's a hint of Usher in Hammill's formidable vocal presence, lit up by the neo-cabaret piano and string arrangement.

'I Who Have Nothing' (Donida/Mogol/Leiber/Stoller)

Here's a partial return to Italian pop, since the English version by Leiber & Stoller was based on an Italian original. This is probably the best-known song on *In Translation*, with celebrated versions by Ben E. King, Tom Jones and Shirley Bassey, among others. What these interpretations miss, however, is the sense that, as Hammill writes in the sleeve notes, 'it's as much the song of a stalker as of an abandoned or lost lover.' Having written a chilling depiction of a stalker in 'Somebody Bad Enough' (*None of the Above*, 2000), it comes as no surprise that Hammill should find a latent creepiness in the way the narrator of this song stares at the object of his desire through the window of a restaurant, all the while insisting that 'he'll never love you the way I love you.' Intoning those last three words in an ominous whisper, Hammill rips the song out of its Radio 2 context and recasts it as a sinister interior drama soundtracked by a descending piano figure.

'Il Vino' (Ciampi/Marchetti)

The last time we met up with Hammill in a bar was in 'Happy Hour' (*Enter K*, 1982). Back then, the narrator, 'fuelled by alcohol,' ended up 'falling … until I wind up on the floor.' Also on his way towards the horizontal is the hero of 'Il Vino', who, drink taken, has 'fallen in the gutter, knee-deep in dirty water' – from which perspective he is, at least, able to look up at the stars. In this rousing hymn to the joys of the grape, acoustic and electric guitars dance around lively organ tones and sparkling touches of glockenspiel. Hammill has great fun making the kind of lusty declarations you might expect someone who has over-imbibed to come out with, ending in a wordless singalong: 'Life goes on day after day … is there any hope left, is it hopeless?'

'Lost To The World' (Mahler/Rückert)

The album draws to a close with this sumptuous reading of a song by Mahler, a setting of a poem by Friedrich Rückert that attracts a new, charged resonance in the middle of a global pandemic. If, as Hammill suggests in the sleeve notes, most of the songs on *In Translation* 'are to do with measures of dislocation, of loss, of an imagined future which didn't arrive', it's in 'Lost To The World' that we find the record's clearest indication of where humankind stands in 2020-21: 'you might as well say I've flown away from here … I find myself oblivious to all the manic rough and tumble of the world.' Rising in pitch and intensity, Hammill's voice takes on a magical airborne quality, carried by a ravishing chamber music arrangement. The last line, 'If love is lifelong, the song lives on', serves as an affirmation not only of this project but of Peter Hammill's life's work.

Live albums

Sadly, there are no official live albums of Hammill in the 1970s. The songs from this period on the 1995 *Peel Sessions* CD, plus a recently unearthed, three-song performance from Swiss TV in 1974, confirm the magisterial form he was in at the time. The K Group era is better represented, but live albums were still rarities until the early 1990s. The lack of any official live album of the 1994-96 PH Quartet is another regrettable omission. In recent years, however, Hammill has extensively documented his solo and duo performances.

The Margin/The Margin + (1985/2002)

An essential set of recordings from 1982 and 1983, documenting the short but vital existence of the K Group. The original double album from 1985 is squeezed onto the first CD of the 2002 reissue, minus one track. It shows the group in concert mode, somewhat formal and airless; the lack of audience noise doesn't help in this regard. The second CD is taken from an excellent quality bootleg, *The Secret Asteroid Jungle*, and more closely reflects the full-on energy of the live K Group experience.

Room Temperature (1990)

In 1990 Hammill embarked on a tour of North America, accompanied by Stuart Gordon on violin and Nic Potter on bass. *Room Temperature* is a fine document of that tour. Revisiting songs from all phases of Hammill's career, the drumless trio format takes the songs in wild and unexpected directions. It's a sobering thought that neither of Hammill's bandmates on this album is still with us.

There Goes The Daylight (1993)

Hammill took to the road in 1993, on the back of that year's studio album *The Noise*. For whatever reason, lead guitarist John Ellis, who had provided many of that record's finest moments, didn't join him on tour, leaving Stuart Gordon (who had originally been a guitarist, but had dropped the instrument in favour of the violin) to double up on guitar and violin alongside Hammill, Potter and drummer Manny Elias. The resulting live album wisely steers mostly clear of material from *The Noise*, focusing instead on energetic renditions of some of the more aggressive tracks from the PH and Van der Graaf back catalogues.

The Peel Sessions (1995)

Another essential live album, albeit not one recorded in front of an audience. The CD contains BBC radio sessions from 1974, 1977, 1979 and 1988 (the last of these was actually recorded for Richard Skinner, not John Peel). The versions of the *In Camera* tracks 'Faint-Heart and the Sermon' and 'No More (The Sub-Mariner)' from 1974 are worth the price of the album by themselves.

The Union Chapel Concert (1997)

In 1996 Hammill, Guy Evans and a group of associates played a one-off concert in London that included an unannounced, one-song reunion of the classic VdGG line-up playing 'Lemmings', the first time the four of them had played together in twenty years. This seismic event – as well as the rest of the concert – was captured in less than pristine sound quality on a double CD.

Typical (1999)

An immaculately recorded double live CD taken from a run of European solo shows in 1992. It replicates the shape of a 'typical' Hammill solo concert, which consists of two keyboard sets interspersed with a guitar set. But what makes this album unusual is that Hammill plays electric, rather than acoustic, in the guitar set; as a result, many of the guitar songs are warped significantly out of shape. The version of 'Modern', in particular, is extraordinary.

Veracious (2006)

As noted in the chapter on *Out of Water* (1990), Stuart Gordon frequently played with Hammill, both in the studio and onstage, until his untimely death in 2014. *Veracious* is an excellent document of the intense duo shows that the pair regularly performed together from about 1998 to 2006 – the tracklisting was chosen to include songs that had not previously been released on live albums. The album is named after Gordon's violin, which he affectionately called Vera.

In The Passionskirche (2009)

Another double live CD of 1992 solo performances, this time taken from a single concert in Berlin. This release is worth it for the inclusion of the 'Usher Suite', unavailable anywhere else. The same material is also available on DVD, one of the few live pro-shot Hammill concert performances.

Pno Gtr Vox (2011) / Pno Gtr Vox Box (2012)

This is a complicated one. *Pno Gtr Vox* is another double live CD of solo performances, but with the first CD consisting solely of piano songs and the second CD of guitar songs (acoustic, not electric, this time). The idea had its basis in a 2010 tour of Japan, where some of the shows followed this prescription. A year later, Hammill followed it up with *Pno Gtr Vox Box*, a 7CD box set containing the two CDs from the original release plus five others, all solo recordings from 2010 and similarly arranged along thematic lines. The full box was a limited edition of 2000 copies, and is now one of the rarest Hammill solo releases.

Live at Rockpalast – Hamburg 1981 (2016)

As noted above, there's a dearth of pro-shot Hammill concert footage. This is a treat from the Rockpalast archives, a full K Group concert including a transcendent version of 'Flight'. The package contains the same material on DVD and double audio CD.

X/Ten (2018)
A track-by-track solo recreation of the *From The Trees* album recorded at various concerts in 2017 and 2018.

Not Yet Not Now (2019)
A mammoth 8CD box set collecting live performances of no fewer than 101 different songs, all of them taken from a sustained period of solo touring in 2017-18. There is surely no other artist at work today who is able to call on such an extensive back catalogue, playing successive concerts with no songs at all repeated from one evening to the next.

Skeletons of Songs (1978/1992)
Bootlegs are outside the scope of this book, but I'm making an exception for this essential recording of a 1978 solo show in Kansas City, USA. The original vinyl LP is fabulously rare, but the album was later released on a 'grey area' CD out of Italy. The sound quality is middling, but the performances are some of the greatest on any Hammill live album – this is brutal, edge-of-the-seat stuff. Hammill acknowledged the importance of *Skeletons of Songs* by including several songs from it as bonus tracks on the 2006 reissues of four 1970s solo albums.

Collaborations

Hammill's work with other musicians is extensive, ranging from full-scale artistic collaborations to guest appearances on vocals, guitar and keyboards, lyric-writing, translation and production work. The list of these activities is long, and beyond the scope of this book. On the five albums below, Hammill makes significant creative contributions not only as a performer but also as a composer. These albums do not, however, form part of his main canon of solo work.

Spur of the Moment (1988)

In 1988, Hammill and VdGG drummer Guy Evans got together in Hammill's home studio to record an album of instrumental improvisations. Hammill played acoustic guitar, piano and keyboards, while Evans played acoustic and electronic percussion kits. The resulting recordings were then sequenced, mixed and treated to produce the eleven tracks we hear on the CD. Although intermittently interesting, the album is a long way not only from Hammill's normal run of solo work but also from his previous experimental album, 1983's *Loops and Reels*. The overall mood is glitchy and unnerving, with brief flurries of melody coalescing around furtive strands of percussion.

On the opening 'Sweating It Out', Hammill's insectoid piano scurries in and out of Evans' restrained, fluent beats. The elegant 'Surprise' is a calm interlude driven by ripples of acoustic guitar. Here and there, as on 'Little Did He Know' and 'You Think Not?', the album calls to mind the glistening surfaces of Tangerine Dream. Otherwise, highlights are few and far between, with little of the raw inspiration that one associates with the finest improvised music. Hammill and Evans performed a few tracks from the album at concerts in 1988 and at the one-off Union Chapel concert in 1996.

The Appointed Hour (1999)

Hammill and composer Roger Eno (brother of the more famous Brian) had met when they both played at a festival in Lanzarote in 1989. Several years later, Eno contacted Hammill to float the idea of a collaboration, the result of which was *The Appointed Hour*. At Hammill's suggestion, the 'art glue' binding the project together was that both men should improvise on guitar, piano and keyboards in their respective studios for exactly an hour at the same time on the same day – 1 April 1999. Other than agreeing to start in the key of D minor, no prior arrangement was made as to what should be played. The two tapes were then mixed together without any further overdubs. The result is a highly listenable, almost alchemical sixty-minute drift work in which Eno's ambient leanings are disrupted by Hammill's astringent piano and guitar melodies.

Although the music is continuous, the CD is divided into 20 tracks for reference purposes. Reflecting the date of recording, April Fool's Day, the titles of the tracks are lines cut up from 'Fools Rush In', the popular song made famous by Frank Sinatra.

Other World (2014)

This album is a one-off collaboration with American guitarist and composer Gary Lucas, best known for his tenure in Captain Beefheart's Magic Band in the early 1980s. Hammill sings, plays guitar, wrote the lyrics and co-wrote the music, while Lucas plays guitar and co-wrote the music. It's a patchy, largely undistinguished affair. Never having been one to privilege virtuosity at the expense of expressive power, it's dispiriting to hear Hammill cede ground to Lucas, whose playing, while technically impressive, lacks the volatile force we have come to expect from Hammill and his collaborators. The most compelling moments are 'Spinning Coins' and 'Of Kith and Kin', two beautiful acoustic numbers that cast wintry shadows over the early part of the album and carve out a folk/roots sensibility unlike anything else in Hammill's work. Towards the end, the haunting '2 Views' returns to a familiar Hammill theme: 'look forward, don't look back, have no regrets.' Elsewhere, though, the more uptempo tracks 'This Is Showbiz' and 'Black Ice' fail to convince, while instrumentals like 'Built From Scratch' and 'Attar of Roses' founder on Lucas' effects-laden approach. With fourteen tracks and a running time of an hour, the album is something of a trudge.

In Amazonia (2019)

The first of two highly enjoyable collaborations with the Swedish neo-prog outfit Isildurs Bane. The lyrics and vocals are all Hammill's, while the music was co-written with group leader Mats Johansson. As recounted by Hammill in a 2019 journal entry, the seeds of the collaboration were sown when he played live with the group at the 2017 Gouveia Art Rock festival in Portugal. The following year the group floated the idea of a joint recording project, a proposal that resulted in the *In Amazonia* album.

As is so often the case these days, Hammill was never in a room with the group during the recording of the album, which progressed instead by means of file-sharing between Sweden and Wiltshire. Nevertheless, there's an epic, sweeping atmosphere to the record that stands in marked contrast both to Hammill's recent solo albums and to his post-2005 work with VdGG. Consisting of five longish tracks and a short instrumental coda, the album explores mythical and visionary states of mind even as it imparts a sense of primal unease with the state of the planet: 'time's come adrift, you're balanced over tectonic shift' ('Under The Current'). The music of Isildurs Bane is a beguiling mix of melodic progressive rock, spaced-out transmissions and knotty Radiohead-esque drama, over which Hammill sings with a scouring intensity.

In Disequilibrium (2021)

The follow-up to *In Amazonia* is, if anything, even more impressive than its predecessor. Whereas there was a certain exotic quality to the first collaboration, signified in part by the koto of guest musician Karin Nakagawa,

In Disequilibrium trades that global reach for a troubling sense of interior disintegration. The music is harder and meaner this time, energised by the powerhouse stickwork of guest drummer Pat Mastelotto (moonlighting from his day job with King Crimson) and the bristling fire of Hammill's vocals.

The album consists of two side-long suites, 'In Disequilibrium' and 'Gently (Step by Step)'. The story goes that Isildurs Bane leader Johansson sent instrumental demos of both sides to Hammill, who then searched for parts within the music where he could most effectively incorporate his vocal lines. The texts themselves, noted Hammill, were 'the first lyrics I came to write while the world was in the grip of the Covid pandemic, and this undoubtedly had some influence on the way these turned out.' Indeed there's a simplicity and directness to the lyrics that feels entirely appropriate to these times. Stripped of metaphor and wordplay, they seem to come from a place where eloquence is no longer a viable option. 'What were you thinking,' rages Hammill, 'if you were really thinking at all?'

Compilations

For an artist with such a daunting back catalogue as Hammill's, a compilation can be a useful entry point. There are several here to choose from.

Vision (1978)

Long out of print, this US and Canada-only compilation was intended as an introduction to solo Hammill for the North American market. Notable for a Hammill poem printed on the back cover, which has not been published anywhere else; and for the back cover photo of Peter manhandling a rather surprised-looking cat.

The Love Songs (1984)

In one of his occasional attempts to enter the realms of the commercially successful, Hammill re-recorded many of the love songs from his previous solo albums for this set, which occupies a position halfway between compilation and new work. 'Just Good Friends' (from *Patience*, 1983) was re-recorded from scratch and released as a single, while the other tracks were given new lead vocals and additional arrangements. The new versions, while undeniably listener-friendly, lack the grit of the originals. Sadly, neither album nor single managed to scrape into the charts.

The Calm (After The Storm)/The Storm (Before The Calm) (both 1993)

As noted in the chapter on *The Noise* (1993), Virgin released these themed compilations in response to Hammill's (temporary, as it turned out) separation of his studio albums into the *BeCalm* and *A Loud* series. *The Calm (After The Storm)* compiled reflective songs from the Charisma/Virgin years, while *The Storm (Before The Calm)* was a selection of more raucous material. With a generous 35 songs spread over the two compilations and useful sleeve notes by PH himself, these are among the best introductions to Hammill's work.

After The Show (1996)

Another compilation of the Charisma/Virgin years, with a fairly scattergun track listing and a bizarre cover shot of Hammill on a tourist visit to Alcatraz prison.

Past Go: Collected (1996)

An early selection of songs from Hammill's releases on his own Fie! label.

The Thin Man Sings Ballads (2002)

In an unusually strongly-worded 2002 newsletter, Hammill expressed frustration at his continued lack of visibility, particularly in the UK: 'I still have the feeling that a wider (if never exactly mainstream) audience would find my stuff approachable if only they were exposed to it or even knew of its existence.' *The Thin Man Sings Ballads* (the title nods to Dylan, and to Hammill's perpetually slim appearance) was an attempt to rectify the problem by putting out another selection of reflective material in the vein of *The Love Songs*. Did it work, then? In the next newsletter, tongue planted firmly in cheek, Hammill reported that 'I am now unable to enter a supermarket without hordes of admirers clustering around my trolley.'

Miscellany

Here are three albums that are not part of the main run of solo albums but which didn't seem to fit into any of the other categories.

Offensichtlich Goldfisch (1993)

A compilation of songs from prior albums sung in German, released on Hammill's German label Rockport. The album had been anticipated by the release the previous year of an EP, *A Fix on the Mix*, two of the songs on which would later be included on the album. The vocals were re-recorded and added to the original instrumental mixes, with the exception of 'Schlaft nun' ('Sleep Now'), which was a re-recording. The texts were translated into German by the writer Heinz Rudolf Kunze, who provided a telling insight into Hammill's work with the comment (quoted by Hammill in a 1993 newsletter) that 'nobody writes songs like this in German'. As Hammill wrote in the same newsletter, it's 'strange, for a culture so philosophical and analytical in a literary sense, that this should be so.'

The songs chosen for treatment *auf Deutsch* were a disparate bunch from the 1980s and 1990s: one from *And Close As This*, two from *In A Foreign Town*, one from *Out of Water* and four apiece from *Fireships* and *The Noise*. The unifying thread, according to Hammill, was that 'the subject matter of these songs seem to have at least some specific reference to German culture, or that their sentiments could run in happy parallel in the language.' But of the twelve songs here, only two ('Auto' and 'Kaufhaus Europa') refer directly to Germany, leaving the other ten to draw out the philosophical and analytical tendencies so prominent in Hammill's work.

Sonix (Hybrid Experiments 1994-1996) (1996)

A collection of largely instrumental pieces, mostly written for film and dance, that bears some relation to *Loops and Reels* (1983). Several of the pieces here were written for *Emmène-moi*, a film by the French director Michel Spinosa, although only the graceful main theme ended up being used in the film. This is presented in two versions, with swooning violin and viola by Stuart Gordon. The other pieces composed for the film are shorter and of only marginal interest.

On the other hand, there are a couple of pieces here that really make you sit up and take notice. The first of these is 'Four to the Floor', a highly effective experimental skirmish written and performed by Hammill with drummer Manny Elias. Murky and claustrophobic, it combines sinister industrial loops with dense tribal beats. 'Dark Matter' is another highlight, a hellish noisescape constructed from improvised electric guitar. Finally, there is the 26-minute 'Labyrinthine Dreams', commissioned to accompany a dance piece for the Catania Festival in Sicily in 1996. This is an intricate work for solo piano with hazy vocal sections that drift in and out of the piece.

Unsung (2001)

A collection of fourteen short instrumental pieces, this is the third in a loose series that began with *Loops and Reels* and continued with *Sonix*. As Hammill puts it in the sleeve notes, these are 'pieces [that] began their lives as potential songs, but went self-deterministic on me and refused to be made into songs as such.' The album is one for the committed fan, although there are certainly a few tracks here that repay further investigation. Four of the pieces – 'gated', 'gateless', '1 meg loop' and 'eyebrows' – were, as Hammill notes, 'written or discovered in a comparatively conventional fashion.' On these four, the second of which seems to be a variation on the first, treated and reverbed guitars thread their way lightly through spare touches of percussion to hypnotic effect.

Elsewhere, Hammill comes as close as he ever has to Cageian indeterminacy on the linked tracks 'handsfree' and 'the printer port'. As he explains in the sleeve notes, these came about when he attempted to print something and accidentally sent the print command to his MIDI set-up, which responded with various sounds which were used to generate the two pieces. Pulsating and scattering like transmissions from a distant planet, these two tracks show Hammill in the grip of the 'serious fun' that has always been central to his work.

On Track series

Tori Amos – Lisa Torem 978-1-78952-142-9

Asia – Peter Braidis 978-1-78952-099-6

Barclay James Harvest – Keith and Monica Domone 978-1-78952-067-5

The Beatles – Andrew Wild 978-1-78952-009-5

The Beatles Solo 1969-1980 – Andrew Wild 978-1-78952-030-9

Blue Oyster Cult – Jacob Holm-Lupo 978-1-78952-007-1

Marc Bolan and T.Rex – Peter Gallagher 978-1-78952-124-5

Kate Bush – Bill Thomas 978-1-78952-097-2

Camel – Hamish Kuzminski 978-1-78952-040-8

Caravan – Andy Boot 978-1-78952-127-6

Cardiacs – Eric Benac 978-1-78952-131-3

Eric Clapton Solo – Andrew Wild 978-1-78952-141-2

The Clash – Nick Assirati 978-1-78952-077-4

Crosby, Stills and Nash – Andrew Wild 978-1-78952-039-2

The Damned – Morgan Brown 978-1-78952-136-8

Deep Purple and Rainbow 1968-79 – Steve Pilkington 978-1-78952-002-6

Dire Straits – Andrew Wild 978-1-78952-044-6

The Doors – Tony Thompson 978-1-78952-137-5

Dream Theater – Jordan Blum 978-1-78952-050-7

Elvis Costello and The Attractions – Georg Purvis 978-1-78952-129-0

Emerson Lake and Palmer – Mike Goode 978-1-78952-000-2

Fairport Convention – Kevan Furbank 978-1-78952-051-4

Peter Gabriel – Graeme Scarfe 978-1-78952-138-2

Genesis – Stuart MacFarlane 978-1-78952-005-7

Gentle Giant – Gary Steel 978-1-78952-058-3

Gong – Kevan Furbank 978-1-78952-082-8

Hawkwind – Duncan Harris 978-1-78952-052-1

Roy Harper – Opher Goodwin 978-1-78952-130-6

Iron Maiden – Steve Pilkington 978-1-78952-061-3

Jefferson Airplane – Richard Butterworth 978-1-78952-143-6

Jethro Tull – Jordan Blum 978-1-78952-016-3

Elton John in the 1970s – Peter Kearns 978-1-78952-034-7

The Incredible String Band – Tim Moon 978-1-78952-107-8

Iron Maiden – Steve Pilkington 978-1-78952-061-3

Judas Priest – John Tucker 978-1-78952-018-7

Kansas – Kevin Cummings 978-1-78952-057-6

Led Zeppelin – Steve Pilkington 978-1-78952-151-1

Level 42 – Matt Philips 978-1-78952-102-3

Aimee Mann – Jez Rowden 978-1-78952-036-1

Joni Mitchell – Peter Kearns 978-1-78952-081-1

The Moody Blues – Geoffrey Feakes 978-1-78952-042-2

Mike Oldfield – Ryan Yard 978-1-78952-060-6

Tom Petty – Richard James 978-1-78952-128-3

Porcupine Tree – Nick Holmes 978-1-78952-144-3

Queen – Andrew Wild 978-1-78952-003-3

Radiohead – William Allen 978-1-78952-149-8

Renaissance – David Detmer 978-1-78952-062-0

The Rolling Stones 1963-80 – Steve Pilkington 978-1-78952-017-0

The Smiths and Morrissey – Tommy Gunnarsson 978-1-78952-140-5

Steely Dan – Jez Rowden 978-1-78952-043-9

Steve Hackett – Geoffrey Feakes 978-1-78952-098-9

Thin Lizzy – Graeme Stroud 978-1-78952-064-4

Toto – Jacob Holm-Lupo 978-1-78952-019-4

U2 – Eoghan Lyng 978-1-78952-078-1

UFO – Richard James 978-1-78952-073-6

The Who – Geoffrey Feakes 978-1-78952-076-7

Roy Wood and the Move – James R Turner 978-1-78952-008-8

Van Der Graaf Generator – Dan Coffey 978-1-78952-031-6

Yes – Stephen Lambe 978-1-78952-001-9

Frank Zappa 1966 to 1979 – Eric Benac 978-1-78952-033-0

10CC – Peter Kearns 978-1-78952-054-5

Decades Series

The Bee Gees in the 1960s – Andrew Mon Hughes et al 978-1-78952-148-1

Alice Cooper in the 1970s – Chris Sutton 978-1-78952-104-7

Curved Air in the 1970s – Laura Shenton 978-1-78952-069-9

Fleetwood Mac in the 1970s – Andrew Wild 978-1-78952-105-4

Focus in the 1970s – Stephen Lambe 978-1-78952-079-8

Genesis in the 1970s – Bill Thomas 978178952-146-7

Marillion in the 1980s – Nathaniel Webb 978-1-78952-065-1

Pink Floyd In The 1970s – Georg Purvis 978-1-78952-072-9

The Sweet in the 1970s – Darren Johnson 978-1-78952-139-9

Uriah Heep in the 1970s – Steve Pilkington 978-1-78952-103-0

Yes in the 1980s – Stephen Lambe with David Watkinson 978-1-78952-125-2

On Screen series

Carry On... – Stephen Lambe 978-1-78952-004-0

David Cronenberg – Patrick Chapman 978-1-78952-071-2

Doctor Who: The David Tennant Years – Jamie Hailstone 978-1-78952-066-8

Monty Python – Steve Pilkington 978-1-78952-047-7

Seinfeld Seasons 1 to 5 – Stephen Lambe 978-1-78952-012-5

Other Books

Babysitting A Band On The Rocks – G.D. Praetorius 978-1-78952-106-1

Derek Taylor: For Your Radioactive Children – Andrew Darlington
978-1-78952-038-5

Iggy and The Stooges On Stage 1967-1974 – Per Nilsen 978-1-78952-101-6

Jon Anderson and the Warriors – the road to Yes – David Watkinson
978-1-78952-059-0

Nu Metal: A Definitive Guide – Matt Karpe 978-1-78952-063-7

Tommy Bolin: In and Out of Deep Purple – Laura Shenton 978-1-78952-070-5

Maximum Darkness – Deke Leonard 978-1-78952-048-4

Maybe I Should've Stayed In Bed – Deke Leonard 978-1-78952-053-8

Psychedelic Rock in 1967 – Kevan Furbank 978-1-78952-155-9

The Twang Dynasty – Deke Leonard 978-1-78952-049-1

and many more to come!

Would you like to write for Sonicbond Publishing?

We are mainly a music publisher, but we also occasionally
publish in other genres including film and television. At Sonicbond
Publishing we are always on the look-out for authors, particularly for
our two main series, On Track and Decades.

Mixing fact with in depth analysis, the On Track series examines
the entire recorded work of a particular musical artist or group. All
genres are considered from easy listening and jazz to 60s soul to 90s
pop, via rock and metal.

The Decades series singles out a particular decade in an artist or
group's history and focuses on that decade in more detail than may
be allowed in the On Track series.

While professional writing experience would, of course, be
an advantage, the most important qualification is to have real
enthusiasm and knowledge of your subject. First-time authors are
welcomed, but the ability to write well in English is essential.

Sonicbond Publishing has distribution throughout Europe and
North America, and all our books are also published in E-book form.
Authors will be paid a royalty based on sales of their book.
Further details about our books are available from
www.sonicbondpublishing.com. To contact us, complete the
contact form there or email info@sonicbondpublishing.co.uk